Abstract Painting, Once Removed

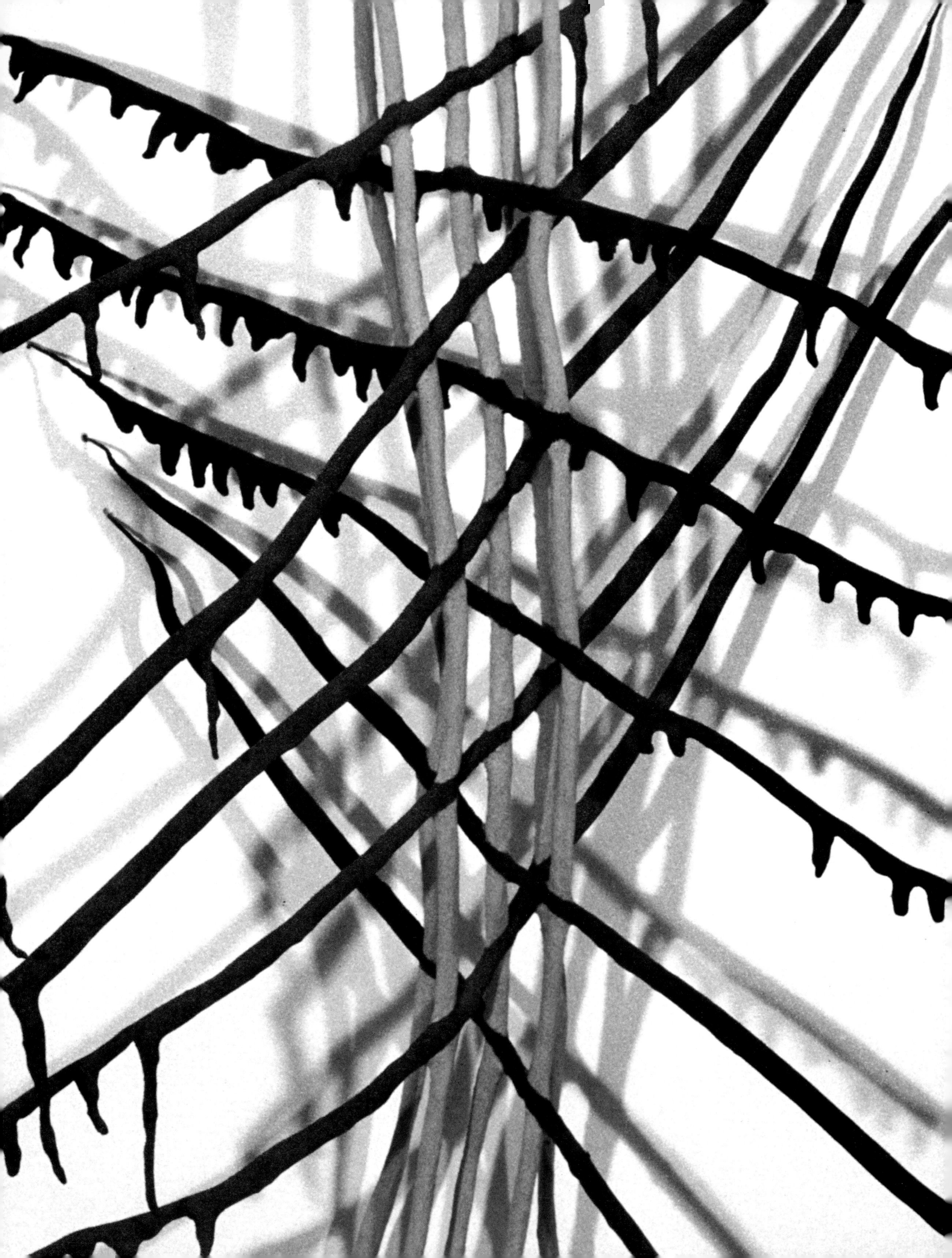

Abstract Painting
Once Removed

DANA FRIIS-HANSEN

with essays by

DAVID PAGEL

RAPHAEL RUBINSTEIN

PETER SCHJELDAHL

Contemporary Arts Museum, Houston

This catalogue has been published to accompany the exhibition
"Abstract Painting, Once Removed"
organized by Dana Friis-Hansen, Senior Curator,
Contemporary Arts Museum, Houston

Exhibition Itinerary
Contemporary Arts Museum, Houston, Texas
October 3 – December 6, 1998

Kemper Museum of Contemporary Art, Kansas City, Missouri
April 23 – July 18, 1999

"Abstract Painting, Once Removed" has been supported by grants from The Brown Foundation, Inc., and the Contemporary Arts Museum's Major Exhibition Fund contributors:

Patron
Ms. Louisa Stude Sarofim

Benefactors
George and Mary Josephine Hamman Foundation
Mr. and Mrs. I.H. Kempner III
Mary Lynch Kurtz
Fayez Sarofim & Co.
Mr. and Mrs. Marvin H. Seline
The Susan Vaughan Foundation

Donors
American General
Arthur Andersen LLP
Mr. and Mrs. A.L. Ballard
Max and Isabell Smith Herzstein
Rob and Louise Jamail
Michael and Jeanne Klein
Mary Lawrence Porter
Shell Oil Company Foundation
Stephen D. Susman

Special support has been provided by The British Council.

front cover:
Aaron Parazette, *Tournament*, 1998 (detail), p. 75

back cover:
Scott Richter, Untitled, 1994, p. 80

end papers:
Fabian Marcaccio, *560 Conjectures For a New Paint Management*, 1996 (detail), p. 68

frontispiece:
Sally Elesby, *Motive Painting #3*, 1997 (detail), p. 56

Library of Congress Catalogue Card Number
98-73230
ISBN 0-936080-44-2

Printed and bound in the United States of America.

Contemporary Arts Museum, Houston
5216 Montrose Boulevard
Houston, Texas 77006–6598
phone: 713/284–8250 fax: 713/284–8275
www.camh.org

Contents

Lenders to the Exhibition

Sheridan Brown, Los Angeles
Cindy and Tony Canzoneri, Malibu, California
J. Scott Caruthers, Houston
Mark D. Cole, Dallas
Sally Elesby, Los Angeles
Jeff Elrod, Houston
Ellen Katzman, Los Angeles
Jeanne and Michael Klein, Houston
Rachel Lehmann
Victoria Montelongo and Bob Sullivan, Dallas
Eileen and Peter Norton, Santa Monica, California
Ron and Ann Pizzuti, Columbus, Ohio
Monique Prieto, Los Angeles
Howard E. Rachofsky, Dallas
David Reed, New York
John Robertshaw, New York
Dr. Roberta Smith, Pacific Palisades, California
Susan Margules Steinhardt and John Steinhardt
Stephen D. Susman, Houston
Dean Valentine, Beverly Hills, California
Pae White, Pasedena, California
Private Collections

The Bohen Foundation
The British Council
The Museum of Fine Arts, Houston
Saatchi Collection, London
The SunAmerica Collection, Los Angeles
Tate Gallery, London
Walker Art Center, Minneapolis
Yvonne Force, Inc.

ACME., Los Angeles
Pamela Auchincloss Arts Management, New York
CRG Gallery, New York
D'Amelio Terras Gallery, New York
Gorney Bravin & Lee, New York
Haines Gallery, San Francisco
Shoshana Wayne Gallery, Santa Monica, California
Texas Gallery, Houston

Foreword

The Contemporary Arts Museum is proud to present "Abstract Painting, Once Removed," an especially timely exhibition documenting the work of one of the most interesting new directions in contemporary art at the verge of the new millennium. The show follows a distinguished record of exhibitions mounted by the Museum since 1948 identifying and documenting the diverse ways in which artists of the last fifty years have captured the intellectual, emotional, and cultural tenor of their times.

On October 31, 1948, the fledgling Contemporary Arts Association opened its first exhibition, "This is Contemporary Art," to the city's culture-hungry public. In the years since, an explosion in artistic activity, in institutions presenting that activity, and in the size of the audience has taken place, and the Contemporary Arts Museum has been a major player—regionally, nationally, and internationally—in that expansion.

In 1997, after a major renovation, the Museum looked back at its past through the window of an exhibition called "Finders/Keepers." In 1998, as we celebrate the institution's fiftieth anniversary—and the support and loyalty of its audience—we look forward once again. Senior Curator Dana Friis-Hansen at first proposed an exhibition modeled on "This is Contemporary Art" (which had encompassed painting, sculpture, photography, architecture, and design), but it soon became evident that the parameters of art activity have grown too large and diverse to be accommodated in one exhibition. Instead, Friis-Hansen now proposes to present five exhibitions over the next several years that document various themes and media that seem pivotal in the arts at the dawn of the twenty-first century. All will be successors to the first show, and all will focus on the most critical developments in art at the present moment. The first of these exhibitions, "Abstract Painting, Once Removed," is focused on the current resurgence of painting as a pivotal medium for new ideas.

Friis-Hansen's thesis for "Abstract Painting, Once Removed" is that the practice of, and critical discussion about, abstract and non-objective painting has been invigorated and broadened by the injection of ideas, forms, processes, tools, and materials from outside the spiritual, expressionistic and/or formalist strands that heretofore dominated twentieth-century abstraction. Focusing on recent work by twenty-one artists from the United States, England, Scotland, Brazil, and Japan, the exhibition documents some of the new approaches that are guiding these emerging artists in their work today—ideas that engage the audience in new ways of looking at, and communicating about, the art of our time.

The exhibition focuses on work from the past five years by artists who are wrestling with the boundaries of both the idea of painting as an art practice and the form and meaning of the resulting object. A painting has traditionally been defined as a two-dimensional work of art made by an artist using pigment in some kind of binder (oil or acrylic resin, for example) on a regularly-shaped support (such as canvas or wood) to create a wall-bound work that embodies an image and/or idea. Certainly, the parameters of the object, as well as its purpose, have changed over the last five or six hundred years. But until the 1970s, a painting was at least recognizable as something other than a sculpture or a drawing or a work of architecture. As artists of the 1970s expanded and pushed at the boundaries of art-making—in media, form, and content—the object itself, the painting, became less and less distinguishable as a distinct visual form. By the end of that decade, most critics, curators, and art historians had come to the conclusion that a work of art was basically what the artist called it. If a three-dimensional work was called a painting by its maker, perhaps because of the formal issues or the visual traditions from which it arose (or was created in reaction to), then it was a painting: the artist classified the object and the rest of us chose to abide by the artist's definition, much as we choose to accept the title given to a work by its creator.

It is fortunate that we are accustomed to doing so, because the artists in this exhibition have extended the explorations of the 1970s and 1980s even further, assuming a conceptual position that reacts, critically and intellectually, to the Modernist tradition. In fact, their reexamination and reevaluation of the medium extends throughout Modernism's by now century-long history, resulting here in work that is physically, emotionally, or conceptually distanced from the abstraction of earlier twentieth-century movements—it is *once removed* from its heritage, its family, its base.

Interestingly enough, the geographic centers that would have dominated in the 1948 exhibition—Paris and New York come immediately to mind—are greatly expanded in the present exhibition and now extend beyond France and the United States, beyond Europe and the Americas. This reflects the decentralization of the art world that began in the 1970s as artists were able to live and work outside Western art capitals and still remain part of the critical dialogue. The present decade has seen increasing attention to artists working in all parts of the world as the internationalization of art has been accelerated and intensified by the ease and frequency of international travel and the daily effects of electronic communication. Today, information and its dissemination are truly instant and truly global. Modernism has been disseminated, digested, and, perhaps, superseded worldwide.

We are very grateful to the authors of this catalogue. In addition to Dana Friis-Hansen, we are pleased to publish essays by David Pagel, an art critic for the *Los Angeles Times;* Raphael Rubinstein, associate editor of *Art in America;* and Peter Schjeldahl, a long-active and astute writer who is currently the art critic for *The Village Voice*. They have provided thought-provoking and insightful contributions to this publication, placing the exhibiting artists and the new abstraction in the context of history, culture, and the Modernist period.

The Contemporary Arts Museum has been at the forefront of the art of the moment for fifty years in large part due to the loyalty, generosity, adventurousness, and leadership provided by members of its Board of Trustees. The current members are listed on page 110 and we are grateful for their abiding and enthusiastic support as well as that of their predecessors.

Exhibitions presented in The Brown Foundation Gallery are made possible by the generous and substantial contributions from supporters of the Contemporary Arts Museum's

Major Exhibition Fund. This cadre of enlightened individuals, foundations, and corporations has provided the considerable resources necessary to organize this exhibition and the other four projects to be presented in The Brown Foundation Gallery during the fiftieth anniversary season. The Brown Foundation—without which, I'm certain, the Museum would not be celebrating its longevity—has given a generous grant in support of "Abstract Painting, Once Removed." The British Council has ensured our ability to transport the London loans.

After its presentation at the Contemporary Arts Museum, the exhibition will travel to the Kemper Museum of Contemporary Art in Kansas City, Missouri. I'm grateful to our colleagues there, Director Daniel Keegan and Curator Dana Self, for their enthusiastic response to the project and for their commitment to sharing it with their audiences. A lovely coincidence is that the buildings of both institutions were designed by the Illinois architect Gunnar Birkerts—our building in 1972 and the Kemper in 1994.

On behalf of the Board of Trustees of the Contemporary Arts Museum, I extend our gratitude to each and every lender to the exhibition. As a non-collecting institution, the Museum is totally dependent on loans for its exhibitions and programs and, therefore, relies on the generosity of lenders who agree to share valued works of art with our audiences.

A final word of thanks is due the artists included in the exhibition; their work is the origin of the exhibition's thesis and forms its reality.

Marti Mayo
Director

Acknowledgments

An exhibition of this scale and complexity cannot move forward without the generous cooperation and enthusiastic collaboration of the kind I have received throughout the organization of "Abstract Painting, Once Removed." I have been blessed with the support of the entire staff of the Contemporary Arts Museum, who made many efforts beyond the call of duty to ensure that this exhibition and its catalogue achieved its promise—to broaden the understanding and appreciation of new directions in contemporary art and abstract painting. This exhibition grew out of a desire to reexamine key issues raised by twentieth-century art and to look toward the future through the art being made today.

I am grateful to Director Marti Mayo, who encouraged this project from the start and offered invaluable feedback along the way. Assistant Curator Alexandra Irvine has been indespensable in managing the myriad details of the production and presentation of the exhibition and its catalogue. Together with Curator Lynn M. Herbert who herself tracked illustrations and offered sound advice and assistance, they elegantly managed the efficient production of yet another major publication for the Museum. Registrar Tim Barkley arranged for the safe transport of a spectrum of some unusual and fragile art objects from all points of the world with professional proficiency, and Preparator Pete Hannon and his team supervised a complicated installation with due care and all good spirits. Curator of Education Meredith Wilson, with Education Assistant Paula Newton, developed innovative interpretive materials and events for adults and children, which will help to broaden the public's accessibility to the art and ideas considered here. Director of Public Relations and Marketing Kelli Dunning, with the assistance of intern Wesley Miller (Sarah Lawrence College), ensured that the public would know about and feel welcome in the exhibition. Director of Development Karen Skaer Soh and the Development Office staff cheerfully ensured financial support for the project.

This catalogue also had a special team. The Museum is honored to publish the ideas of David Pagel, Raphael Rubinstein, and Peter Schjeldahl in new essays that broaden our context for understanding the artists selected for the exhibition. In addition to my curatorial colleagues, I am grateful to our curatorial interns, beginning with Stephanie Smith (Rice University), who did initial research, followed by Jenny Jasinski (University of Houston), Amanda Shagrin (University of Texas), and Liz Riddle (The Kincaid School), who compiled the artists' bibliographies and exhibition histories for the catalogue and chased down stray facts. Copy editing tasks for the entire book were expertly handled by Polly Koch, while Paula Webb provided insight into shaping (and shortening) my essays. The entire package was pulled together by Don Quaintance, Public Address Design, who maintained his fine touch and sense of humor throughout a complicated production process.

Even before this exhibition project began, and even more so after I began my active research, I enjoyed a lively dialogue about the current state of abstract painting with many friends and colleagues from around the world. Especially valuable have been my discussions with Susan Brades, David Bonetti, Kerry Brougher, Susan Cahan, Sheryl Conkelton, Lynne

Cooke, Lisa Corrin, Michael Darling, Olivia Georgia, Lynn Gumpert, Madeleine Grynsztejn, Laura Hoptman, Hudson, Chryssie Isles, Maaretta Jaukkuri, Marjory Jacobson, Isobel Johnstone, Katy Kline, Ivo Mesquita, Fumio Nanjo, David Pagel, Ron Platt, Helaine Posner, Raphael Rubinstein, Tom Solomon, Nicholas Serota, William F. Stern, Robert Storr, Anne Umland, and Lynn Zelevansky. Thanks are also due to Mark Holzbach for his encouragement and patience.

The artists' dealers and representatives devoted considerable time and energy to ensure that important works were available for the exhibition and that documentation about the artists was accurate and complete. The dedication of the following individuals and their gallery staffs was simply invaluable: Randy Sommer and Robert Gunderman, ACME., Los Angeles; David McAuliffe and Lynn Sharpless, Angles Gallery, Santa Monica, California; Pamela Auchincloss, Pamela Auchincloss Arts Management, New York; Tim Blum and Jeff Poe, Blum & Poe, Santa Monica, California; Karen Bravin and John Post Lee, Gorney Bravin & Lee Gallery, New York; Marcantonio Vilaça, Galeria Camargo Vilaça, São Paulo, Brazil; Carla Chammas, Richard Desroche, and Glenn McMillan, CRG Gallery, New York; Chris D'Amelio and Lucian Terras, D'Amelio Terras Gallery, New York; Anthony d'Offay and Mark Fletcher, Anthony d'Offay Gallery, London; Hudson, Feature, Inc., New York; Sean Kelly and Annabella Johnson, Sean Kelly Gallery, New York; Shoshana Blank, Shoshana Wayne Gallery, Santa Monica, California; Ian Glennie and Fredericka Hunter, Texas Gallery, Houston; and Edward Thorp and Ashley Fowler, Edward Thorp Gallery, New York. Additional assistance was provided by Jeffrey Deitch, Deitch Projects, New York; Rose Lord, Frith Gallery, London; Caren Golden, Caren Golden Fine Art, New York; Cheryl Haines and Gina Findlay, Haines Gallery, San Francisco; Ghislaine Hussenot, Galerie Ghislaine Hussenot, Paris; Tomio Koyama, Tomio Koyama Gallery, Tokyo; Doug Lawing, Lawing Gallery, Houston; Sarah Watson, Patrick Painter, Inc., Santa Monica, California; and Helaine de Franchis, Studio la Cittá, Verona, Italy.

I wish to add my voice to the director's in thanking all who provided financial support for the project; to the museums, collectors, foundations, agencies, artists, and galleries that are lending work; and to all who helped coordinate these loans so this work could be seen in a new context and enjoyed by a wider audience.

Finally, I extend my wholehearted appreciation and admiration to the artists in this exhibition, who responded with warmth, wit, intelligence, and no small amount of patience to our persistent questions about their work and ideas. They proved to be crucial resources for the exhibition histories published at the end of this catalogue. Most important is their visually and intellectually stimulating work, which has prompted a rethinking of abstract painting—not only helping to find closure for the art of this century, but also looking forward with enthusiasm to the new ideas we are sure to see in the art made in the next.

Dana Friis-Hansen
Senior Curator

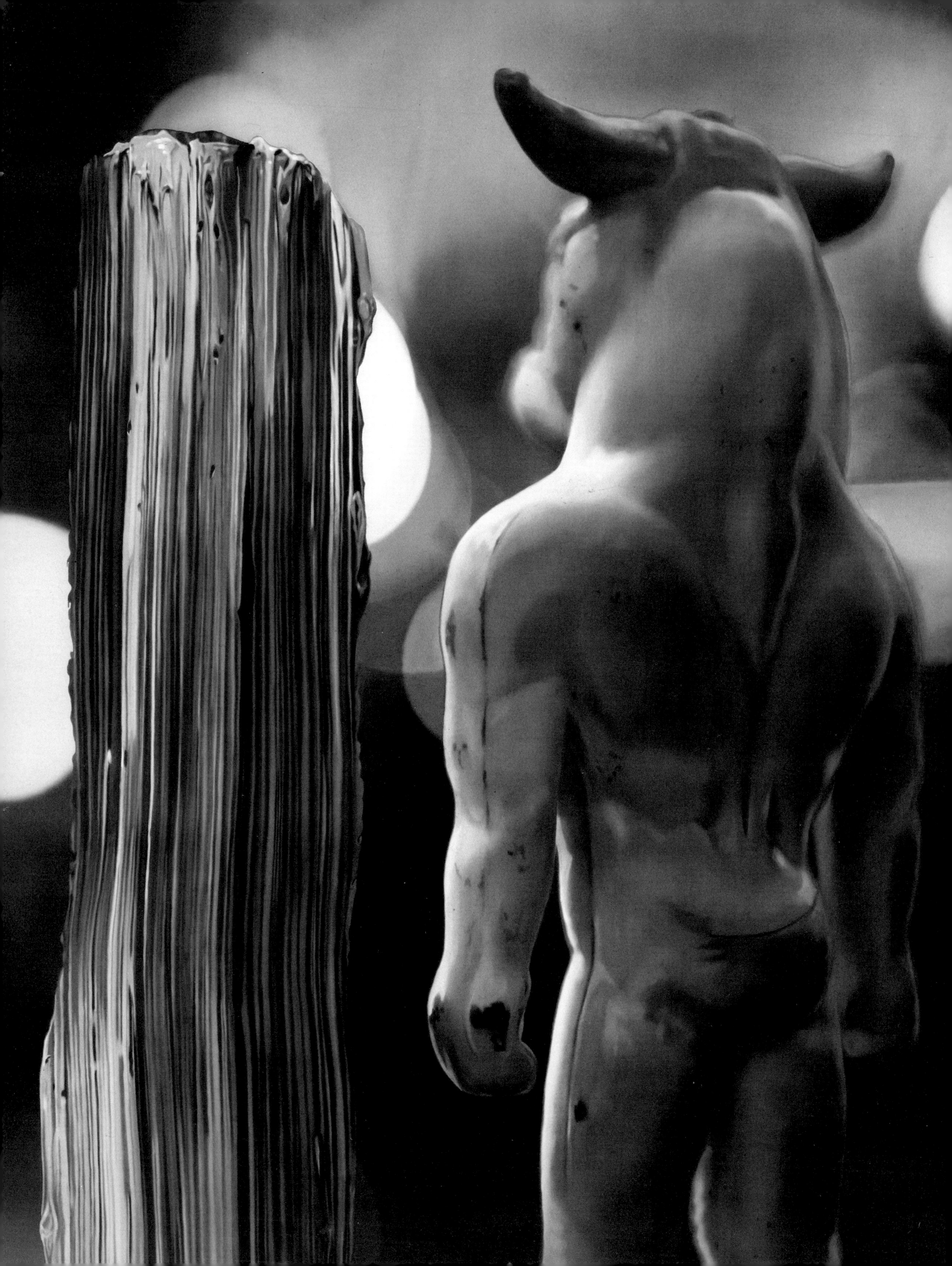

Where do we come from? What are we? Where are we going?
Abstract Painting, Once Removed

Dana Friis-Hansen

Painting has enjoyed a privileged position over sculpture and architecture in much of art history since the Renaissance; furthermore, abstract and non-objective painting[1] held the defining position throughout the history of Modernism from its beginnings in Impressionism into the 1970s. Abstract painting has even been declared "the Modernist medium *par excellence*,"[2] as it was so well suited to spiritual quest, self-expression, and formalist invention, issues that shaped the culture of the late nineteenth century and much of the twentieth. In the past three decades, however, contemporary art has been broadened and enlivened by artists working in the new forms of performance, installation, public art, video and film, digital media, and the Internet, and it seemed as if our electronic age no longer had patience for, let alone interest in, new ideas and approaches to abstract painting. This exhibition draws together the work of twenty-one artists who are injecting fresh energy and ideas into contemporary art by exploring issues of abstract painting, a medium considered by many to be a dead end. By bringing new, open attitudes to this medium, they dramatically reposition abstract painting for the next century.

The rich and heavy history of abstract painting, together with persistent critical debate denying its relevance in a Postmodern world, nearly extinguished serious efforts to pursue new forms of abstract painting. But as we approach the end of this century, exciting new critical bodies of abstract painting by artists around the world are emerging from, connecting with, and contributing to the broader spectrum of contemporary art in the 1990s.[3] Whether these artists actually paint on a canvas support—or make three-dimensional objects, photographs, or installations that relate to the process or history of abstract painting—they all work in a climate where painting is no longer more important than any other medium. But on their newly leveled playing field, these artists have started a whole new ballgame with what was arguably this century's dominant art form.

"Abstract Painting, Once Removed" is, in many ways, a "family" dialogue. In genealogical terms, the expression "once removed" denotes a difference of one generation between related family members; while children and their parents are technically once removed, the expression is most often used for a more remote relationship, such as first or second cousins. This group of artists is related—or distanced—in one, two, or more degrees of remoteness to the inventors and pioneers of Modernist abstraction.

Abstract painting's "family values" were defined elegantly early on by nineteenth-century French poet and critic Stéphane Mallarmé: "Paint not the thing, but the effect it produces."[4] One of American abstraction's most vocal proponents, critic Clement Greenberg, writing in 1946, felt Modernist painting must "identify itself with its material vehicle, with paint and canvas, surface, and shape."[5] The [Greenbergian] critical discourse shaping late Modernist painting stressed a kind of collective inquiry from within, painting into painting in an effort to exhibit what painting itself is. Under its own Modernist self-analysis, painting would be "rendered pure."[6]

1. Richard Patterson
***Young Minotaur*, 1997**
Oil on canvas
82¼ x 48¼ inches
Collection Yvonne Force, Inc.

Today painting is no longer the sacred calling it once was but merely one choice of medium among many. The artists in this exhibition make provocative works that are physically, emotionally, or conceptually distanced from the "pure" abstraction of earlier periods. Most came to this medium in the late 1980s and early 1990s, developing their interests and attitudes in an era when painting was *not* paramount; indeed, many educational institutions treated painting as a marginal, retrograde activity. Conceptualism's formidable open-ended questioning and Postmodernism's skepticism conspired to refute the tired dogma of painting as the all-transcendent form of artmaking. The artists here have responded to the "gods" in the family history [i.e., Piet Mondrian, Jackson Pollock, Willem de Kooning, and Frank Stella, among others] and to their alter egos [Marcel Duchamp, Robert Rauschenberg, Andy Warhol, Gerhard Richter, Sigmar Polke, and so on] even as they charted their own courses. Significantly, the positive, comfortable approach to painting these artists take results from both a broader view of painting's possibilities and a study of models *outside* painting.

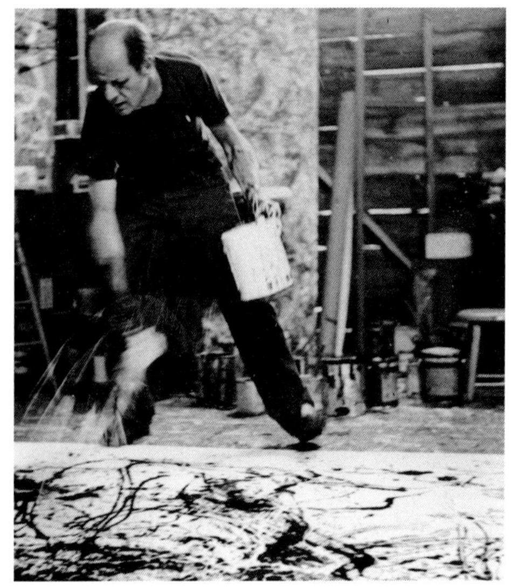

2. Hans Namuth
Jackson Pollock, 1950
Courtesy Collection Center for Creative Photography, The University of Arizona

Challenges to the primacy of abstract painting

Whether a holy ceremony, as celebrated by Pollock in full swing in the pages of *Life* magazine and Hans Namuth's photographs (fig. 2), or a quest via the tragic and timeless subject matter of Mark Rothko, by mid century, the act of painting had become spectacle. In the United States, large-scale, energetic expressionistic works or deep, brooding canvases were exorcising postwar existential angst. Yet the truth is, as triumphant as Abstract Expressionism was, only a few showed true genius; in the following decades, as second and third generations followed in the footsteps of the originators of this increasingly popular approach, less and less first-rate work was produced. By the 1960s, even Greenberg admitted its decline. "Abstract Expressionism," he observed, "turned into a school then into a manner, finally into a set of mannerisms. Its leaders attracted imitators, many of them, and then some of those leaders took to imitating themselves."[7] Perhaps the territory was over-grazed, or perhaps the artists had become fatigued, but by the late 1950s and 1960s, many younger artists felt the field was too narrow for innovation. Roy Lichtenstein, reflecting upon the crisis that prompted his break from Abstract Expressionism, seemed desperate when he lamented, "There was no space between Milton Resnick and Mike Goldberg."[8] Beyond Lichtenstein's move to Pop, reconsideration of the grand paintings of Abstract Expressionism, the Modernist *art objet par excellence,* prompted the avant-garde to seek refuge (and their potential) in other fields, including performance and Happenings, Fluxus, New Dance, and experimental music. All extended aspects of the painter's physical and psychological energies beyond the edge of the canvas.

Challenges to the primacy of painting are nothing new, nor is the ringing of its death knell. It began over a century ago with the advent of photography, when Paul Delaroche, one of the leading academic history painters of Paris, declared, "From today, painting is dead,"[9] the first time he saw a daguerreotype. And it continues into our own time, with the development of Postmodernism and its attendant pluralistic, democratic assertion that no one medium shall dominate. This "death of painting" (best interpreted as the medium's loss of relevance as part of advanced contemporary art practice and theory) has been proclaimed often enough, but actually the prominence of painting has continually reasserted itself. Despite the visibility of many other media, since the 1970s, we have witnessed Lyrical Abstraction, New Image Painting, Pattern and Decoration, "Bad Painting," Neo-Expressionism, "Neo-Geo," and many other variants of abstract painting.

"The quintessential painting" and the dematerialized object

Artists are continually rethinking what painting is, is not, and might be.[10] One key element of Modernism has been the impulse to absorb, digest, and sometimes desecrate what has gone before in order to go further, to launch a more progressive, if linear, trajectory. This path resulted in a reductivist tendency toward "the quintessential painting," a concept that Thomas McEvilley has traced to its beginnings. Russian Suprematist Kasimir Malevich referred to his works, including *Black Square*, 1915, and *White on White*, 1918, as "the ultimate paintings, the last two-dimensional artworks,"[11] while New York School painter Ad Reinhardt, who by the 1960s was producing his delicate black monochromes, declared, "I am simply making the last paintings which can be ever made."[12] McEvilley himself refers to Rothko's Chapel paintings in Houston as "the last great monument of Modernism and the abstract sublime."[13] Following the self-referential thread that runs through Modernism to its dissolution in the diverse practices of the Conceptualist artists, McEvilley goes on to observe:

> . . . the monochrome has from its beginning asserted a critique of previous types of painting . . . and it was natural to engage the monochrome idea in Conceptualism's relentless critique of painting in the late 1960s and 1970s. Both [Yves] Klein's and [Piero] Manzoni's oeuvres featured Conceptualist irony. Klein's exhibition of "invisible paintings" . . . foreshadowed many Conceptual works that carried the inflated idea of the "last painting" *ad absurdum*.[14]

Marcel Duchamp was an especially influential figure in New York well into the 1960s. Not only did his 1914 introduction of the readymade challenge the barrier between the mass-produced product and art that emphasized the hand of the artist, but his calculated use of found objects, appropriated imagery, punning language, and mythologies of self and gender in multiples, publications, public events, and installations had wide resonances for how generations of artists considered the art object. Duchamp himself had stopped painting early in the century. "I wanted to get away from the physical aspect of painting," he said. "I was interested in ideas—not merely in visual products," and he never hesitated to show his disdain for painting, frequently reminding interviewers of the French phrase "*bete comme un peinteur* [as stupid as a painter]."[15]

The development of photography as an art form presented another challenge to Modernist painting—not in the way that it threatened portraiture and history painting in the nineteenth century, but as a critical alternative. Only recently has technology allowed photographic images to carry the scale, color, and presence of a major Abstract Expressionist painting,[16] but the key issue attracting artists in the 1970s and 1980s was that photography was *not painting*. German theorist Walter Benjamin's now classic essay "The Work of Art in the Age of Mechanical Reproduction"[17] posited photography and film as challengers to the authority of the original work of art—its "aura"—freeing it from place and time. Through publication and wide distribution, photographic images became immensely more accessible, and art was thereby reactivated as a socially useful tool for employment in new contexts. These ideas prompted artists to explore how pictures functioned in mass media and the place of mechanical reproduction—its imagery, its look, its processes—in contemporary art.[18]

In the 1960s, a new generation of artists sought other ways to purge the widely-perceived emphasis on all that was represented by traces of the artist's hand, and to eventually shift formalist investigations away from the material of paint itself, endowed as it was with such a long and dominant history. For example, it can be argued that Stella, Donald Judd, Sol LeWitt, and others took the simple forms of monochrome painting and moved them toward serial systems. This was one of the paths which led to Conceptualism—an umbrella term for opened-up

3. John Baldessari
EVERYTHING IS PURGED FROM THIS PAINTING BUT ART, NO IDEAS HAVE ENTERED THIS WORK, 1966-68
Acrylic on canvas
67¾ x 55⅞ inches
Sonnabend Collection, New York

practices as diverse as Body Art, Earth Art, installations, Arte Povera, and especially works that used language, mathematics, or social systems, all evolving far from the painter's easel. For example, during 1967–68 John Baldessari created an important set of paintings using texts painted by a professional sign painter on a stretched canvas ("the only art signal I wanted was the canvas"[19]) under Baldessari's direction. Typical of that series, *EVERYTHING IS PURGED . . .*, 1966–68 (fig. 3) presents a conundrum facing contemporary painting. LeWitt and Lawrence Weiner, also pioneers of Conceptualism, provided other critiques of the cult of the (portable, saleable, resaleable) painting with their temporary wall works—penciled line drawings and painted texts, respectively, applied directly to the wall either by the artist or, with equal validity, by another person following the artist's instructions. Art became depersonalized, the anonymous hand was valued for allowing a more direct connection to the idea that originated the work. Ann Goldstein and Anne Rorimer, curators who recently organized a survey of this investigatory practice from 1965–75 for The Museum of Contemporary Art, Los Angeles have written:

> The initial phase of Conceptual art can be characterized by its studied dismantling of, and ultimate break with, the Western tradition of Modernism. The self-referentiality of Minimalism becomes in Conceptual art a self-examination of the machinery of a work of art. Numerous new questions are raised through this work: What is the function of this work? How is its meaning constructed? Where and when does the work exist? Why does it take the form it does? To whom is it addressed?[20]

These questions became essential to artists who were interrogating the power and place of painting in the late 1960s. By their example, the artists of today are, increasingly, responding to these questions by making paintings.

Shifting practices

The *practice* of art has changed since the late 1960s as the line of Modernism was abandoned for more pluralistic paths. The boundaries of paint on canvas are now long gone, and an increasingly higher proportion of artists and critics has focused their investigations in media other than paint. Unlike earlier generations, when the avant-garde lived and learned at society's fringe, in the past few decades younger artists have increasingly sought to join a class of university-educated professionals.[21] Since the 1960s, and especially during the 1980s art boom, the expansion of the art market and gallery system, together with a proliferation of new contemporary art museums, prompted a large spawning of art schools offering graduate level programs. Advanced university degree programs required artists to develop their critical thinking, speaking, and writing skills, as well as their hands and eyes, and this intellectual milieu greatly influences the art being made by the artists in this exhibition.

Today's artists consider experiments, practices, and theories from *any* field, even those outside art, as relevant to their practice. In the late 1960s at the newly opened California Institute for the Arts (CalArts) in Valencia, Baldessari offered a course called "Post-Studio Art" intended to be "a catchall to anyone who wasn't doing straight painting and straight sculpture."[22] At CalArts and other schools, an emphasis on ideas and issues took precedence over training the hand of the artist in the discipline of a craft. Beyond learning *to paint*, per se, they learned *about painting*—its histories, its theories, and its context among other practices. The legacy of Modernist painting could not be ignored by even the driest of Postmodern academics, and to deny its pleasures and problematics was foolhardy, but as they were warned by Duchamp, it is all too easy to fall in love with the smell of paint for its own sake.[23]

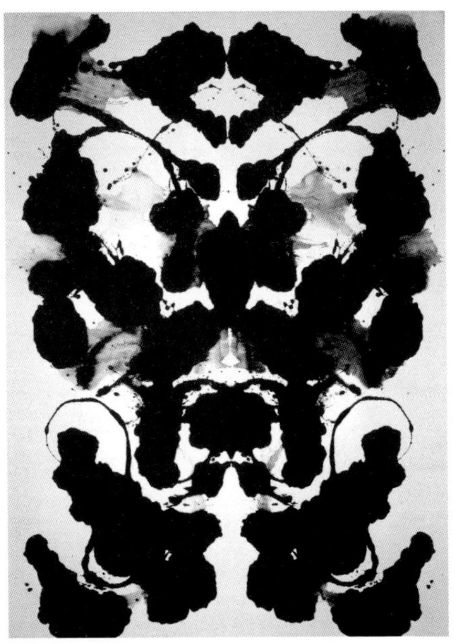

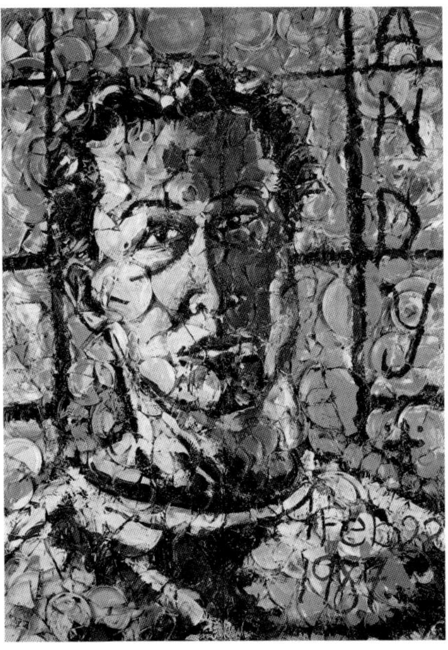

4. Andy Warhol
***Rorschach*, 1984**
Synthetic polymer paint on canvas
165 x 119 inches
The Andy Warhol Museum, Pittsburgh
Founding Collection, Contribution The Andy Warhol Foundation for the Visual Arts, Inc.

5. Julian Schnabel
Self Portrait in Andy's Shadow, 1987
Oil, Bondo, and plates on wood
103 x 72 inches
The Eli and Edythe L. Broad Collection

Postmodern painting

As the artists in this exhibition grapple with the dominant issues of Modernism, they add to several decades of Postmodernist painting. In the 1960s and 1970s, social movements including feminism and multiculturalism, plus a general decentralization in the art world—all those university-educated artists spreading themselves out across the United States opened up new "regionalist" possibilities—led to a broadening of the critical discourse to a wider range of voices and visions. This new liberalism helped to open abstract painting up to different approaches, considerably changing attitudes about the subject and object.

Pop artists have been especially influential to the current generation. Lichtenstein's 1965–66 graphic Brushstrokes series condenses the bravura of de Kooning's or Franz Kline's large, confident gestural sweeps into comic book motifs.[24] In the 1980s, Warhol turned to various methods beyond silkscreening to make "abstract paintings," adopting some anti-intellectual processes not based on artistic skill, like folding a paint-smeared canvas in half to create Rorschach-like inkblots (fig. 4) or having associates urinate onto canvases covered with metallic paints to produce colorful patinas.

In Europe, two key figures in the current explorations of abstraction, Richter and Polke, emerged in the late 1960s, and they have continued to create important bodies of painting that wrestle with issues of originality, high and low culture, the mass media, and the sources and materials of artmaking. Their influence internationally is now beginning to be broadly felt.[25]

In the early 1980s, Europe and the United States witnessed a resurgence of painting in the form of Neo-Expressionism, with artists from Italy and Germany as well as New York exploring a heroic, humanist imagery that ranged from the rough to the esoteric. A wide range fell under this rubric (so wide it was also called "transavantgarde"), including spiritualist mythmakers such as Francesco Clemente and Enzo Cucci; those confronting history such as Anselm Kiefer or Jörg Immendorf; contemporary figurative scenemakers such as Eric Fischl and Robert Longo; and those drawing upon urban graffiti such as Jean-Michel Basquiat and Keith Haring. Each were in conversation with past Modernist painters while contributing to the current dialogue about what role painting could play in contemporary art. For example, Julian Schnabel's paintings over broken plates crumpled up the old idea about the flat picture plane, opening new possibilities for thinking about space, surface, materials, and the human gesture. Schnabel shows his truly Postmodernist appetite by including among his influences the flatly colored geometric panels of German artist Blinky Palermo, the animated "scraffito" of Cy Twombly, and even the media-mirror Warhol, who shares the frame with Schnabel in *Self Portrait in Andy's Shadow*, 1987 (fig. 5).

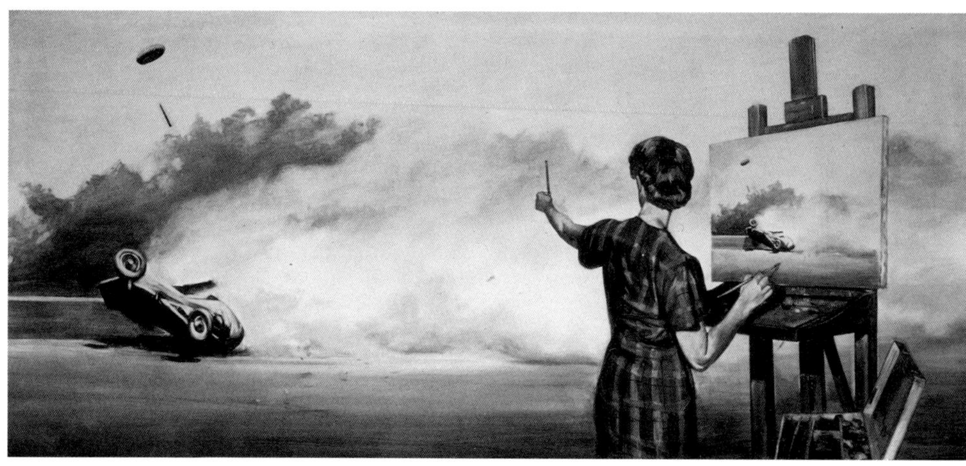

6. Mark Tansey
***Action Painting,* 1981**
Oil on canvas
36 x 78 inches
Courtesy Curt Marcus Gallery, New York

In counterpoint to the boisterous energy of 1980s Neo-Expressionist painting, other artists followed the conceptual and political threads initiated by theorists such as Benjamin, Roland Barthes, and Jean Baudrillard. Mark Tansey used the style of 1940s and 1950s photopictorial magazines to produce pseudo-allegorical paintings, such as *Action Painting,* 1981 (fig. 6), which wryly re-picture moments from recent art history. Other artists, among them Peter Halley, David Reed, Philip Taaffe, and Christopher Wool merged pictorial patterning with theoretical reflections on art and contemporary life. Sherrie Levine destabilized the authenticity and power of the artist as "author." By rephotographing, repainting, or recasting original works of art from the canon of Modernism, she undermined the cult of the art object and the hand of the "artist-god." For her own (handmade) paintings begun in 1985, she chose simple generic motifs (stripes, checkerboards, and backgammon patterns) and dull materials (wood, lead, and casein paint) at a modest scale, so she could connect to the seductive nature of painting and its "potential for reconciliation."[26]

A decade ago, an important part of the discourse within contemporary art focused on the body and its politics, whether it be feminist and psychoanalytic explorations of the representation of gender, sexuality, and race; responses to the AIDS epidemic; or the tangled issues surrounding the withdrawal of support for work by artists such as Andres Serrano, Robert Mapplethorpe, or Karen Finley. This period inspired only limited abstract painting addressing issues surrounding the body, with the exception of Byron Kim's important *Synecdoche,* 1991–92, flat monochrome panels in oil and wax based on the skin color of friends and family; without insight into their source, these might be mistaken for classic non-objective Color Field painting.

Part of the fallout of the politicized late 1980s and early 1990s was a wider discussion of, and greater sensitivity towards, sensuality, pleasure, and beauty. Beauty, it was declared by art critic Dave Hickey, would be "The Issue of the Nineties."[27] With its rich color, its fluid, malleable possibilities, and its intoxicating scent, there are few more sensuous materials with which to make beautiful objects than paint. Today's artists—far from being politically correct—are more willing to be seduced by the pleasures of painting, and if they are, they take pleasure in sharing that enjoyment with the viewer.

Currents among twenty-one tributaries

In which directions will the current generation lead abstract painting? As we pass from the 1990s into the next century, is painting once again reborn? Stillborn? Still dead? Was it ever dead? Just as the artists in this exhibition are repositioning abstraction away from Painting with a capital "P" and its self-reflective, isolationist path, critic and philosopher Arthur C. Danto declares, "I see the end of the exclusivity of pure painting as the vehicle of art history." [28] He offers an apt metaphor for this transition away from the hegemony of Modernist painting. From a succession of art historical periods and movements, we move to the contemporary era of the last few decades where, Danto observes:

> . . . there are countless directions for artmaking to take, none more privileged, historically at least, than the rest. . . . That painting was no longer the "key" did not mean that something else was to take over from it . . . It was as if a great river had now resolved itself into a network of tributaries.[29]

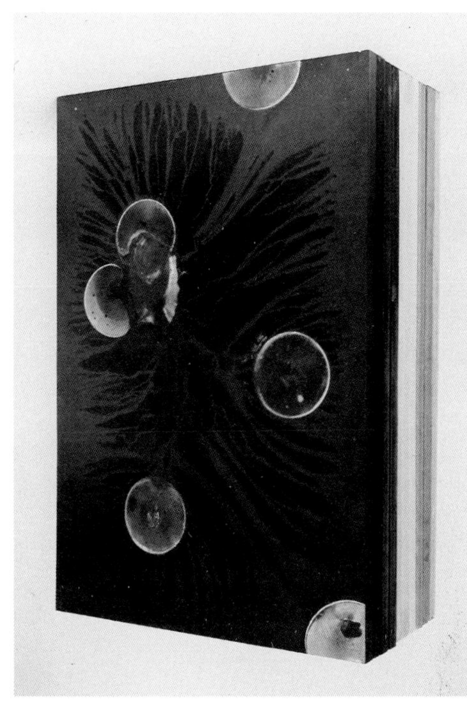

7. Emil Lukas
***Buffer*, 1998**
Canvas, wood, paper, mixed paints, organic material, thread, glass, and pencil
Five panels: 80 x 54 x 5½ inches (overall)
Courtesy the artist and Gorney Bravin & Lee, New York and Haines Gallery, San Francisco

The twenty-one artists in "Abstract Painting, Once Removed" embrace this freedom by charting their courses along twenty-one different tributaries, tapping into various strategies to carry abstract painting into new visual, physical, and intellectual territories. The work of these artists all respond (positively or negatively) to certain core values of abstract painting (painterly brushstrokes, purity of surface, or flatness, for example), but they are also united in their position once removed. With each day we get farther and farther away from the era when painting was Painting; most of these artists could be grandchildren of the Abstract Expressionists and thus have a different relationship with Modernist painting. Reviewing an exhibition by Monique Prieto, critic Michael Darling wrote:

> Sooner or later, the scourge of contemporary art discourse—formalist, Greenbergian painting—had to return for a fresh reappraisal. . . . it should be no surprise that artists too young to have forged any steadfast ideological aversion to painting theories of the nineteen fifties and sixties might also be able to contribute new interpretations of now archival material.[30]

One aspect of artmaking these artists are eager to explore is the physical—rather than solely the retinal, spiritual, or conceptual—aspects of painting and its tools. By isolating the elements of the language of painting—the drip and the stroke, canvas, palette, stretcher, etc.—for examination, celebration, or deconstruction, they freshen our understanding of what painting can be. The Expressionist drip and brushstroke are key icons for Ingrid Calame, Sally Elesby, Fabian Marcaccio, Takashi Murakami, Aaron Parazette, and Richard Patterson, who address paint's primary syntactical form in diverse ways. Instead of brushes, Tad Griffin makes customized squeegees to pull paint across a surface.

Other artists shift the space or place for painterly activity or painting-objects. Scott Richter uses the palette table, rather than a wall-mounted canvas, as the ground for his layered paintings. Polly Apfelbaum and Pae White shift the focus to the floor, but bounce color up onto adjacent walls. Emil Lukas stacks, or stands upright, his painted or otherwise manipulated double-sided membranes (fig. 7). Jim Hodges pulls the real-time activities of the world into his canvas-mounted mirrors (fig. 8).

The increasing presence of technology in our world, and in contemporary art, has found its way into the paintings of the 1990s. Kevin Appel, Jeff Elrod, Parazette, and Prieto use the computer as a limitless sketchpad with an array of electronic tricks to generate or manipulate

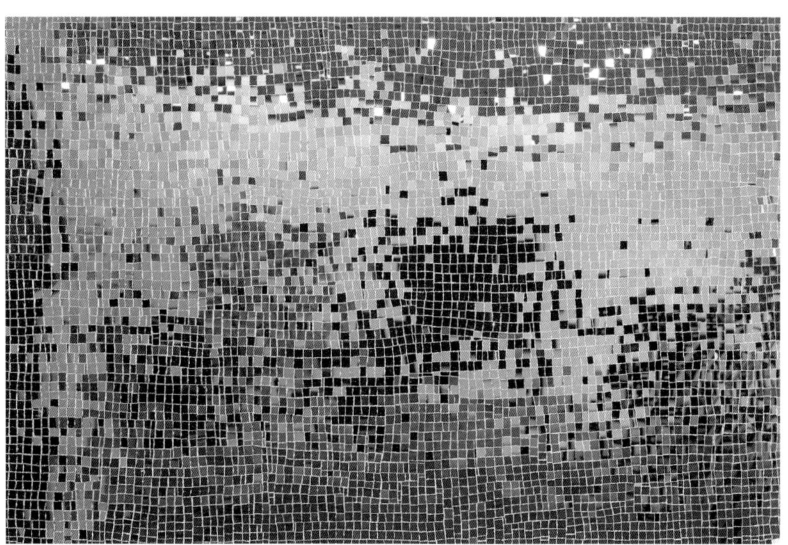

8. Jim Hodges
***On Earth*, 1998**
Mirror on canvas
40 x 60 inches
Collection Ron and Ann Pizzuti

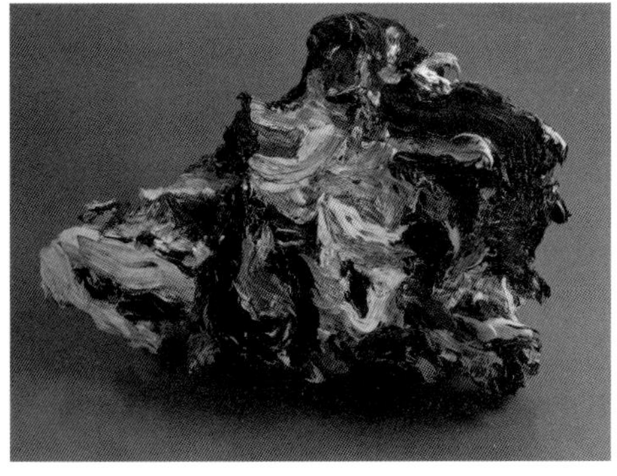

9. Glenn Brown
***Never Forever*, 1995**
Plaster, acrylic and oil paint, and chicken wire
14 x 12 x 12
Saatchi Collection, London

images, which they then render by hand in paint on canvas. Griffin finds fascination with the imagery of the ephemera of electronic data (sonar scans, bar codes, and fax machine misfeeds) to find a new universal visual language. Fandra Chang layers photomechanical reproductions onto plastic sheets and aluminum panels to create interference patterns which seem to hum like video. Elesby is inspired as much by the Internet as by Pollock's field paintings as a structural model to describe contemporary space.

Disregarding hard classification between media or styles, these artists feel free to straddle categories, to take creative risks by inhabiting hybrid territories. For example, Appel, Glenn Brown, Parazette, and Murakami mix representational painting with issues of abstraction. Photography is part of the production, or even the final product, in the work of Uta Barth, Brown, Chang, and Patterson, who use the camera as a tool to address issues of abstraction in painting. The idea of painting-as-object is part of the Modernist painting legacy, but 1970s Postminimal sculpture and Postmodernist installation art also played a key role in shaping the work of Apfelbaum, Elesby, Hodges, Callum Innes, Lukas, Marcaccio, and White. The traditional sculpture processes of casting or modeling are formative stages in the work of Mark D. Cole and Brown (fig. 9). One doesn't necessarily need to put paint on canvas to contribute to the dialogue about painting.

Challenging the stereotype of painters isolated in their garret studios, the artists of "Abstract Painting, Once Removed" are not removed from the wider issues and images of society. Calame collects the shapes of her pseudo-Expressionist drips and splashes from the streets of Los Angeles, Murakami translates imagery from Japanese *manga* (comic books) into painterly graphics, and Beatriz Milhazes blends both everyday and celebratory motifs from Rio de Janeiro and from the different regions and peoples of Brazil into her abstractions. With his explosions of flowers and shattered mirrors, Hodges explores the iconography of loss and, by extension, the tragedy of the AIDS epidemic.

With its fall from grace and rumors of its death, abstract painting's reputation and attractiveness became more than a little tarnished. It has taken a few decades, but recently artists have been feeling more comfortable, less threatened, to experiment with this medium; now the search for the quintessential painting has been abandoned, rigid stylistic categories have been jettisoned (along with divisions between media), and formal cues and content can come from a rich range of sources. When this century began, Modernist art was fueled by Utopian visions which are now long played out. The artists in "Abstract Painting, Once Removed" show that as we approach the next century, the possibilities that abstract painting offers today are as rich and rewarding as a century ago—and fan out in innumerable directions.

Notes

1. The term *abstract* implies an image extrapolated or transformed from the real world, while *non-objective* or *non-representational* painting comes from the artist without observation and has no basis in seeing. The distinction has not been maintained throughout Modernist painting's history, so in this text and the artist entries, *abstract* is meant to imply both works that "abstract from" reality and those that are completely non-objective from the start.

2. Thomas McEvilley, "Introduction: Painting's Exile and Return," in *The Exile's Return: Toward a Redefinition of Painting for the Post-Modern Era* (Cambridge: Cambridge University Press, 1993), p. 6.

3. In the past few years, numerous important exhibitions in museums and commercial galleries have focused on new approaches to abstract painting, including "Painting—The Extended Field," Rooseum Center for Contemporary Art, Malmö/Magasin 3 Stockholm Konsthall, Sweden; "Painting Outside Painting," The Corcoran Gallery of Art, Washington, D.C.; "Face-to-Face," MIT List Visual Arts Center, Cambridge, Massachusetts, and others. See Selected Readings, p. 109.

4. *Piendre non la chose mais l'effet qu'elle produit.*

5. Clement Greenberg, quoted in Arthur C. Danto, "Painting and the Pale of History: The Passing of the Pure," in *After the End of Art* (Princeton, N.J.: Princeton University Press, 1997), p. 106.

6. Clement Greenberg, "Modernist Painting," in *Modernism with a Vengence, 1957–1969 [The Collected Essays and Criticism, vol.4]*, edited by John O'Brian, (Chicago: University of Chicago Press, 1995), p. 85.

7. Clement Greenberg, "After Abstract Expressionism, 1962," quoted in Danto, "Painting and the Pale of History," p. 103.

8. Roy Lichtenstein, interview with John Coplans, *Artforum*, October 1963, reprinted in *Roy Lichtenstein*, edited by John Coplans (New York: Praeger Publishers, 1972), p. 15. Milton Resnick, born 1917, was a first-generation Abstract Expressionist, and Michael Goldberg, born 1924, was part of the second generation; in the 1950s both painted large gestural works.

9. Paul Delaroche, quoted in "Painting and Photography," *International Center of Photography's Encyclopedia of Photography* (New York: Crown Publishers, 1984), p. 375.

10. See Raphael Rubinstein's account of various established and lesser-known artists' attempts to rethink painting from the 1920s to the 1980s, pp. 28–33.

11. Thomas McEvilley, "Seeking the Primal through Paint: The Monochrome Icon," in *The Exile's Return*, p. 20.

12. Ad Reinhardt, quoted in McEvilley, "Seeking the Primal through Paint," p. 44.

13. McEvilley, "Seeking the Primal through Paint," p. 47.

14. Ibid., p. 55.

15. Marcel Duchamp, quoted in Calvin Tomkins, *The World of Marcel Duchamp* (New York: Time Incorporated, 1966), pp. 8–9.

16. Uta Barth recently used billboard ink-jet technology to print seamless images 11 x 17 feet for the monumental lobby walls of the Museum of Contemporary Art, Chicago.

17. Written in 1936, this current university seminar classic was not popularized until 1963 in Germany; translated into English in 1968, it became widely read in universities and art schools in the late 1970s and 1980s.

18. Many artists who emerged in the 1980s, including David Salle, Troy Brauntuch, Tom Lawson, Jack Goldstein, Robert Longo, and Gretchen Bender, made "paintings" derived from photographs.

19. John Baldessari, statement in *John Baldessari* (Eindhoven: Stedelijk van Abbemuseum and Essen: Museum Folkwang, 1981), p. 6.

20. Ann Goldstein and Anne Rorimer, "Introduction," in *1965–1975: Reconsidering the Object of Art* (Los Angeles: The Museum of Contemporary Art, 1995), p. 14.

21. Of the artists in this exhibition, more than half have MFAs or have completed some graduate study.

22. John Baldessari, interview with Nancy Drew, in *John Baldessari: Work 1966–1980* (New York: The New Museum, 1981), p. 64.

23. Marcel Duchamp, quoted in Tomkins, p. 9.

24. Ironically (though no irony was intended), these are actually enlarged projections of Lichtenstein's own painted gestures, loaded brushstrokes of black Magma paint on the repellent surface of acetate. See John Coplans, "Chronology of Imagery and Art," in *Roy Lichtenstein*, p. 45.

25. As more exhibitions and publications travel outside Germany, they have had increasing influence on artists internationally. Younger European artists whose work has been shaped in part by these two figures include Philip Akkerman, Karen Kneffel, and Luc Tuymans.

26. Sherrie Levine, quoted in Lilly Wei, "Talking Abstract, Part Two," *Art in America*, December 1987, p. 114.

27. Dave Hickey, "Enter the Dragon: On the Vernacular of Beauty," *The Invisible Dragon: Four Essays on Beauty* (Los Angeles: The Foundation for Advanced Critical Studies, 1993), p. 12.

28. Arthur C. Danto, "Painting, Politics, and Post-Historical Art," in *After the End of Art* (Princeton: Princeton University Press, 1997), p. 148.

29. Ibid., p. 136.

30. Michael Darling, "Monique Prieto at ACME.," *Art issues.*, January/February 1996, p. 41.

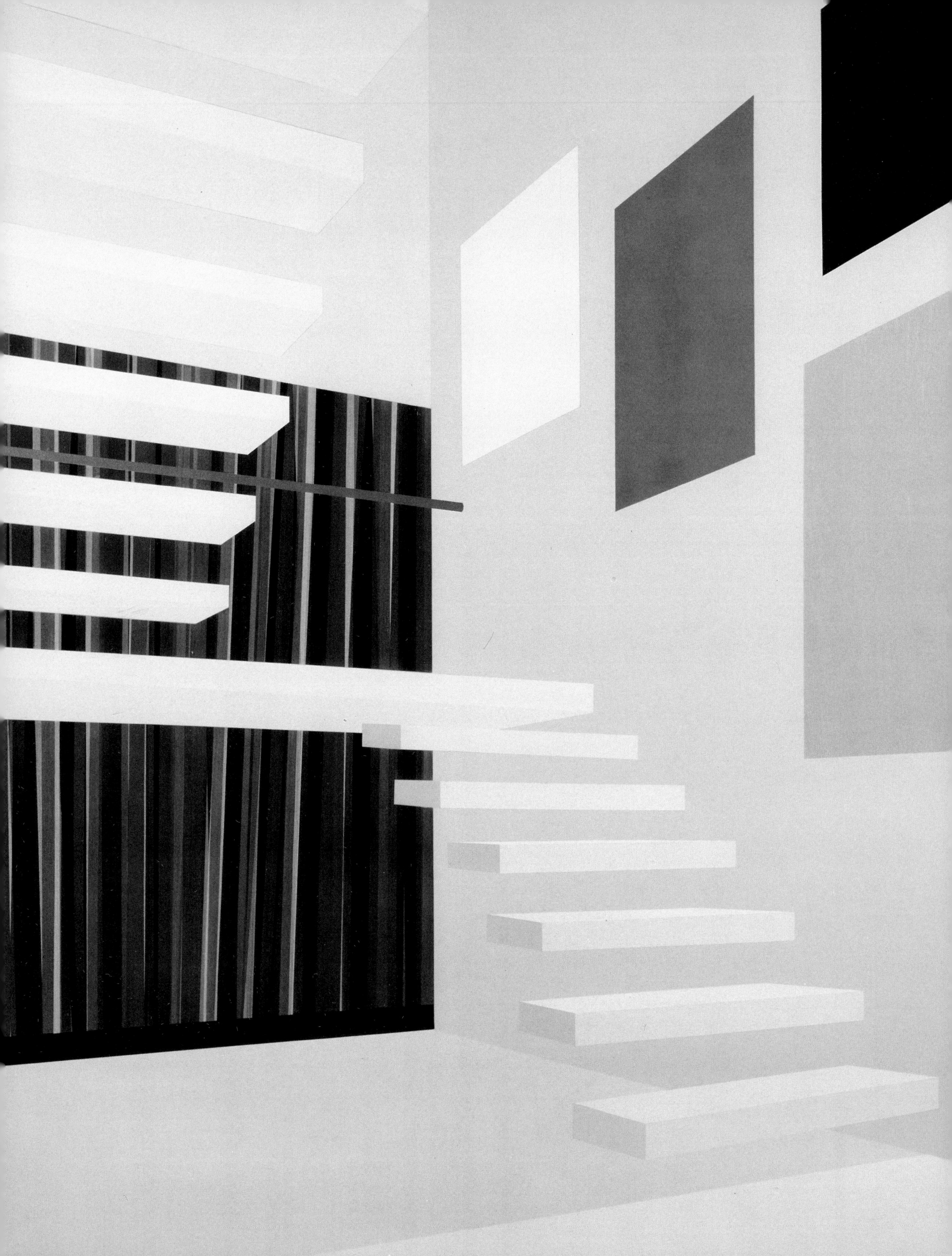

Once Removed from What?

David Pagel

The first question one might ask in surveying the diverse works that make up "Abstract Painting, Once Removed" is: Once removed from what?

As a Los Angeles-based critic—who's particularly sensitive to the ways in which New Yorkers talk about abstract paintings made out here as opposed to those made back there—I immediately answered this question geographically: "Abstract Painting, Once Removed from New York." Adding this prepositional phrase to the show's title accounts for the geographic distribution of the twenty-one artists in the exhibition, only four of whom live in the New York area (Polly Apfelbaum, Jim Hodges, Fabian Marcaccio, and Scott Richter). By featuring seven artists currently residing in Los Angeles (Kevin Appel, Uta Barth, Ingrid Calame, Fandra Chang, Sally Elesby, Monique Prieto, and Pae White), *Abstract Painting, Once Removed* is, to my knowledge, the first U.S. museum survey of contemporary abstraction in which artists who made their reputations in L.A. outnumber those who did so in New York. It is certainly the first show of its type in which as many artists reside in Texas (Mark D. Cole, Jeff Elrod, Tad Griffin, and Aaron Parazette) as in the environs of New York. The rest of the roster includes two painters from London (Glenn Brown and Richard Patterson), as well as one each from Edinburgh (Callum Innes), Tokyo (Takashi Murakami), Rio de Janeiro (Beatriz Milhazes), and Pennsylvania (Emil Lukas). It's significant (and refreshing) that none of the artists' works is called upon to represent its maker's national or cultural identity. Instead, viewers are invited to consider all of these works on equal footing with one another—at one remove, as it were, from the tendency of critics and curators to treat art forms from other places as signs of their environments, rather than as multilayered objects that shape their surroundings as much as they're shaped by them.

Since Manhattan is no longer the undisputed center of art-making, and since most of the critics, curators, editors, and educators working there continue to act as if it still were, it seems sensible to conclude that today any ambitious painter, working anywhere in the world (including New York), must feel that he or she is painting at one remove—outside the loop (of what used to be called the dominant discourse). What's happening now in studios all over the world generally goes against the grain of what has taken place so far in the postwar era—or at least is at odds with what has been written about that era of art. What distinguishes this generation from previous ones is that its painters are perfectly content to be working at one remove. It's commonly felt that passing through New York is no longer a necessary stage in an artist's career. If Los Angeles stands as an example, staying out of New York may be more fruitful since it often gives a developing artist more room to experiment on his or her own, testing results and exploring possibilities that would be ruled out in a more traditional rule-bound context.

At the same time, it must be emphasized that establishing an antagonistic relationship with the mystique and reputation of New York is not an essential component of contemporary painting either. The most exciting painters working today neither seek the establishment's approval, nor go out of their way to reject its protocols and assumptions. Instead, artists of this

10. Kevin Appel
***Landing*, 1998** (detail)
Oil and acrylic on canvas over panel
72 x 64 inches
The SunAmerica Collection, Los Angeles

11. Uta Barth
***Ground #52*, 1995**
Color photograph on panel
9¾ x 12 inches
Private Collection

generation simply carry on with their work as if the old center of the art world didn't really matter. Spite drives none of the works in this exhibition. After all, making compelling paintings is not a zero-sum game, and what happens in Manhattan does not have to be addressed for artists to pursue their own projects. Consequently, it seems that many of the best paintings being made today inhabit something like a parallel universe—one that is remarkably similar to New York's often provincial art world but fundamentally different in every detail. One of the most startling characteristics of this universe is that works thriving in one locale are often invisible or incomprehensible in another. To take Los Angeles as an example again, no matter how ambitious or original a particular work from here may be, when shown in New York, it often barely registers as a blip on that city's critical radar screen. Usually, this says less about the art's merits than about New York's tightly focused (i.e., constrictive) frame of reference and the difficulty of breaking habits or seeing beyond established horizons.

Of course, contemporary painting is not only geographically removed from New York. It's also conceptually removed from many of the self-conscious strategies that have dominated the past decade, when institutionally affiliated arts professionals filled the vacuum created by the crash of the overheated international art market at the end of the 1980s. It's important to distinguish what's going on in abstract painting today (as indicated by this exhibition) from the once prevalent Postmodern notion of art-in-quotation-marks. The primary purpose of the latter's predominantly abstract works was to make grand (tongue in cheek) propositions, and then by means of a sly wink, knowing nudge, or ironic twist, let insiders know that such goals were ridiculously overblown, even dangerously authoritarian. This insistence on making a mockery of Modernism, first by turning the history of American abstraction into a simplistic cliché, and then by attacking this straw target, goes hand-in-hand with the idea that form and content are separable and that artists' intentions are easily translated to objects. It cynically treats the contemporary world as an incidental footnote to a vaunted history from which artists and viewers have become irredeemably alienated. This passive-aggressive approach to artmaking often prevails where a surfeit of historical precedents is available, but current works have no vital connection or living relation to precedents—and have a hard time coming to terms with that fact.

Although paintings based on this Postmodern strategy appear to be operating at one remove, it would be a mistake to think that they share much with the works in this exhibition. Too eager to close the gap between the past and the present by claiming a position of centrality for themselves, their willingness to be once removed is an empty pretense, based less on maturity and willful humility than on juvenile self-aggrandizement. These defensive painterly surrogates merely act as if all of history were a sham in order to be seen, themselves, as "historically important." Linked so closely to earlier works, they never risk being seen as inconsequential, being misunderstood, or being not seen at all. In that light, it's useful to append the show's title with another prepositional phrase: "Abstract Painting, Once Removed from Postmodern Quotation." By taking a step back from such glib historicism, the painters in this exhibition find themselves in the thick of things once again. Strange as it may seem, putting some distance back into art brings it more intensely into the present, where the here-and-now has a chance to measure up to the long ago and faraway.

Finally, the question "Once removed from what?" must be answered in terms of expressive intentions. "Abstract Painting, Once Removed from Self-Expression" situates the works in this exhibition far from the old-fashioned yet still prevalent idea that abstract painting is the perfect vehicle by which "creative" individuals spill their guts and tell their personal, angst-laden stories, whose unique pains and torments could not be conveyed by any other means. More than any other artform, abstract painting has been burdened with a history of misreadings, many of which put forth the hoary cliché that this art's primary purpose is to communicate one dysfunctional individual's interior life to another—as vividly, dramatically, and bombastically as possible. Rather than deriving a variety of social pleasures from a painting's forms and context, viewers beholden to this approach "read" paintings as authentic signs of another's psyche, which has been so traumatized by modern life that it cannot speak in less difficult, more conventional terms, but needs abstract painting to register its "uniqueness."

All of the works in "Abstract Painting, Once Removed" sidestep such sappy sentimentality. Preferring to pay more attention to the social spaces paintings actually occupy than to the psychological depths many viewers presume to read into their surfaces, they favor insistent superficiality. They cultivate a public that demands that art be regarded in terms of the effects it has on people who actually live in the world rather than merely read about it in books. With these works, speculation about particular gestures, flecks, and smears of paint never leads back to an originating consciousness. Instead, the activity of paying close attention to the peculiarities of each piece leads viewers beyond the shroud of privacy and into the world of shared social space, where arguments can be made openly and aggressively without compromises being made for personal "feelings." Throughout the show, cool detachment, intellectual rigor, and material veracity take precedence over urgent expressivity and inward-turning emotionalism. Paradoxically, keeping such overwrought theatrics at arm's length gives viewers more room to maneuver. It also accounts for the open-ended generosity of these restrained yet profoundly non-secretive works.

All three answers—removed from New York, removed from Postmodernism's smug historicism, and removed from self-expression—put a premium on distance. Contrary to expectations, distance in art is not the same as distance in life, where it provides a margin of safety, putting sufficient space between an object (or a person) and the rest of the world by creating a comfortable buffer zone. In contrast, "Abstract Painting, Once Removed" prioritizes the space between things in order to emphasize the *here* and *now* over the *there* and *then*. Whether measured spatially or temporally (i.e., geographically or historically), the distances implied by "once removed" are not vast, daunting, or impossible to traverse. In fact, they suggest only a slight degree of separation, one in which connections, echoes, similarities, and affinities play as important a role as do differences and distinctions. What distinguishes these works from their immediate predecessors is that they do not derive the bulk of their power or forcefulness from negating or criticizing previous works, recent styles, or current social practices. With this generation of abstract artists, one-dimensional oppositions such as this fade far into the background. Apposition, rather than opposition, is their modus operandi.

Until very recently, if an artist was a woman who also made abstract work, it was assumed that she was being ironic and that her art offered a critical commentary on the obvious macho problems posed by Minimalism, Abstract Expressionism, and other unfriendly styles from which women have been traditionally excluded. Because abstraction looked content-free, and also appeared to be easy (if you didn't look very carefully), it was often treated as an empty vessel into which impatient, well-meaning artists could insert whatever content they chose. Whether politically motivated or personally driven, such narrative-oriented abstractions almost always began with recent art historical masterpieces (the most popular being works by Jackson Pollock and Richard Serra, followed closely by Carl Andre and Donald Judd) to which the next generation appended a variety of self-conscious revisions, which were often called feminist. "Correcting" the mistakes of their forebears' apparently misanthropic works, they softened these works' hard edges, ameliorated their authoritarian natures, and generally shifted their emphasis from heavy industry to body-scaled domesticity. Viewers were thus subjugated to tedious lectures by artists eager to transform the present into a time to do penance for the sins of the past. Religion and reeducation dovetailed as the possibility that art—and the present—might hold something different was squeezed out of the picture. (Today it appears that such academic exercises were insufficiently feminist, and it remains to be seen whether they gave feminisim such a bad name that young artists will have nothing to do with it, at least until they put some distance between this episode and their own work.)

Over the past four or five years, some of the best abstract painting in Los Angeles has been made by women. With remarkable consistency, these young painters do not begin with art enshrined in major museums but with works that have been critically dismissed and, after enjoying their fifteen minutes of fame, now are consigned to basement storage bins (or are still on display in regional museums whose acquisition budgets were cut long ago). Rather than starting with recent art history's triumphant success stories, such artists as Calame, Prieto, and White (along with New Yorker Apfelbaum) start with recent art history's biggest failures and defeats. They make 1960s Color Field painting look interesting again, transforming Formalist Abstraction, which had been written off as Modernism's biggest dead end, into a fresh beginning. Filled with verve and vitality, the works by these women redeem a style of painting that was so far out of fashion that no one gave it serious consideration—at least not in public.

Calame's enamel-on-aluminum panels and monochromatic cartographies on vellum give Helen Frankenthaler's vacuous stain paintings an aggressive edginess in which the persistent amateurism of paint-by-number kits lurks not far in the background. Prieto's buoyant blobs of crisp color, stacked like odd architectural elements, highlight the gravity-defying lightness of Jules Olitski's early compositions by marrying their hovering forms to Tom Wesselmann's sexy Pop palette. And White's dazzling slabs of highly reflective Plexiglas infuse DeWain Valentine's giddy, candy-colored confections with diabolical intensity, transforming physically weighty (if conceptually lightweight) decorations into shimmering instances of blazing immateriality, whose hellishness is pointedly evoked by the double-edged title *The Inconsolable Wailing of the Damned*, 1994. For their part, Apfelbaum's installations of countless dots and splotches of color stained into elongated swatches of stretch velvet put Larry Poons' ellipses

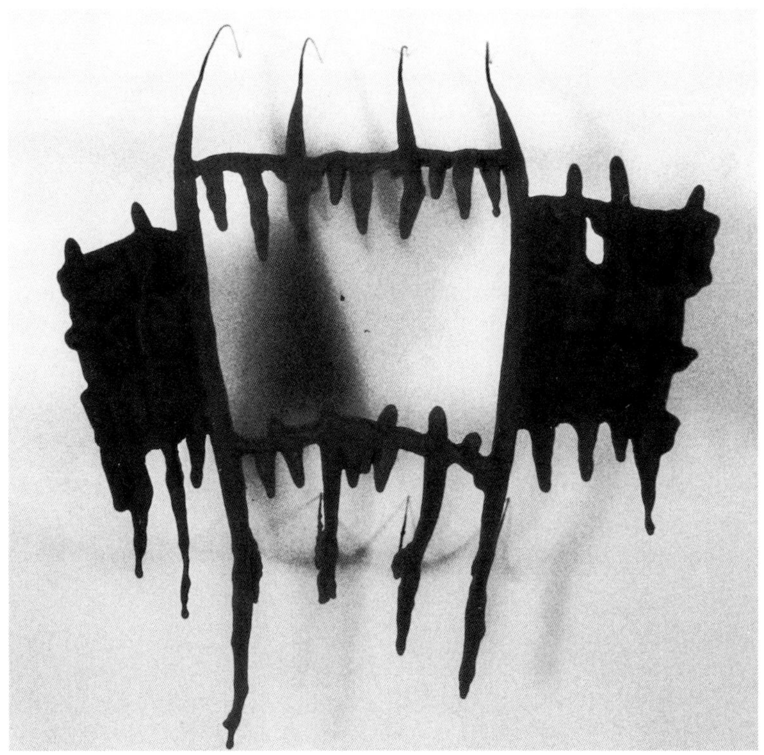

12. Sally Elesby
***Blue Painting Opened Up*, 1996**
Wire, colored glue, and oils
14 x 15 x 6 inches
Private Collection

underfoot, where they function like paintings that have undergone molecular melt-downs. To step into one of these installations is to imagine that you're in a big printed picture whose Benday dots are on acid (which is a lot different from being on acid yourself).

Likewise, Appel's subtly subversive interiors travel back to David Hockney's intentionally distorted rooms and Southern California backyards only to take viewers into the future, where computer-generated fictions are at once seductive and suffocating, both strangely alien and hauntingly familiar. In a related manner, Barth, Chang, and Elesby scrutinize human perceptual processes by interrogating abstract painting's links, respectively, to photography, to prints (both silkscreen and digital), and to sculpture. By foregrounding what transpires between our eyes and our minds whenever we look at the world, these three artists open the exploration of perception that began with the Light and Space movement to even more untraditional materials and newly developed processes, persuasively demonstrating that *what* something is made of isn't nearly as interesting as *how* it works. As a group, all of the artists in "Abstract Painting, Once Removed" belong to what may be the first generation since the late 1960s for whom the label "formalist" is not an outright insult. Having been off limits for several generations, formal exploration has become once again a rich—and open-ended—area of inquiry. Perhaps the most exciting aspect of painting today is that it is equally indebted to Pop Art's exploitation of mechanical reproduction and High Modernism's focus on the embodied effects of aesthetics.

This is doubly curious because Pop Art began as a critique of museum art—in the name of more accessible commercial exchanges unsanctioned by highbrow institutions. It took about ten years (from the early 1960s to the early 1970s) for Pop to be transformed from a democratic indictment of elitism into an elitist critique of popular forms—all in the name of Marxist academics (whose tenure at prestigious institutions made their endorsements attractive to museums, which sought to distinguish their programs from the commercial world). Today, after both of these tendencies have run their course, the techniques and procedures of each run together in works that cannot be accounted for by either. For those who have been in power, this is undoubtedly bad news. But for those of us whose interests have not been served by the status quo, what could be better?

The Life and Afterlife of Painting: A Descriptive Chronology of Six Decades (1920–1980)

Raphael Rubinstein

The following chronology is not meant to be an exhaustive account of its subject, nor is it an attempt to simply ferret out historical precedents for today's innovations in abstraction. Instead, the aim is to suggest that abstract painting has always been a fluid category, a point of perennial departure, rather than an article of aesthetic orthodoxy.[†] Ironically, the most oblique of all the entries may be the first one, Man Ray's *Dust Breeding*. This 1920 photograph might seem distant from the realm of abstract painting, but it raises a number of issues that resonate in the work of many contemporary artists. With his glass diagram of the "bachelor-machine" universe, Duchamp struck off at a tangent from painting, and by photographing the *Large Glass* in its dust-covered, horizontal state, Man Ray broached the notion of "objecthood" decades before the advent of Minimalism. Here, then, in one seventy-eight-year-old image, painting is positioned in relation to photography and horizontality—two issues that resonate throughout "Abstract Painting, Once Removed."

In putting together this chronology, I wanted to make room for artists not usually included in the Modernist canon. These range from a forgotten figure of the 1940s American scene, Thomas Wilfred, to overlooked Europeans such as Giuseppe Pinot-Gallizio, Jean-Michel Sanejouand, and Patrick Saytour. As T. S. Eliot long ago pointed out, the aesthetic reality of any given moment will affect how the past is seen; the changing nature of artistic production impels us to keep revising our understanding of art history. Another of my concerns, evident toward the end of this chronology, is to recall the 1970s work of American painters such as David Reed and Jack Whitten, whose early achievements have been occluded by the long shadow of Gerhard Richter. It also seemed important to reexamine, albeit glancingly, the 1970s work of artists such as Judy Pfaff and Richard Jackson, whose extrapolations of painting today seem more relevant than ever.

† My sources for this chronology are too many to credit individually, but I would like to mention two especially useful volumes: Bruce Altshuler's *The Avant-Garde in Exhibition* (1994) and Kristine Stiles and Peter Selz's *Theories and Documents of Contemporary Art* (1996).

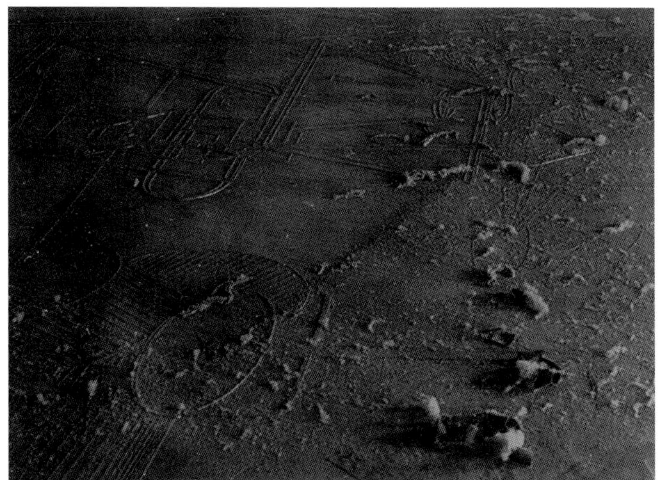

13. Man Ray

***1920*—Man Ray** photographs a section of the still unfinished *The Bride Stripped Bare by Her Bachelors, Even,* which Marcel Duchamp has been working on since 1915. Duchamp's paint-on-glass experiment has been lying on trestles for three months and is covered with dust particles, hence the title of Man Ray's photograph, *Dust Breeding* (fig. 13).

***1933*—Kurt Schwitters**, collagist extraordinaire, completes *Der Merzbau*, a walk-in installation of irregular planes and forms on which he has been working for thirteen years.

***1946*—Marcel Duchamp** inserts *Paysage fautif* [*Faulty Landscapes*] (inscribed "For the sculptress Maria [Martins]") into one of the "deluxe" copies of his *Boîte* edition, the *Boîte-en-valise*. The picture's fluid biomorphic shape has been "painted" onto a ground of black satin with ejaculated semen, presumably the artist's own.

***1946*—Jean Dubuffet** invents a medium he calls *haute pâte* [high paste], a mortarlike compound of paint, sand, and tar to which he sometimes adds pebbles, glass, and string. The year before he has declared, "All you need is mud, nothing but a single monochrome mud, if you really want to paint, and not just color some silk neckerchiefs." In 1953, he will begin to use butterfly wings in collages. Throughout the decade, he will use various debris and organic material in his paintings, including dried leaves, papier mâché, and aluminum foil.

***1949*—Lucio Fontana**, who throughout the 1930s and 1940s has been a sculptor, makes his first paintings: monochrome canvases that he perforates multiple times to create loose patterns. For the rest of his life, Fontana will develop this idea in a series titled Concetto spaziale [Spatial Concept], slashing and puncturing the canvas, studding it with colored stones and glitter, and painting biomorphic shapes on it.

***1950*—Alberto Burri**, who made his first burlap-sack painting the year before, grows mold on canvas for his Muffe [Mold] series. He also begins using tar, sewing together burlap and other kinds of rough cloth, and adding glue, pieces of broken pottery, roughly patched tears and holes, and irregular armatures that warp the surface of the painting.

1920 — 1954

***1935*—Marcel Duchamp** creates *Rotorelief*, an edition of multiple sets of colored cardboard discs designed to be placed on a revolving gramophone. At a certain speed, an illusion of depth is created by the spiral lines on each disc.

***1941*—Thomas Wilfred** makes *Vertical Sequence, Op. 137*. As in subsequent works by this Danish-born American artist who died in 1968, several of them in the collection of The Museum of Modern Art, New York, *Vertical Sequence* consists of colored electric lights projected onto a translucent screen. The changing abstract projections of *Vertical Sequence* are calibrated to run in fifty-hour cycles.

***1947*—**"I believe the easel picture to be a dying form . . . ," writes **Jackson Pollock** in a Guggenheim application.

***1949*—Raymond Hains** and **Jacques de la Villeglé**, who will later participate in the Nouveau Realisme movement, collaborate to create *Ach Alma Manetro*, a long, narrow section of ripped and torn posters that they have salvaged from a Parisian wall (fig. 14). The title is derived from typographical fragments visible in the work.

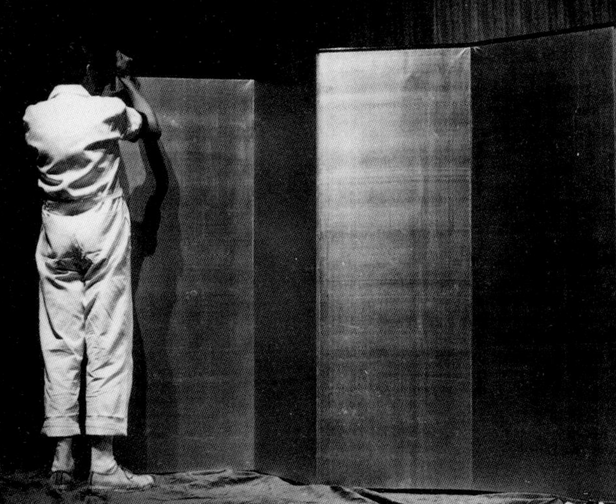

15. Robert Rauschenberg

***1954*—Robert Rauschenberg** produces his first Combine painting in which everyday objects are attached to densely painted, vividly colored supports to create a fusion of three-dimensional sculpture and two-dimensional painting. The series will go on to include the early, predominantly red works such as *Minutiae*, 1954, the well-known *Bed*, 1955, and *Monogram*, 1955–59, and it will culminate with *Gold Standard*, 1964, a freestanding six-panel work that the artist will create in public during a 1964 performance in Tokyo called "Twenty Questions to Bob Rauschenberg" (fig. 15).

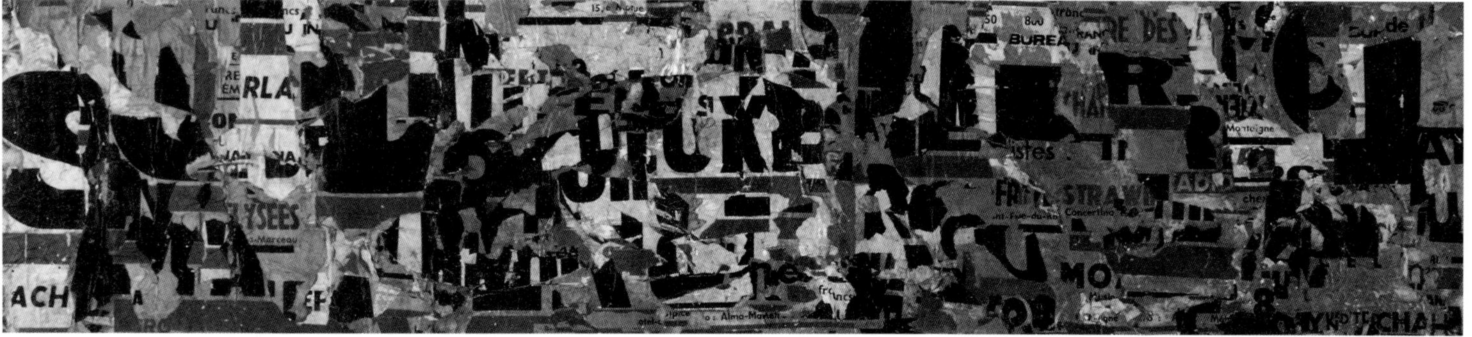

14. Raymond Hains and Jacques de la Villeglé

1954—Italian painter **Mimmo Rotella** abandons brush and canvas. Using a technique he terms *décollage*, he begins to make paintinglike objects from the torn posters he finds around the Piazza del Popolo in Rome.

1955—For the first exhibition of the avant-garde Japanese group Gutai, one of its twenty-three members, **Kazuo Shiraga**, creates a work partly inspired by Pollock's paintings: eliminating actual object-making from "action painting," Shiraga thrashes around in a ton of wet clay for twenty minutes. The following year, he will have himself suspended from a rope in order to make a painting with his feet. At an outdoor exhibition, another Gutai participant, **Shozo Shimamoto**, will suspend a large piece of red plastic in some trees and splatter it with paint fired from a homemade cannon. In 1957, **Akira Kanayama** will make a mural-size painting by attaching a can of paint to a remote-controlled model car and directing it to disperse drips around a large canvas laid out on the floor.

1956—**Burri** makes his first Combustione works: canvases covered with burned and melted plastic.

1959—"A pair of socks is no less suitable to make a painting with than wood, nails, turpentine, oil, and fabric," declares **Rauschenberg.**

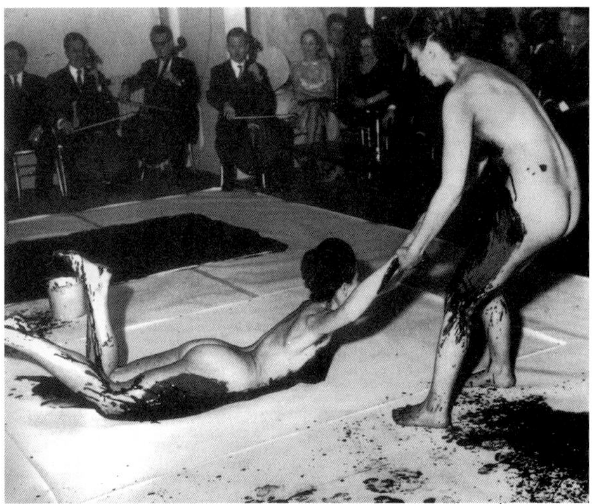

17. Yves Klein

1960—**Yves Klein** mounts his performance *"Anthropométries de l'Epoque Bleue"* in Paris. Before a stylish crowd, he directs three naked women to cover their bodies with blue paint and then to press against and slide along sheets of paper arrayed on the floor and walls (fig. 17). While this is happening, an ensemble of violins, cellos, and voices repeatedly plays Klein's twenty-minute, one-note "Symphonie monotone."

1962—**Giuseppe Pinot-Gallizio** creates *La notte cieca [The Blind Night]*. Trained as a chemist and subsequently making his living as a pharmacist in an out-of-the-way town in Northern Italy, Pinot-Gallizio discovered his calling late in life. In his fifties, he invented what he called "industrial painting," producing long rolls of quasi-abstract canvas through a combination of printed and hand-painted motifs. He also painted a number of dark abstract canvases designed to completely cover the walls, ceiling, and floor of a gallery where viewers were invited to enter, treading over a large section of the painting as if it were carpet (*La caverna dell'antimateria*, 1959, at the Galleria Martano, Turin, and the Galerie René Drouin, Paris).

His masterpiece, however, which will find a home in the collection of the Georges Pompidou Center, Paris, is *La notte cieca*, a roughly 7 x 32-foot canvas that the artist paints while blindfolded (fig. 19). During the three-day creation of the work, the canvas is laid out on the floor with cans of black, white, yellow, and red paint along its length. The hardest part, Pinot-Gallizio confides to a friend, is not looking at the work until it is finished. "It's worse than trying not to smoke," he exclaims.

1954 — 1963

1959—**Piero Manzoni** begins his Achromes, a series of works in various mediums that are generally white and have rectangular formats (fig. 16). The early works employ stretched canvas that has been altered to make horizontal creases across the white painting. A group of Achromes from 1961 will sport lavish manes of white fiberglass resembling feathers or wool.

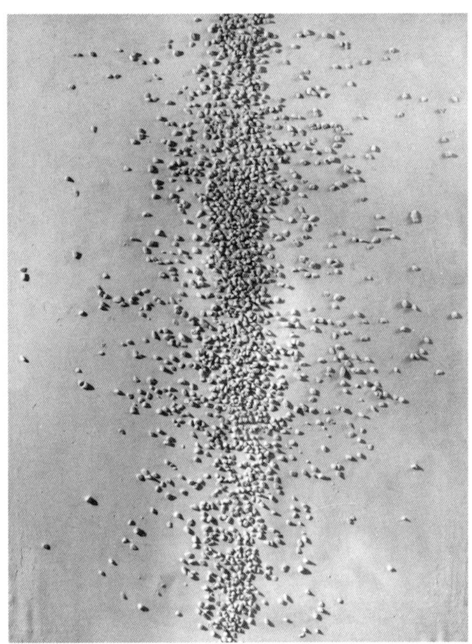

16. Piero Manzoni

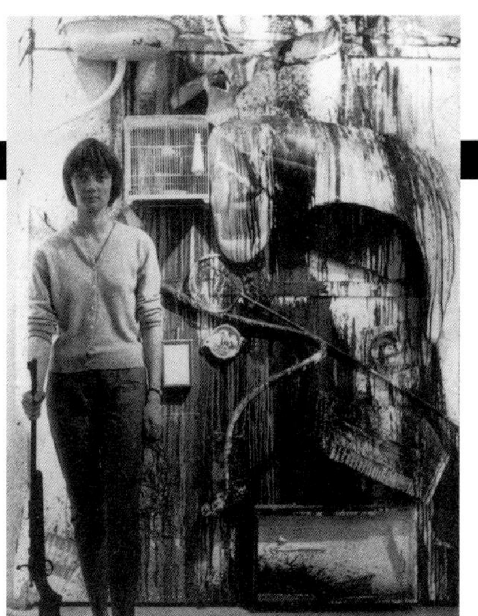

18. Niki de Saint Phalle

1960—**Niki de Saint Phalle** creates her first Tir, an assemblage to which balloons of paint are attached. The artist, or an invited surrogate, shoots at the balloons with a rifle. When they are hit, the colored paint inside bursts out onto the previously white sculpture (fig. 18).

1961—"Pictures are no longer dungeons, where mind and body are shackled together, but mirrors whose powers affect man, streams freely pouring forth into space, not ebbing but flooding," writes **Otto Piene** in "Paths to Paradise."

1960–61—German artist **Günter Uecker** stretches canvases over wooden boards and shoots arrows into them.

1962–63—**Arakawa** makes a pair of painting-sculpture hybrids that carries the descriptive title *Bottomless*. They are six-sided steel structures suspended from the ceiling. The tops and bottoms are open, allowing the viewer to poke his or her head into the center of the work. On one side is a mirror, on another is an abstract acrylic painting, on another is clothing that has been stretched out and flattened, and on another is steel mesh. In 1963, with his collaborator **Madeleine Gins**, Arakawa begins the series Mechanism of Meaning. This central monument of Conceptual Painting consists of dozens of 96 x 68-inch canvases that use abstract forms, stenciled text, and everyday objects to exhaustively explore the nature of visual signification. **Arakawa/Gins** will complete Mechanism of Meaning in 1973.

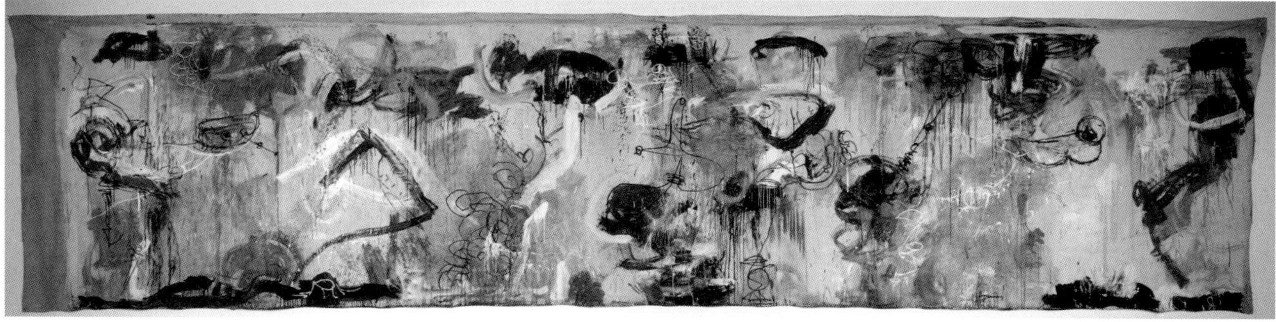

19. Guiseppe Pinot-Gallizio

1964—As part of his project of exploring abstraction through readymades, French artist **Jean-Michel Sanejouand** leaves untouched a roughly 5 x 4-foot sheet of linoleum with a dense pattern of colored flecks and spots. The title, *Linoleum Pointilliste*, evokes the art-historical echoes of its composition. The same year Sanejouand begins a series of monochrome canvases covered with wire mesh. In another 1964 work, the artist stretches striped awning fabric over a conventional painting stretcher and screws two wheels to the bottom edge of the painting, allowing it to be easily moved.

1964—**Richard Artschwager**, who has been using the paper-composite material Celotex as a painting support because it gives his work a photographic graining and blurring, makes *Triptych II*, a sculptural object that evokes the history of painting. Measuring nearly four feet high and eight feet wide, the work consists of three panels of wood-grain Formica that are hinged together in imitation of a Renaissance altarpiece.

1965—**Roy Lichtenstein** takes aim at the pieties of Abstract Expressionism with his Brushstroke paintings such as *Little Big Painting* in which scaled-up cartoonish images of isolated or overlapping brushstrokes are shown in a field of Benday dots (fig. 20).

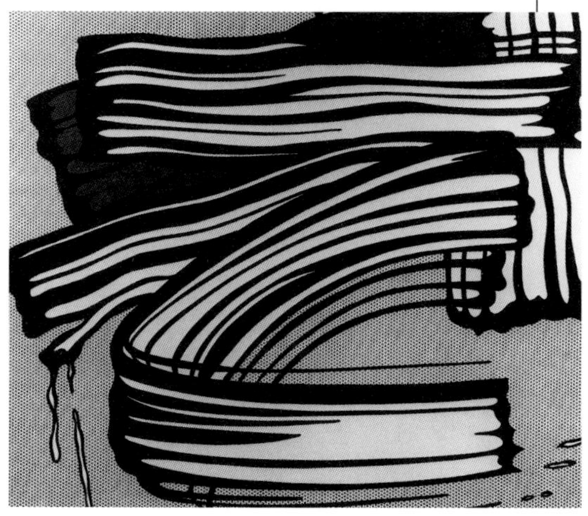

20. Roy Lichtenstein

1965—"Half or more of the best new work in the last few years has been neither painting nor sculpture," writes **Donald Judd** in "Specific Objects," *Arts Yearbook* 8.

1965—"If painting is too much for you now, fuck it—quit. If drawing gives some pleasure—some satisfaction, do it—go ahead. It might also lead to a way other than painting, or at least painting in oil," writes **Eva Hesse** in a February 5 diary entry.

1966—Invited by a Tokyo newspaper to create a "sky painting," **Sam Francis** hires five helicopters to release trails of colored smoke—blue, magenta, yellow, red, and white—above Tokyo Bay. In 1967, at the Japanese ski resort of Naibara, Francis will have skiers carrying smoke canisters create an ephemeral painting on the side of a mountain. A few years later, he will conceive of a plan that involves sending rockets into the stratosphere where they would release ionized compounds to create a visual display visible for thousands of miles. Francis will submit the project to NASA, which will balk at the project's estimated $1 million price tag.

1967—**Patrick Saytour**, a member of the French Supports/Surfaces group, makes a series of works titled Brulages. Each consists of a wide strip of commercially produced floral fabric that has been methodically singed or burned. The darkened spots or charred holes in the cloth form a pattern that closely echoes and sometimes partially obliterates the printed design. For exhibitions, the Brulages will be attached at their top edges to the wall and left to hang free like vertical scrolls.

1964 — 1968

1968—**Sigmar Polke** adorns a 59 x 49-inch canvas with a variety of whitish gestures and lines and a purple splatter against a black background. Around the edges of the black ground is a thin white border, slightly wider along the bottom, which gives the entire painting the look of an art postcard. The mocking title of this generic abstract painting is written along the bottom margin: *Moderne Kunst* [*Modern Art*].

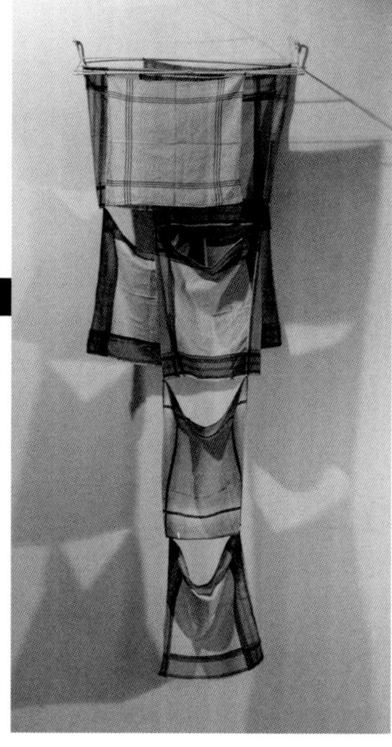

21. Noël Dolla

1968—**Noël Dolla,** another participant in Supports/Surfaces, creates *Structure à la tente d'indien* by hanging on a multipronged towel rack, attached to the wall, several pieces of cloth, each of which he has stained partly or wholly with color (fig. 21). The cloths range in nature from dish towels to a scarf with a gaudy pattern. *Etendoir aux mouchoirs*, another work from the same year, features ten handkerchiefs, partially dyed yellow and pink, again suspended from a store-bought rack. The handkerchiefs are sewn together to form two strips of unequal length, each of which hangs free in space. Pursuing what might be called "painting by other means," Dolla's flimsy, quotidian inventions sneak up on the heritage of artists such as Vladimir Tatlin, Barnett Newman, and Morris Louis.

***1968*—Walter Redinger**, a Canadian artist based in London, Ontario, makes *Spermatogenesis Study*, a white cast-fiberglass wall relief in which a tonguelike form droops down from a rectangular support. The support suggests a cast taken from a thick stretched canvas. Positioned somewhere between painting and sculpture, the oozing monochrome relief carries an erotic charge tinged with malignancy.

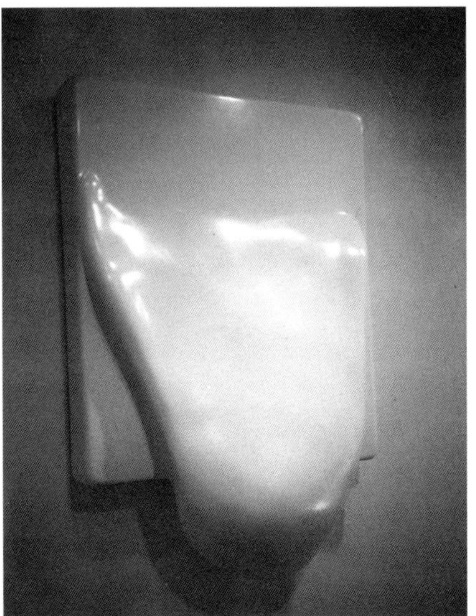

22. Walter Redinger

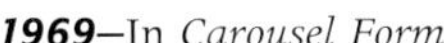

***1969*—**In *Carousel Form II*, **Sam Gilliam** suspends his large, vividly stained and splattered canvases from the ceiling, attached to wires at several points along their length. The paintings are arranged in a series of graceful swags and peaks, forms that Gilliam will continue to explore.

***1970*—James Rosenquist**, known chiefly for his syntactically fractured Pop paintings, makes *Horizon, Home Sweet Home*, an unconventional installation of abstract elements. The work consists of twenty-eight tall, narrow panels (half of them painted in monochrome hues and half covered with reflecting silver mylar) that are surrounded with billowing white clouds pouring out of a dry ice machine.

***1970*—David Deutsch** begins making works described by Fidel Danieli in *Contemporary Artists* (1977) as follows: "sheets of plastic are stapled onto the wall, draped into folded garments; dye is then injected into the space between the plastic and the wall. The plastic is removed. The dye dries as runs of paint and shapes formed into fold 'impressions.'"

***1974*—Jack Whitten** shows a group of paintings at the Whitney Museum of American Art, works created by pulling a heavy scraper across wet oil paint. The colored striations and interrupting marks created by objects strewn around the canvas produce a blurred, strangely photographic, yet resolutely abstract image.

***1975*—David Reed** has his first solo show (Susan Caldwell Gallery, New York) featuring the Stroke paintings, tall canvases in which stacks of similar black or red brushstrokes combine process and image, intention and accident (fig. 24). Reviewing the show for *Art in America*, Peter Schjeldahl observes, "The stroke—the hand-made mark—is as much the hero of these pictures as of a de Kooning, but Reed abstracts it through repetition, making no special claims for it.

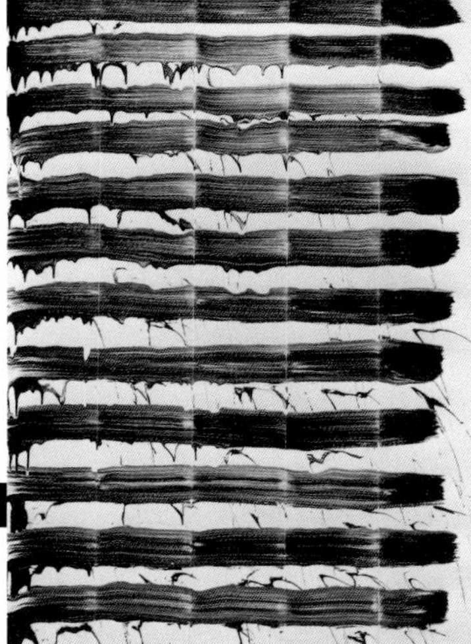

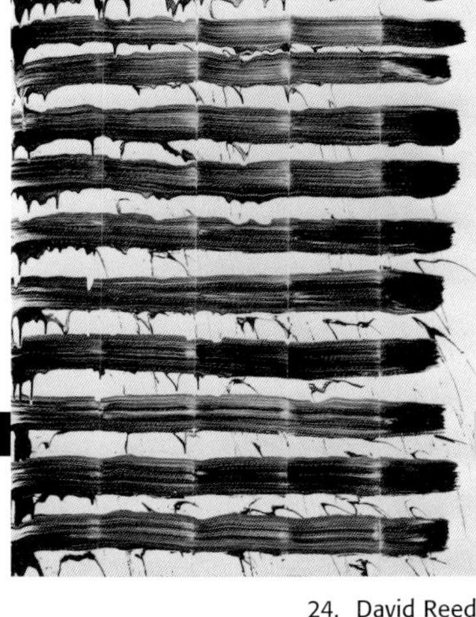

24. David Reed

1968 **1977**

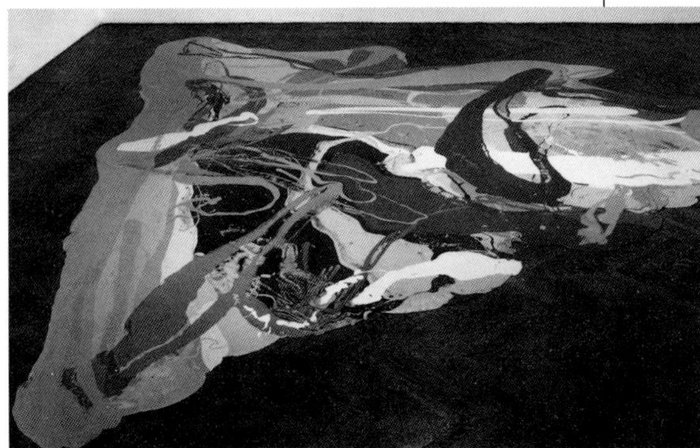

23. Lynda Benglis

***1969*—Lynda Benglis** makes a number of poured latex paintings including *Contraband* and *Bounce* (Bykert Gallery, New York) (fig. 23). The pigmented liquid latex, which includes fluorescent and day-glo colors, spreads out like a stretch of polychrome river. Following the latex pours, Benglis will make extended wall reliefs by spreading polyurethane foam over armatures. When the foam has dried, the armatures are removed, leaving shapes that a later critic (Carter Ratcliff) says, ". . .whispered bat wings, Spanish moss dripping from branches, and slithery reptilian creatures."

***1973*—Miriam Schapiro** begins to combine fabric collage and acrylic paint to make abstract compositions (femmages) that address feminist issues. In 1976, she will exhibit *Anatomy of a Kimono*, a fifty-foot-wide work made with this technique.

***1974*—Günter Uecker**, who since the 1950s has been centered on driving nails into paintinglike supports, makes two works, *Skin Tumor* and *Nail Corner*. Unprimed canvas is stretched over wood and an array of long nails are partly driven into the upper right corner of the stretched canvas, creating a porcupinelike growth that seems to be erupting from the frame. Also in 1974, Uecker constructs his *Painting Machine* in which long cords hanging from a rod near the ceiling are dragged back and forth through a three-foot wide and nearly ten-foot long pile of white powdered pigment.

***1977*—Gerhard Richter** begins his Abstrakte Bilder series. From 1977 to 1980, these will consist of abstract paintings that are precise copies of Richter's small-scale sketches, giving the works the paradoxical status of being abstract images made with a representational method. After 1980, Richter will dispense with this copying method and create the Abstrakte Bilder works by more direct means (fig. 25). A couple of years later he will observe, "Everything made since Duchamp has been a readymade, even when hand-painted."

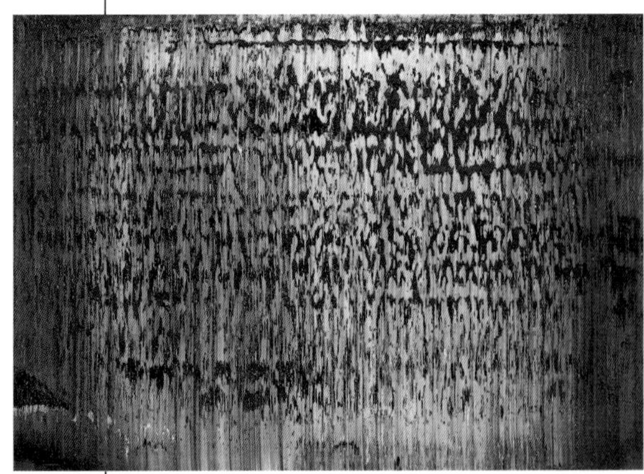

25. Gerhard Richter

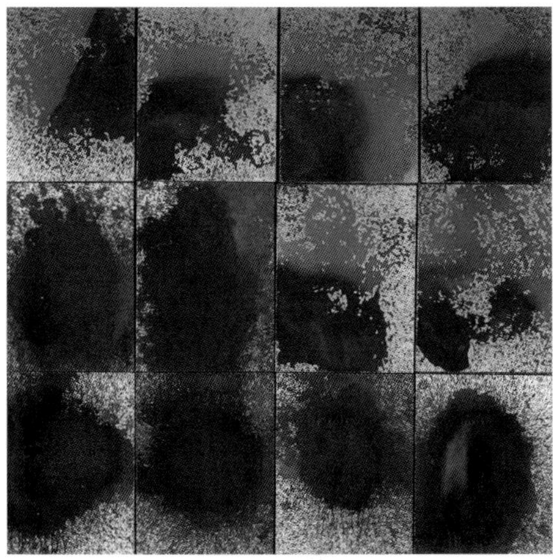

26. Andy Warhol

***1978*—Andy Warhol** makes the Oxidation series of paintings, canvases onto which the artist invites associates to urinate (fig. 26). Bronze or copper metallic paint added to the paintings interacts with the urine to create a variety of dribbles, blobs, and clouds. Works in the series reach mural-like dimensions as large as 9 x 27-feet.

1978—Bringing together aspects of process painting, installation, and performance, **Richard Jackson**'s untitled work at Rosamund Felsen Gallery in Los Angeles consists of a 30 x 19-foot diamond-shaped canvas placed on stilts of different heights (fig. 27). At the far end, the tilted canvas touches the ceiling, while closer to the entrance to the space, it reaches to the floor. To complete the work, paint is applied to a second large, rectangular canvas which, turned painted side down and still wet, is pushed across the diamond-shaped canvas, creating a wide smear of orange, yellow, green, and red paint.

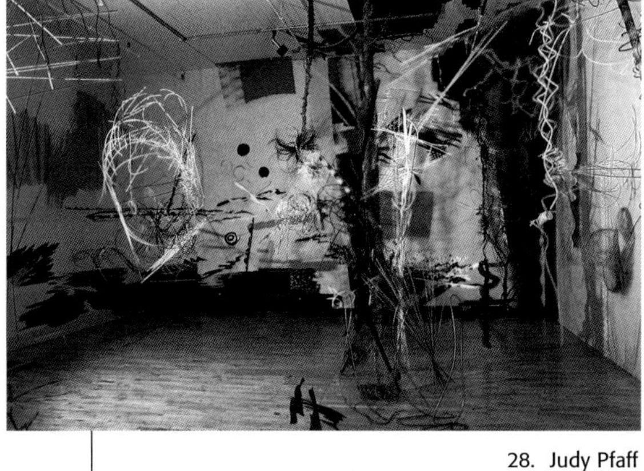

28. Judy Pfaff

1980—The **Judy Pfaff** installation *Deepwater,* at Holly Solomon Gallery, New York, seems to invite the viewer to step inside an abstract composition (fig. 28). The installation is bound by walls and ceiling painted with vivid fields and splotches of color and with errant lines and fragmentary patterns. Numerous clumps of colored plastic tubing and wires and an occasional tree branch or bundle of reeds are suspended from the ceiling, attached to the walls, or allowed to rest on the floor. Acknowledging Pfaff's debt to painting, *Art in America* reviewer Wade Saunders comments on the fact that *Deepwater* "is loaded with thousands of snap decisions and details, and [that Pfaff] makes ample use of the abstract painter's vocabulary of color and shape."

1978 — 1980

27. Richard Jackson

13. Man Ray
***Dust Breeding*, 1920/1964 edition**
Private Collection
©1999 Man Ray Trust/Artists Rights Society, NY/ADAGP, Paris

14. Raymond Hains and Jacques de la Villeglé
***Ach Alma Manetro*, 1949**
Collection Musée National d'Art Moderne, Paris

15. Robert Rauschenberg
***Gold Standard*, 1964**
Oil, paper, printed reproductions, clock, cardboard box, metal, fabric, wood, string, shoe, and Coca-Cola bottles on gold folding Japanese screen, with electric light, rope, and ceramic dog on bicycle seat and wire-mesh base
84¼ x 142 x 51 inches
Collection The Sogetsu Art Museum, Tokyo
© Robert Rauschenberg/Licensed by VAGA, New York, NY

16. Piero Manzoni
***Achrome*, 1962**
Pebbles on canvas
39⅜ x 31⅛ inches
Courtesy Archivio Opera Piero Manzoni
© Piero Manzoni/Licensed by VAGA, New York, NY

17. Yves Klein
***Anthropométries* performance, March 1960**
Courtesy Yves Klein Archives
©1999 Artists Rights Society (ARS), New York/ADAGP, Paris

18. Niki de Saint Phalle
***Tir de l'Ambassade Americaine*, June 20, 1961**
Wood, miscellaneous objects, plaster of Paris, and color
96½ x 26 x 8¾ inches
Collection of the artist
©1999 Artists Rights Society (ARS), New York/ADAGP, Paris

19. Guiseppe Pinot-Gallizio,
***La notte cieca [The Blind Night]*, 1962**
Collection Musée National d'Art Moderne, Paris

20. Roy Lichtenstein
***Little Big Painting*, 1965**
Oil and synthetic polymer on canvas
68 x 80 inches
Collection Whitney Museum of American Art; Purchase with funds from the Friends of the Whitney Museum of American Art
©Estate of Roy Lichtenstein

21. Noël Dolla
***Etendoir aux mouchoirs*, 1968**
Metal structure and 9 handkerchiefs
67 x 24¾ x 10⅝ inches
Courtesy Brownstone, Corréard & Cie, Paris
©1999 Artists Rights Society (ARS), New York/ADAGP, Paris

22. Walter Redinger
***Spermatogenesis Study*, 1968**
Paint on fiberglass
68 x 44 x 20 inches
Courtesy Mitchell Algus Gallery, New York

23. Lynda Benglis
***Bounce*, 1969**
Poured pigmented latex
161 x 188 inches
Collection Williams College Museum of Art; gift of Nancy and George Rosenfeld
© Lynda Benglis/Licensed by VAGA, New York, NY

24. David Reed
***#64*, 1974**
Oil on canvas
76 x 56 inches
Collection Goetz, Munich

25. Gerhard Richter
***830-2 Abstract Bild, Raps*, 1995**
Oil on linen
55⅛ x 78¾ inches
Courtesy the artist and Marian Goodman Gallery, New York

26. Andy Warhol
***Oxidation*, 1978**
Synthetic polymer paint and urine on canvas
48 x 49 inches
The Andy Warhol Museum, Pittsburgh; Founding Collection, Contribution The Andy Warhol Foundation for the Visual Arts, Inc.
©1999 Andy Warhol Foundation for the Visual Arts/ARS New York

27. Richard Jackson
Untitled, 1978
Acrylic on canvas and wood supports
Courtesy the artist

28. Judy Pfaff
***Deepwater*, 1980**
Mixed media
Courtesy Holly Solomon Gallery, New York

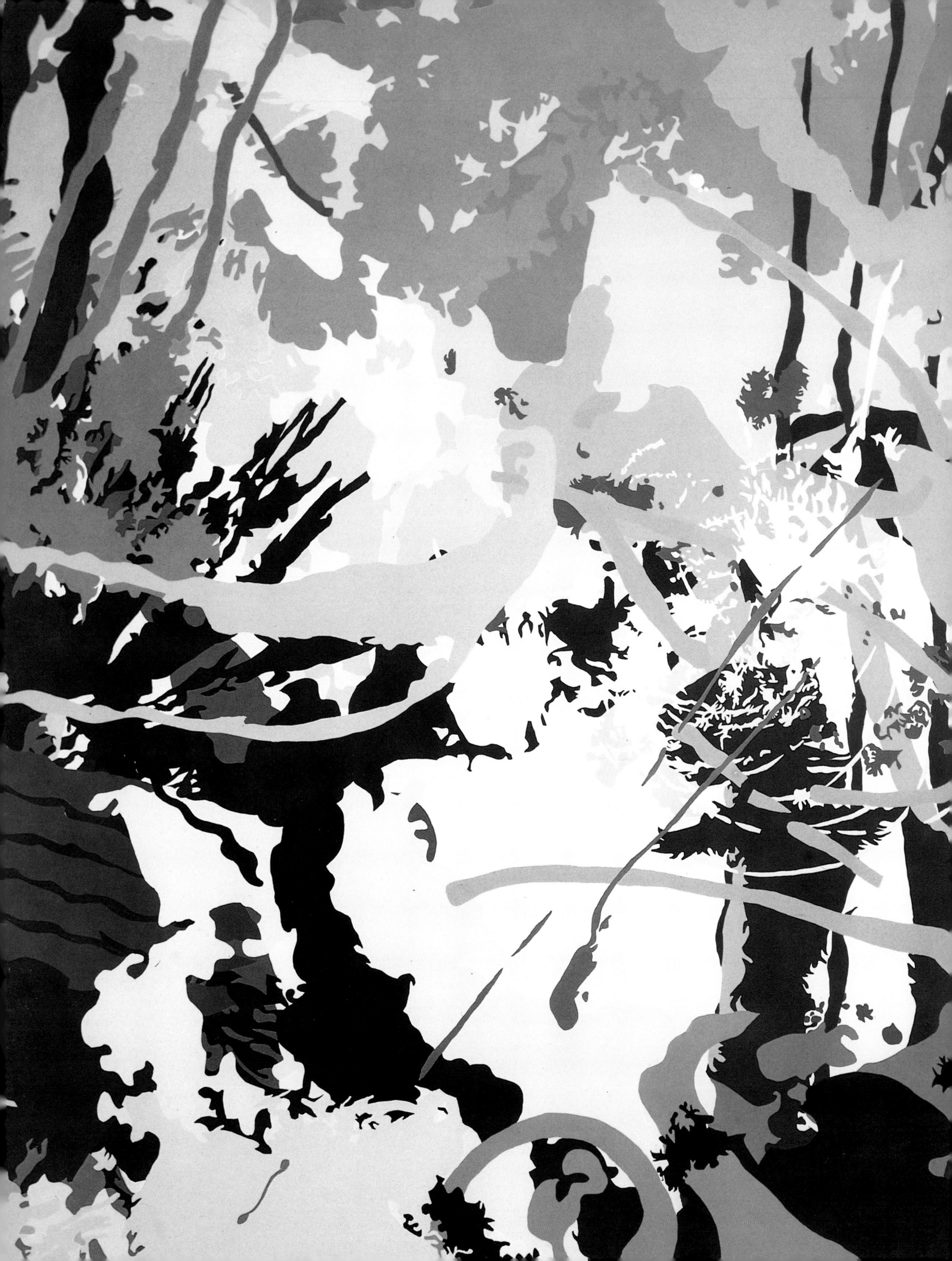

The Rise of Abstraction II

Peter Schjeldahl

Today the painting epoch of Abstraction II gathers ideas and energies, building through trial and error toward a climax that, I rashly predict, will occur around the centenary of Abstraction I.

Abstraction I began with Wassily Kandinsky, et al., a decade into our departing century. It was about purifications: pure essence or pure objectivity, mystical intuition or utopian enthusiasm, rationalization of form or mirror of the soul, hierarchy or anarchy—no matter, so long as the favored intoxicant came straight from some ineffable bottle. Abstraction I hurried to get to the bottom or to the end of things, and its alacrity caused refreshing breezes. Then, in the 1960s, Abstraction I attained the only form of purification that was ever truly available to it: more or less complete sterility.

Abstraction II uses the microbe-free culmination of Abstraction I as a petri dish in which things can grow: selected things, choice contaminants. Abstraction II kicks in after a spell—in the 1970s and 1980s—when dominant sorts of painting more or less threw the exhausted, hypersensitive medium of the modern picture open to the dirty air. Think of Philip Guston, Sigmar Polke, Susan Rothenberg, and David Salle—not Gerhard Richter, who is more a conceptual artist than a painter, though he paints like an angel. The virulence that raged immediately, because its agent had been the one most denied by Abstraction I, was figurational.

It figured, in more ways than one. A furtive secret of Abstraction I from its inception was that its vision quest was no more outside of figuration than Sri Lanka is outside of Asia. Abstraction I just posited special cases of the figurative, limiting its repertoire of forms to the mentally instrumental, like geometry, and the variously ambiguous, produced by arbitrary method, chance, or dreamy association. The crowning feats of Abstraction I—those of Piet Mondrian and Jackson Pollock—introduced systems of marking that are so far removed from normal figuration that they practically circle around to reinvent the figurative from scratch.

There is a sense in Mondrian of architectural or landscape motifs that are both departed from and arrived at by way of an austere code. The situation's encryption frees it of anecdotal features. We behold universal dramas of the horizontal, to which gravity tries to reduce everything, and the vertical, which defeats gravity. Asymmetries in Mondrian's compositions are so many risks of a diagonal—of something falling down—checked by fantastically precise adjustments. Mondrian expresses a universal condition of earthly existence, an *Ur* fact that we grasp with our brains and feel in our guts.

Pollock expresses another condition, that of painting itself: a flat thing, made of stuff. He blows open tacit conventions of every painting ever made. Like Mondrian, he rouses mind and body at once: the most ethereal reach of mentality and the most abject pitch of carnality. What I get from a good Pollock drip is roughly and inextricably (1) the music of the spheres and (2) a dog pissing on a wall. A marriage of extremes, my sense of Pollock

29. Ingrid Calame
***p-CHEEW-chtu-chtu,* 1998** (detail)
Enamel on aluminum
48 x 48 inches
Collection David Reed, New York

brackets the whole possible range of my perceptual experiences. It covers everything. No other art can be wedged in beside it.

After the definitive demonstrations of Mondrian and Pollock, Abstraction I subsisted for a while on piety, hope, and novelty—the triple package of, notably, Frank Stella, who hybridized the two masters in snazzy ways that proved less than overwhelmingly necessary. Meanwhile, the best (Ellsworth Kelly) and the sometimes entertaining worst (Op Art) modes of late Abstraction I frankly addressed abstract painting's function as the last word in secular spiritual ornament. That social use continues in force and exerts a steady and steadying tug on Abstraction II.

I note in passing an important transitional phase of abstract painting after the 1960s: the elegiac, whose knight errant is Brice Marden. Differently practiced by Agnes Martin and Blinky Palermo, among others, this response to the paralysis of Abstraction I poeticized a sense of being orphaned by the death of a parental tradition. It took the appropriate mood of drift as an opportunity to engage viewers in a poignantly lost here and now. Martin's work is like bodiless (gravity-free, outer space/inner space) Mondrian. Marden's nervously corporeal styles are like the eagle of a Pollock with its wings clipped.

The mourning period is over. Away with delicately toned hysterias. History is not only not over, it has reawakened after fever dreams of history. Anyone who does anything now bets on the future. Abstraction is dead. So is the idea that abstraction is dead. No longer ideological causes or independent values, abstract thought and aesthetics are as good as the jobs that they find to do. The jobs are many. First, at this early stage of Abstraction II, comes the imperative to bring abstraction down to equality with other human brainstorms and capacities. No more self-importance. No more fainting fits. In the twenty-first century, everyone and everything must show up for work.

Pragmatism rules. That which succeeds needs no theory. Theory without successful works is dead. The measure is human satisfaction. New art that is really new seeks an original comprehension of what people like. New abstract art seeks such knowledge abstractly, on a plane of predilections: conditions, habits. . . . As viewers of abstract painting, we are invited to be experimental agents of humanity, testing on ourselves certain propositions of how our species operates. This was true also of Abstraction I. Different now is a humbled attentiveness to what people actually and darkly are, not what they ideally and brightly ought to be.

Abstract painting addresses us at root levels of our sincerity: what we most cherish and respect in our respective sensations of being. Abstract painting begs admittance to our inner sanctums of thought and feeling, where we are used to being alone. It is asocial. It takes us away from each other, down into our personal engine rooms—where we may freshly recognize commonalities that predispose us to society. A social function of abstract painting, in the implied program of Abstraction II, is to affirm the coherence (or the manageable incoherence) of citizens' semi-detached minds. It whispers to us that we are not crazy, after all, and so may be fit to have a world together.

Of course, many people never doubt their own sanity, while others are insane. Abstract painting is not for everyone. Nor is it for everywhere. It depends on experience that is framed by highly articulated institutional and decorative conventions. It needs staging. This appalls those who were trained in avant-gardist dogmas of the 1970s, which upheld a principled hostility between art and anything smacking of a cultural status quo. Such hostile types happen to staff much of the art world's current infrastructure. I have heard more than one curator or scholar give vent to bitter incredulity or cynical disdain at painting's increasingly irresistible comeback.

But did they imagine that people would contentedly read wall texts forever? Human eyes are hungry and demanding organs that want exercise commensurate with their ability to discern and discriminate—given an emotional reward that justifies the effort. Intellectual movements of the last quarter century have attacked the cogency and even the morality of any such reward, declaring aesthetic pleasure regressive or elitist. Very well. We have heard out the critiques and will now see exactly how compelling they are in reality. We will do so with the work of painters who know the critical catechism, too, and have internalized its healthy quotient of skepticism. Our common interest is pleasure that doesn't insult our intelligence but isn't insulted by it, either.

I am familiar with only a few of the artists in this timely exhibition and so will not analyze individual achievements here. But it seems to me that all of them give instances of the petri dish cultivation that I take to define Abstraction II. In each case, something of the wide world—some vernacular tone or maverick sensibility—has flown in through the studio window and been caught in paint, where it propagates (see fig. 29). This is the reverse of so-called Postmodern appropriation. Instead of incorporating bits and pieces of received cultural debris in their art, these painters turn their art over wholesale to an inclusive sense of culture.

From the Renaissance until the 1960s, painting has symbolized the ultimate glory, the living end, of Western handiwork. This prejudice lent itself first to the pomposities and preciosities of modern art, then to the critical ridicule that humiliated them. Our new abstract painters seem humiliation-proof. They know that you cannot be knocked off a pedestal if you aren't on one. They paint not because painting is a big deal but because, despite everything, people want to look at paintings. They recover the bizarre human affinity for colored substance deliberately arrayed, not as an arrogant ceremonial function but as an inexhaustible, always potentially thrilling mystery.

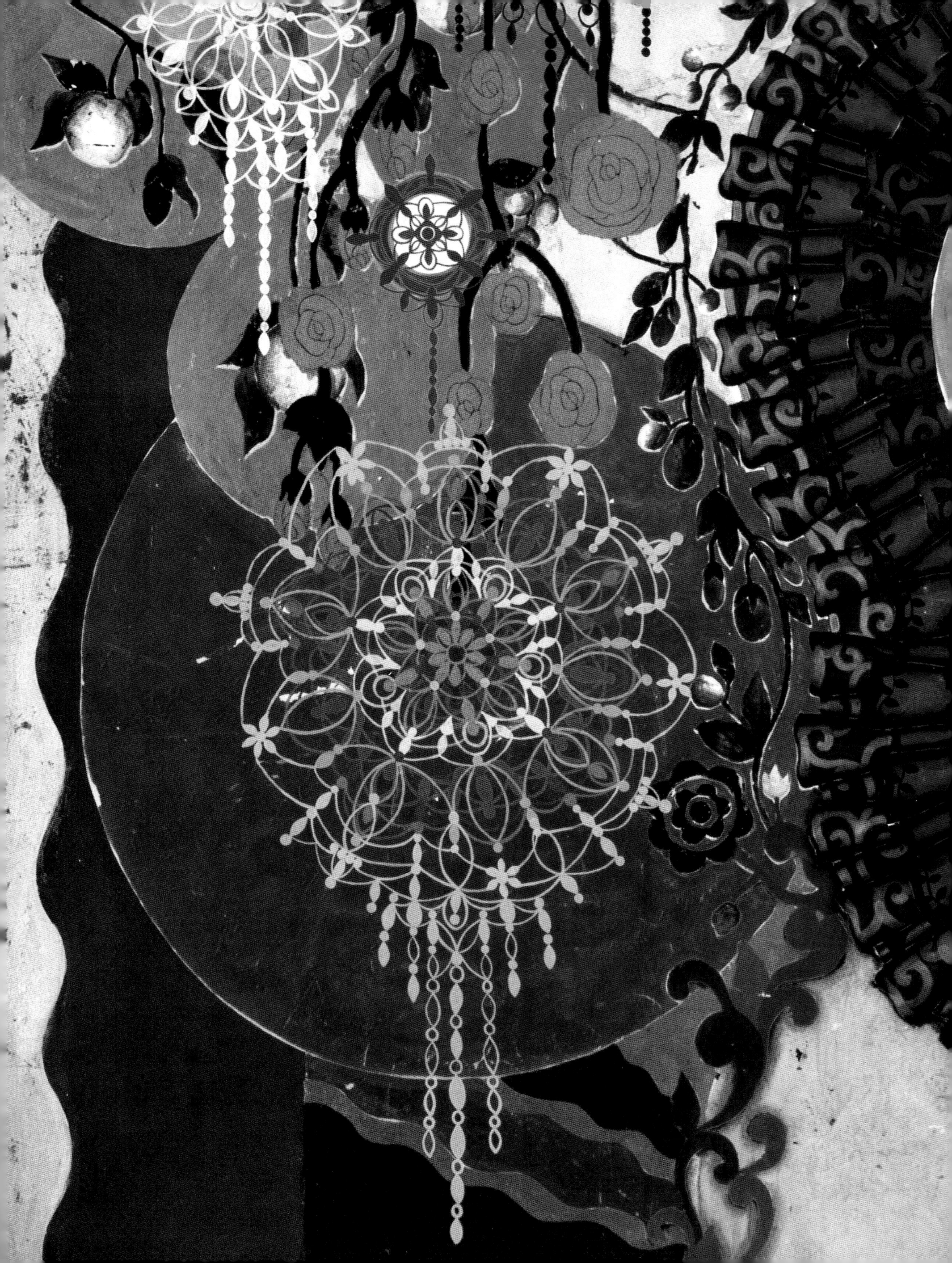

Catalogue Entries and Plates

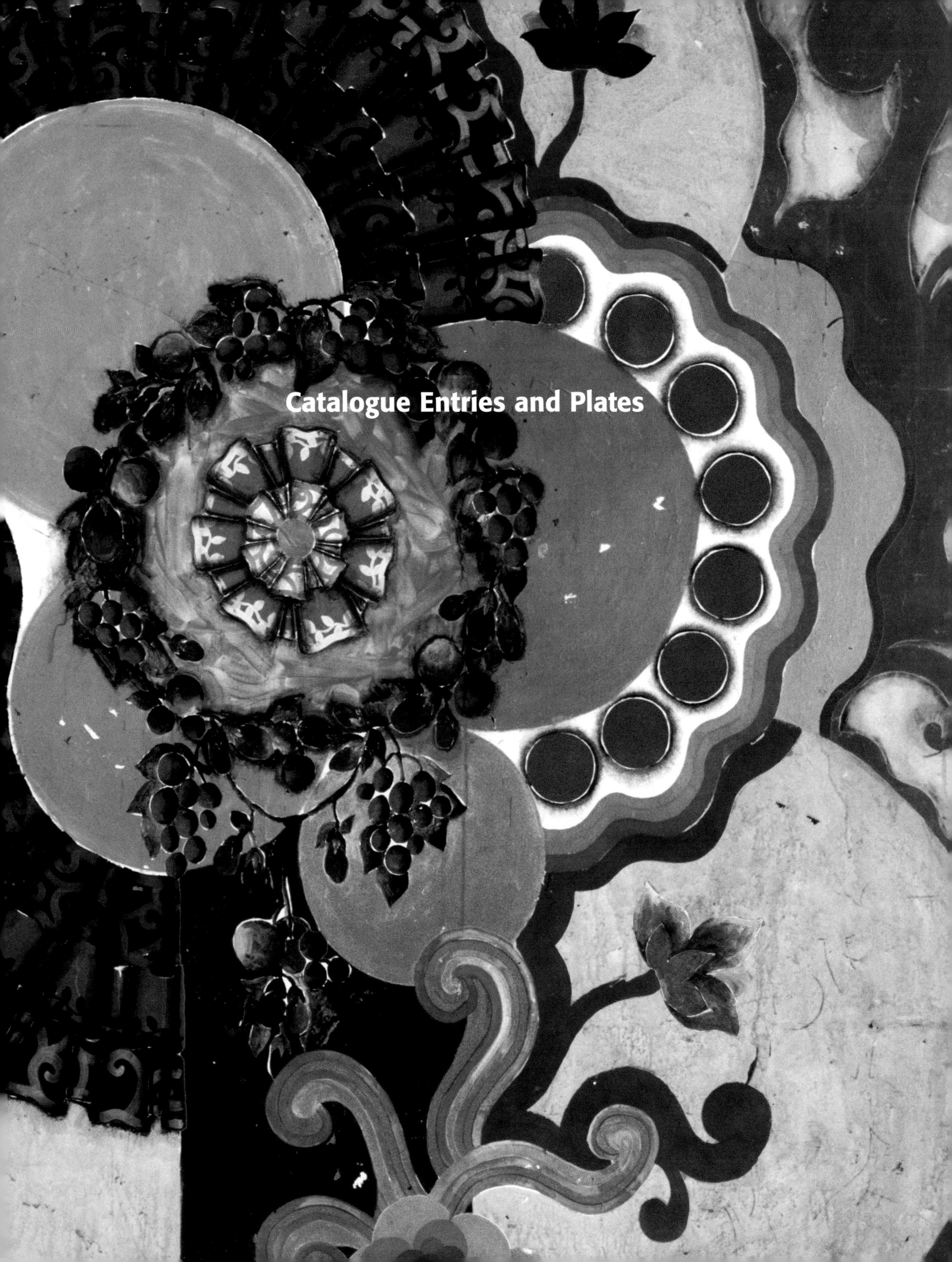

Catalogue of the Exhibition

Dimensions are given in inches, height preceding width preceding depth.

Polly Apfelbaum

***Split*, 1998**
Installation of dyed velvet
Dimensions variable
Courtesy D'Amelio Terras Gallery, New York

Kevin Appel

***Storage System on Two-Toned Wall*, 1997**
Oil and acrylic on canvas
36 x 30
Collection Dean Valentine, Beverly Hills, California

***Interior View (Spring)*, 1998**
Oil and acrylic on canvas over panel
82 x 112
Collection Ron and Ann Pizzuti, Columbus, Ohio

***Landing*, 1998**
Oil and acrylic on canvas over panel
72 x 64
The SunAmerica Collection, Los Angeles

Uta Barth

***Ground #32*, 1994**
Color photograph on panel
12 x 10½
Collection of Ellen Katzman, Los Angeles

***Ground #34*, 1994**
Color photograph on panel
17 x 15½
Collection Jeanne and Michael Klein, Houston

***Ground #47*, 1994**
Color photograph on panel
19½ x 21
Collection Sheridan Brown, Los Angeles

***Ground #43*, 1995**
Color photograph on panel
10½ x 11¼
Private Collection

***Ground #45*, 1995**
Color photograph on panel
27¾ x 34
Collection Dr. Roberta Smith, Pacific Palisades, California

***Ground #52*, 1995**
Color photograph on panel
9¾ x 12
Private Collection

Glenn Brown

***These Days*, 1994**
Plaster, acrylic and oil paint, and chicken wire
8 x 9½ x 8
Saatchi Collection, London

***You Never Touch My Skin in the Way You Did and You've Even Changed the Way You Kiss Me*, 1994**
Oil on canvas
60 x 48
Collection Walker Art Center, Minneapolis; Butler Family Fund, 1994

***Never Forever*, 1995**
Plaster, acrylic and oil paint, and chicken wire
14 x 12 x 12
Saatchi Collection, London

Ingrid Calame

***spalunk*, 1997**
Enamel on trace mylar
228 x 162
Collection Rachel Lehmann

***p-CHEEW-chtu-chtu*, 1998**
Enamel on aluminum
48 x 48
Collection David Reed, New York

Fandra Chang

***Bit Fall #2*, 1994**
Ink on screen, paper, fabric, and plywood
31¼ x 33 x 2½
Collection Cindy and Tony Canzoneri, Malibu, California

***Between Map and Territory 8.2 (rectangular canvas)*, 1998**
Ink on canvas, film-laminated Plexiglas, and anodized aluminum
Seven panels: 39 x 60 (overall)
Courtesy Shoshana Wayne Gallery, Santa Monica, California

Mark D. Cole

***Cast Painting (Gray Diptych)*, 1997**
Polyurethane and pigment
26 x 32 x 1¾
Collection Victoria Montelongo and Bob Sullivan, Dallas

***Cast Painting (American Romantic)*, 1998**
Polyurethane and pigment
79 x 60 x 1¾
Courtesy the artist

Sally Elesby

***Blue Painting Opened Up*, 1996**
Wire, colored glue, and oils
14 x 15 x 6
Private Collection

***Interactive Monochrome Yellow-green/ Lavender-blue*, 1997**
Wire, colored glue, and oils
43 x 46 x 15
Courtesy the artist

***Motive Painting #3*, 1997**
Wire, colored glue, and oils
34 x 20 x 16
Courtesy the artist

Jeff Elrod

***Turning Japanese*, 1998**
Acrylic on canvas
92⅛ x 83⅝ x 2
Collection The Museum of Fine Arts, Houston; Museum purchase with funds provided by Mr. and Mrs. Andrew E. Schneck

***Still-Life*, 1998**
Acrylic on canvas
84 x 72
Courtesy the artist and Texas Gallery, Houston

Tad Griffin

***Echolate 1*, 1994**
Oil on canvas
82 x 72
Courtesy the artist and Texas Gallery, Houston

***Echolate 5*, 1994**
Oil on canvas
82 x 72
Courtesy the artist and Texas Gallery, Houston

Jim Hodges

***No Dust*, 1996**
Mirror on canvas
28 x 22
Collection Dean Valentine, Beverly Hills, California

***Nearing*, 1998**
Plastic, fabric, wire, and pins in 270 parts
50 x 79
Courtesy the artist and CRG Gallery, New York

***On Earth*, 1998**
Mirror on canvas
40 x 60
Collection Ron and Ann Pizzuti, Columbus, Ohio

Callum Innes

***Formed White Painting*, 1995**
Oil on canvas
31½ x 29½
Collection Susan Margules Steinhardt and John Steinhardt

***Exposed Painting, Charcoal Grey*, 1996**
Oil on canvas
39¼ x 38
Collection John Robertshaw, New York

Untitled, 1996
Oil and shellac on canvas
88½ x 87¼
Collection Howard E. Rachofsky, Dallas

Emil Lukas

***Buffer*, 1998**
Canvas, wood, paper, mixed paints, organic material, thread, glass, and pencil in five panels
Dimensions variable; 80 x 54 x 5½ (each panel)
Courtesy the artist and Gorney Bravin & Lee, New York, and Haines Gallery, San Francisco

***Paint Bulge*, 1998**
Plaster, paint, wood, fabric, foam, paper, rubber, and plastic in sixteen sections
Dimensions variable; 57¼ x 9½ x 12 (overall)
Courtesy the artist and Haines Gallery, San Francisco, and Gorney Bravin & Lee, New York

Fabian Marcaccio

***Idiotic Model for Several Types of Realness*, 1991**
Collograph on fabric, burlap, oil, silicon, plaster cast, and wall drawing
84 x 144
Courtesy Gorney Bravin & Lee, New York

Beatriz Milhazes

***Fleur de la Passion: Maracujá* (Passion Flower: Maracujá), 1995–96**
Acrylic on canvas
48 x 78
Collection Stephen D. Susman, Houston

***As Quatro Estações* (The Four Seasons), 1997**
Acrylic on canvas
101½ x 112
Collection The Bohen Foundation

Takashi Murakami

***Cream*, 1998**
Acrylic on canvas on wood panel
96 x 192
Collection of Eileen and Peter Norton, Santa Monica, California

Aaron Parazette

***Beggar's Joys*, 1996**
Oil enamel on canvas
75 x 75
Collection Stephen D. Susman, Houston

***Tournament*, 1998**
Oil enamel on canvas
96 x 72
Collection J. Scott Caruthers, Houston

Richard Patterson

***Painted Minotaur*, 1996–97**
Oil on canvas
82 x 62¼
Tate Gallery, London; Purchased with assistance from Evelyn, Lady Downshire's Trust Fund, 1997

***Young Minotaur*, 1997**
Oil on canvas
82¼ x 48¼
Collection Yvonne Force, Inc.

***Head*, 1998**
Oil on canvas
26 x 26
Collection The British Council

Monique Prieto

***Chronicle*, 1996**
Acrylic on canvas
36 x 48
Collection of the artist
Courtesy ACME., Los Angeles

***Jet Stream*, 1996**
Acrylic on canvas
84½ x 54
Collection Dean Valentine, Beverly Hills, California

Scott Richter

Untitled, 1994
Oil paint, medium, and steel palette table
35 x 33 x 50
Courtesy Pamela Auchincloss Arts Management, New York

***Who's Afraid of Red, Yellow and Blue (for Barnett)*, 1994**
Oil paint, medium, and steel table
64 x 33 x 49
Courtesy Pamela Auchincloss Arts Management, New York

Pae White

***The Inconsolable Wailing of the Damned*, 1994** [Red]
Plexiglas and resin
48 x 96
Collection of the artist

***Vera© Retrospective Series*, 1994/98** [Houston]
Chair, silk scarves, and glass
Dimensions variable
Collection of the artist

Polly Apfelbaum

Born 1955, Abington, Pennsylvania
Lives and works in New York

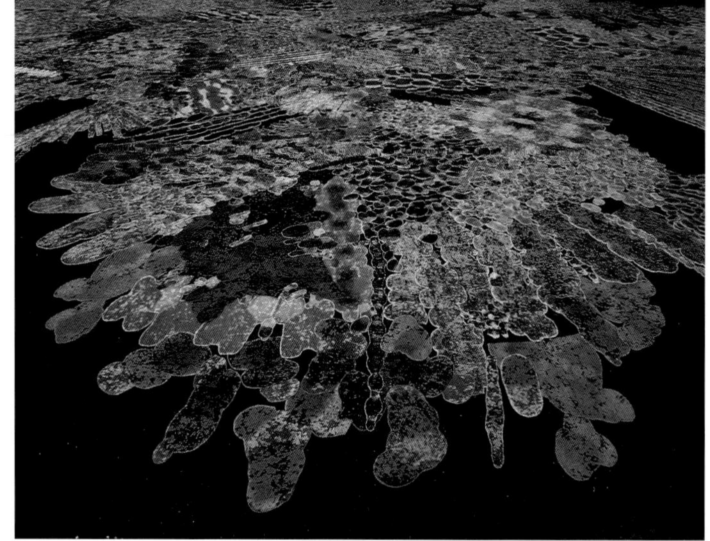

left (detail) *and opposite:*
***Reckless*, 1998**
Installation of dyed velvet
Dimensions variable
Courtesy D'Amelio Terras Gallery, New York
[not in exhibition]

Polly Apfelbaum mixes sophisticated visual play—actually, pleasure—with a range of carefully considered responses to the issues of Modernist painting. At times she sounds like a traditional abstract painter, confessing, "I want to explore different pictorial spaces . . .," but then she betrays her desire to destabilize the common definition of a painting when she adds, "by transferring painting from the wall to the floor to explore fluidity and structurelessness."[1]

Like most painters, Apfelbaum begins a work by imagining its formal structure, which includes color, materials, mark-making strategies, and often its spatial relation to a planned site. But similarities end there. Her work usually takes the form of dyed—not painted—fabric, which is presented whole or cut into shapes.[2] It can be pinned casually to the wall or, more often lately, presented directly on the floor—flat, folded, stacked, crumpled, or arranged in accumulations. She relies on "found" fabrics, choosing old bed sheets bought from Salvation Army stores or new fabric, usually synthetics like stretch crushed velvets in white or fashionable colors, purchased as remnants in New York's fashion district. Dripping, squirting, sponging, or splotching intense color directly onto different types of fabric and allowing it to seep in eliminates any direct trace of the artist's hand and introduces an element of risk, even chance. "All sorts of organic shapes happen—these are the 'brushstrokes' of a piece; they are the building blocks."[3]

The most active part of the creative process is the installation of the work, an intense, intuitive, responsive process. Apfelbaum explains:

> The pieces are dyed and cut out, then set on the floor, ordered and arranged to make more forms. The assemblage of pieces moves through the space like an organic growth—mold or lily pads—like stones in a stream, like liquid spills. Much of the work consists in directing its flow, organizing and looking for new organizations in the liquid movements of fabric and stain.[4]

Split, 1998, has been created for the floor defined by an acute angled corner of the Contemporary Arts Museum's parallelogram-shaped building. In this work the artist returns to the rich pattern of blacks and grays used previously to spectacular effect in *The Night*, 1997; for *Split* she has combined it with a spectrum of 104 dye colors along the work's perimeter. "Edges tend to define my pieces. In this work, I will build the edge differently from the whole. I am always interested in the relationship of whole to part, big to small, as the eye goes back and forth, which enhances a sense of the physicality of the piece."[5]

Apfelbaum pushes the limit between form and formlessness, stability and movement, wet and dry, even pleasure and danger. Clinging to the walls, the amorphous, ambiguous *Split* is cleaved with what seems to be a pathway that invites us deep into its shimmering pool. Its composition recalls both *The Night* and its colorful twin, *Eclipse*, 1997, in the way we imagine the work as floating, amoebic pods bumping into the wall's edge and flattening out. But one could also worry that the viruslike growth might be malign, perhaps able to engulf the visitor who lingers too long in the triangular apex. Its confines are ruffled with a jewel-like spectrum of colors, while the blacks and grays of its core form a spectacular *grisaille* pontillist tapestry. Yet *Split* gives out other signals, too—frostbite, mold, decay. Apfelbaum seems to relish this multiplicity of interpretations, which heightens the viewer's engagement with the work.

The ambiguity of Apfelbaum's work extends right to its categorization. Is it painting, sculpture, or installation? Until the 1970s, walls were the traditional domain for painters, while sculptors were allotted the pedestal or, once the Minimalists dispensed with all such furniture, the floor, which is where this artist lays her flat fields of color, either in the middle of the room or just touching the edges of (the painter's) walls. Artists such as Lynda Benglis, Barry Le Va, or Robert Morris, who in the 1970s used the floor in revolutionary ways with their scattered or poured works, are key precedents. Because fabric and dye are usually associated with women's domestic work, critics have drawn parallels between Apfelbaum's work and the 1970s discourse on feminism and art, noting its connections to household activities, female craft, and the body.[6]

And yet, even though she avoids paint, canvas, and the wall, Apfelbaum is energizing *the activity of painting*. She explores and extends the contributions of painters as diverse as Claude Monet, Jackson Pollock, and Helen Frankenthaler. Tapping into pictorial and procedural legacies common to modern painting since its beginnings, she adapts strategies and attitudes from sculpture, installation, and other Postmodern practices to reposition painting within the critical discourse, unrolling new experiences right at our feet.

1. Polly Apfelbaum, conversation with the author, New York, December 9, 1997.
2. Critics have found in Apfelbaum's organic shapes a whole range of imagery, including lily pads, mold, menstrual stains, scabs, germs, fireworks, footprints, sinister shadows, human organs, Rorschach patterns, aerial views of landscapes, and spilled liquids.
3. Polly Apfelbaum, telephone conversation with the author, July 1, 1998.
4. Polly Apfelbaum, "The Night," in *Polly Apfelbaum* (San Francisco: Walter/McBean Gallery, San Francisco Art Institute, 1997), n.p.
5. Polly Apfelbaum, telephone conversation with the author, July 1, 1998.
6. See Lynn Zelevansky, *Sense and Sensibility: Women Artists and Minimalism in the Nineties* (New York: The Museum of Modern Art, 1994), and Jan Avgikos' review of this exhibition in *Artforum*, October 1994, pp. 98–99.

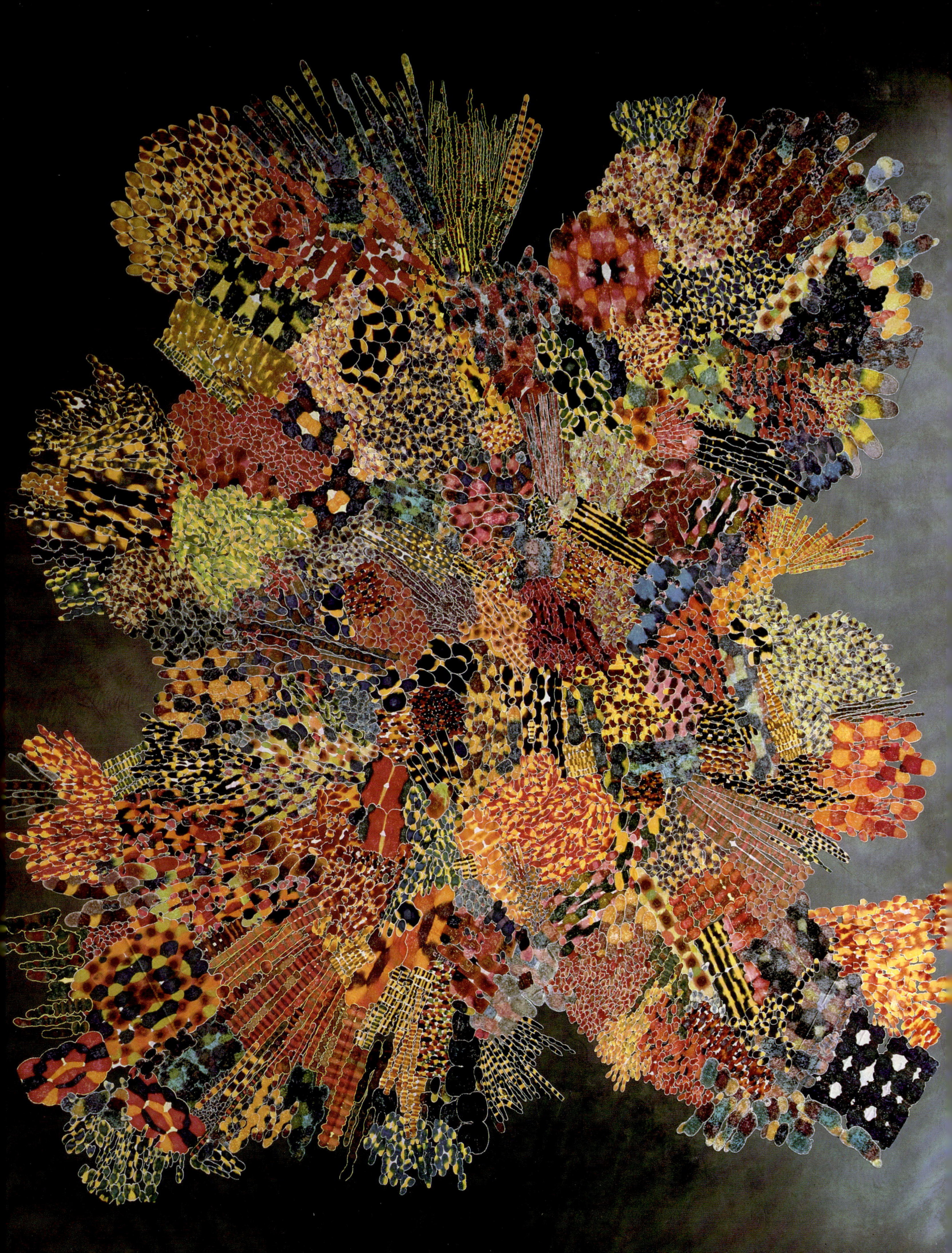

Kevin Appel

Born 1967, Los Angeles
Lives and works in Los Angeles

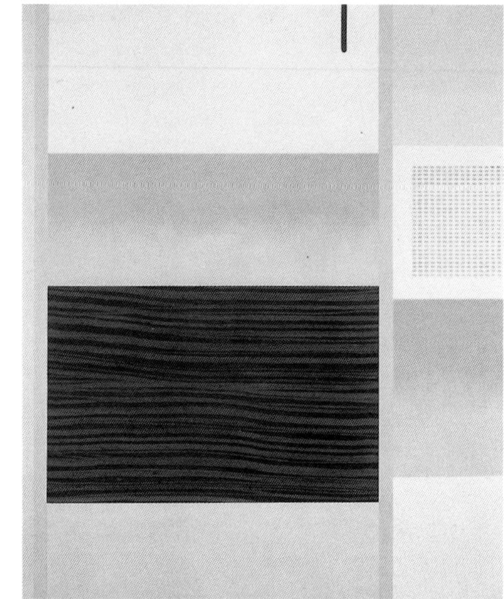

left:
***Storage System on Two-Toned Wall*, 1997**
Oil and acrylic on canvas
36 x 30 inches
Collection Dean Valentine,
Beverly Hills, California

opposite:
***Interior View (Spring)*, 1998**
Oil and acrylic on canvas over panel
82 x 112 inches
Collection Ron and Ann Pizzuti, Columbus, Ohio

Kevin Appel places his paintings in the middle of the classic Modernist tension between illusion and flatness. In his definitive 1960 text "Modernist Painting," Clement Greenberg wrote, "Flatness alone was unique and exclusive to [Modernist] art. . . . What [Modernist painting] has abandoned is the representation of the kind of space that recognizable, three-dimensional objects can inhabit."[1] With their delicately delineated planes of color, Appel's works recall geometric abstractions by artists as diverse as Piet Mondrian and John McLaughlin. Our eyes revel in his crisp edges, his even-handed paint application, and his steady build-up of surfaces, a balanced arrangement of volumes, colors, and textures found only in the finest formalist paintings. But the artist does not slide the door completely closed across the picture plane; these works are actually based on architectural photographs of real, penetrable, three-dimensional spaces. He explains, "I enjoy the fluidity, the slippage between abstraction and a very literal representation of a space. What separates my paintings from being an illustration is the way the surface is addressed."[2]

Raised in a family of architects in a California Modernist home, the artist had an early interest in mid century Southern California architecture, including the important Case Study Houses commissioned by the editors of the journal *Arts & Architecture.* More middle-class, mainstream "do-it-yourself" magazines such as *Sunset* and *Better Homes and Gardens* also provide inspiration and source imagery. To develop the working drawings for his isometric paintings of domestic spaces, Appel often blends aspects of several interiors by scanning magazine photos into a computer, electronically tracing over the lines of the structural and decorative elements, and printing a new, "cleared out" version that he can "redecorate" when he paints the painting.[3] Onto a pristinely prepared white canvas, he builds faceted geometrical shapes, using many layers to produce the painting's delicate surfaces and the illusion of a palpable void. "It is like building a building; different construction or decorative materials require different paint handling."[4]

Some of Appel's paintings parallel wide-angle interior architectural photographs, which open up to a deep space of several rooms. Others focus on household details, offering much flatter, contained views. The computer origin of these compositions not only provides their crispness but also the eerie airlessness of virtual reality—a timeless, bland perfection found in computer renderings but not in our inhabitable real-world space.

Landing, 1998, puts the viewer at the foot of a floating stairway, which brings our eye back into the space, then up and forward again. Tucked into a narrow corner bordered by a luscious blue curtain and a deeply receding picture wall arranged with monochrome quadrangles, the skewed composition tingles with a crisp, almost claustrophobic, clarity.

A more open space, *Interior View (Spring)*, 1998, is based on rooms in a traditional Japanese palace, filtered through Appel's California Modern aesthetic. For example, he has modified the partitions and the *fusuma* sliding doors, and he has transformed such traditional materials as natural wood and paper into painted walls and glass doors, more fitting for a contemporary—or futuristic—space. Appel's springtime tree fascinates the eye and imagination. Its constellation of leaves, each a perfect triangle in different light-green shades of new growth, hovers in midair as if a gust of wind has just sent them into a swirling pattern around its perfect pole, obviously intended to replicate a solid and dependable trunk.

Materials are key to Appel's handmade trompe l'oeil effects, and his almost kitschy faux-finishes are part of the special pleasure found in his paintings of household details. For example, in a work such as *Storage System on Two-Toned Wall*, 1997, it is as if an electronic eye has zoomed in for a close-up of part of some virtual decor. Here the artist mimics a range of effects such as the caning cover of a stereo speaker and the wood grain of a cabinet door, a hybrid surface invented by the artist by combining the textured grain of zebra wood and the color of rosewood.

In his replicated computer-and-paint worlds, Appel negotiates a spectrum of dualities, and it is a formidable challenge. As one critic wrote, "All of these fragments [in Appel's paintings] are flattened and essentialised into a harmonious if unwilling abstraction whose inkling of illusionistic space keeps it in a perceptual purgatory."[5] Appel explores the flow of space from interior to exterior, from Eastern to Western architectural vocabularies, and from the flatness of tightly cropped views of a specific decor to the wide-angle views of several rooms and the deeper space outside. Most significant today is Appel's exploration of the material and immaterial, the fluidity between the computer's virtual reality, which provides a new paradigm for looking at modern spaces, and the flat, handmade facture of Modernist painting.

1. Clement Greenberg, "Modernist Painting," in *Forum Lectures*, 1960, reprinted in *Art and Theory 1900–1990*, edited by Charles Harrison and Paul Wood (Oxford, England: Blackwell, 1992), p. 756.
2. Kevin Appel, telephone conversation with the author, July 6, 1998.
3. Kevin Appel, telephone conversation with the author, April 15, 1998.
4. Kevin Appel, telephone conversation with the author, July 6, 1998.
5. Michael Darling, "Kevin Appel, Angles Gallery," *frieze*, June/July/August 1998, p. 88.

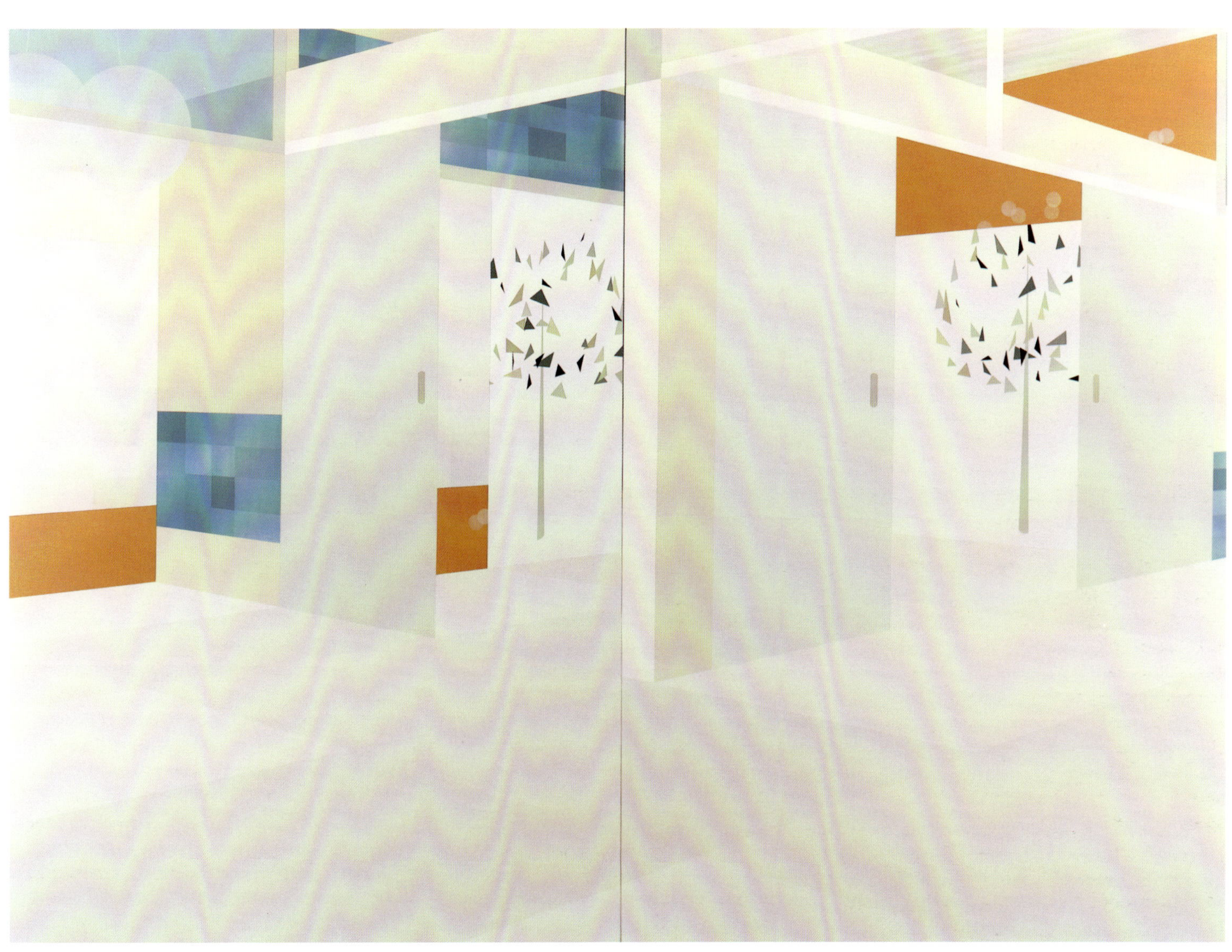

Uta Barth

Born 1958, Berlin, Germany
Lives and works in Los Angeles

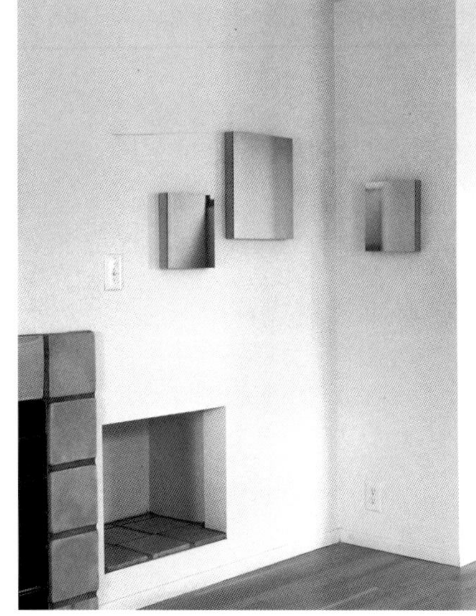

left:
Installation view, 1994
at Domestic Setting Gallery, Los Angeles

opposite:
***Ground #47*, 1994**
Color photograph on panel
19½ x 21 inches
Collection Sheridan Brown,
Los Angeles

Uta Barth's photographs look empty, void of subject, like a non-objective abstraction. To produce her Ground series, the artist initially focuses her camera on a subject in the foreground, then removes the subject before the picture is shot, leaving only the back(ground) in the image. She has explained, "I am interested in what pictures look like; I make photographs in which I take away the 'subject,' so what remains is the surroundings, the container."[1] The resulting image is often partly blurred, the effect of focusing on the foreground within a shallow field, an inherent optical condition of both the camera lens and our eyes.[2]

The artist further confounds our efforts to navigate the space or to immerse ourselves in the image by covering each print with a matte laminate coating, which deadens the surface, frustrating our attempt to focus even on the surface plane. Furthermore, instead of framing the images behind a mat or under glass, which would reinforce the common idea of a photograph as a window, Barth lifts her images a few inches off the wall, mounting her prints onto two-inch thick boxlike forms. Even without that object-like presence, their sparse imagery, taut geometries, and carefully planned arrangements would lead the viewer to think of paintings rather than photographic images.

At the start of this series, Barth looked closely at the conventions of still life, interior, and portrait painting—especially their backgrounds.[3] Critics have marveled at the way that luminosity and architecture become so important within her seemingly "empty" pictures, noting how her works activate the viewing process, proposing Barth as an extension of the essentially Californian Light and Space Art pioneered by Robert Irwin and James Turrell.[4] In an interview, Barth commented, "I am continually interested in visuality and perception. . . . The question for me is how can I make you aware of your own activity of looking, instead of losing your attention to thoughts about what it is you are looking at."[5]

The issue of the work of art as a self-reflexive object intersects concerns of both Modern and Postmodern abstract painting. In his essay "Seeking the Primal Through Paint: The Monochrome Icon," art historian Thomas McEvilley discusses the shift in emphasis from the figure to the ground as the beginning of Modern art. He elaborates upon this idea, noting how the surfaces of J.M.W. Turner's oils become "totally ambiguous in terms of depth or flatness, often seeming almost flat yet to reach back . . . to all directions: every point has become a vanishing point!"; we cannot help but think of Barth when he continues, "Turner has dissolved the figures into the ground."[6] Monochrome painting continued through various cycles of reductivism, but certain visual parallels have relevance to Barth's near-monochrome photographs today. She has addressed this directly:

> There is a curious similarity in the recent photographs of interior environments to a certain kind of minimalist painting. The problems of making these pictures share much of the same territory as those of painting. The subject is removed and one is left with information relating to the edge. Certain questions about figure/ground relationships, about framing and composing, relating information to the edge, etc., are the same in both media. . . . In no way am I interested in making photographs that look like or mimic paintings, but I am interested in the shared territory between the two, which simply arises out of established conventions of picture making.[7]

In the works that are included here, we can easily "read" particular painting languages in the otherwise decipherable common objects found in the spaces Barth has photographed. For example, in *Ground #47*, 1994, roughly a third of the panel is covered in vertical aqua bands, clearly a curtain but equally suggestive of Morris Louis' stained Veil series paintings. *Ground #52*, 1995, flattens three squarish black serial forms (black leather sofa cushions) against a white plane to recall any number of 1960s geometric painters. The two-toned white fields of *Ground #45*, 1995, have the balance and grace of a Barnett Newman painting, although it is diminutive compared to Newman's work, which immerses the viewer in vast areas of color.

Barth doesn't aim for the spiritual aura of painting as Newman did. Instead, she uses the mechanics of the camera to make images of the real and physical world that readdress—from the different angle that conceptual photography offers—topics that have always interested this century's painters, such as figure and ground, subject and object, and the abstracted field. With her thoughtful and thought-provoking photography, Barth brings an exciting freshness to some of the enduring issues of painting.

1. Uta Barth, artist lecture, The Glassell School of Art, The Museum of Fine Arts, Houston, March 1, 1998.
2. The artist has explained: "We do not 'see' [an unfocused blur] unless we make a conscious effort to observe the phenomenon. The camera can 'lock-in' these conditions and give us a picture which allows us to look at (and focus on) out-of-focusness." Uta Barth, quoted in an interview with Sheryl Conkelton, 1996, *Journal of Contemporary Art*, www.thing.net/jca/barth.html.
3. Uta Barth, conversation with the author, Santa Monica, California, February 4, 1998.
4. For discussions of light and space issues in Barth's work, see Elizabeth A.T. Smith, "At the Edge of the Decipherable: Recent Photographs by Uta Barth," in *Uta Barth* (Los Angeles: The Museum of Contemporary Art, 1995), n.p.; Christopher Knight, "Art in All the Right Spaces," *Los Angeles Times*, September 21, 1995, pp. F1, F11; and Julie Joyce, "Images of Anywhere," *Artweek*, August 18, 1994, inside back cover.
5. Uta Barth, conversation with Marilu Knode, *Artlies*, June/July 1995, p. 30
6. Thomas McEvilley, "Seeking the Primal Through Paint: The Monochrome Icon," in *The Exile's Return* (Cambridge, England: Cambridge University Press, 1993), p. 14.
7. Uta Barth, conversation with Knode, p. 30.

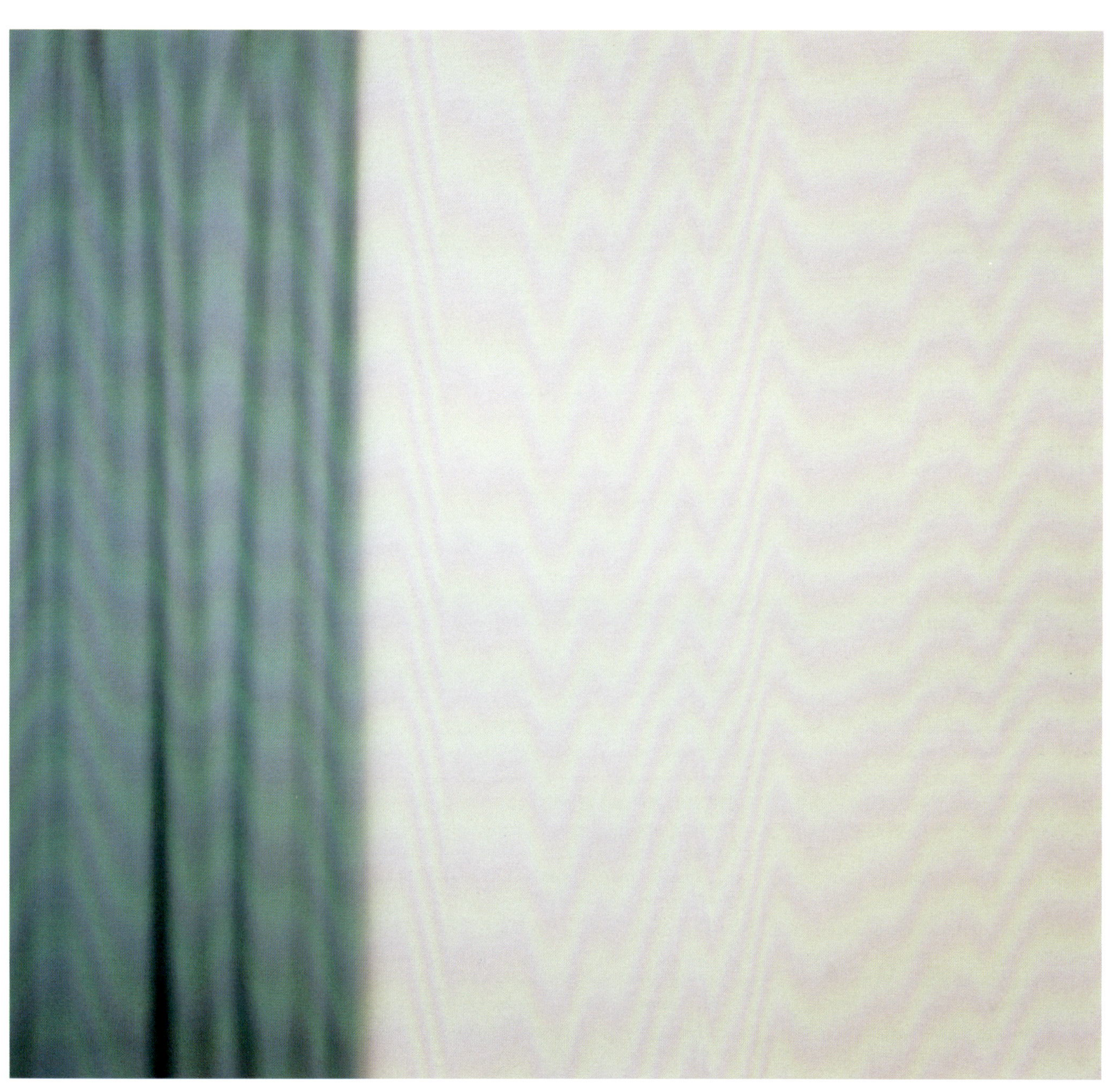

Glenn Brown

Born 1966, Hexham, Northumberland, England
Lives and works in London

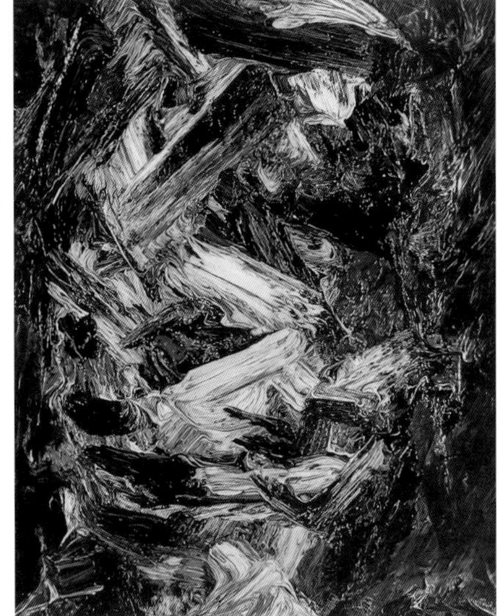

left:
***You Never Touch My Skin in the Way You Did and You've Even Changed the Way You Kiss Me*, 1994**
Oil on canvas
60 x 48 inches
Collection Walker Art Center, Minneapolis;
Butler Family Fund, 1994

opposite:
***These Days*, 1994**
Plaster, acrylic and oil paint, and chicken wire
8 x 9½ x 8 inches
Saatchi Collection, London

Glenn Brown is not interested in painting, photographic reproductions, or sculpture per se, but instead seems more interested in the in-between states of being, the fallout when a real object is translated from one form to another. In his paintings he draws on printed reproductions to create airless, flattened versions of either gestural, painterly Modernist abstractions, hyperreal or surreal images by Salvador Dali, or science-fiction illustrations such as those by Chris Foss. This exhibition focuses on the work of Brown's painting and sculpture based on the British Expressionist Frank Auerbach, whose thickly impastoed, aggressively rendered abstract portraits are considered masterpieces of Modern British painting. As the artist explains, "Auerbach's works are full of the residue of the 'Artist' making the painting through the brushstrokes in a Modernist tradition, an approach described by one exhibition title as 'The Hard Won Image.' "[1]

Brown is especially interested in Auerbach's portraits, and the shift that occurs when the flesh-and-blood subject is transformed into paint by the artist's hand, then again when the painting is photographed, and again when the reproduction is published in a book. The printed versions from which Brown works are always several steps removed from the initial encounter between portraitist and portrayed. Brown describes the betrayal: "The subject, the figure, became helpless, displaced, and lost between Auerbach's interpretation, the photograph, the printed page, and my interpretation. As portraits, [my Auerbach works] represent a hopelessly schizophrenic state, with no single author, so the artist's model is viewed from no one perspective."[2]

Brown's "surrogate paintings," carefully rendered in sharp realist focus from reproductions of Auerbach's work, are disturbing displacements of what our eyes would lead us to expect, the physical trace of thick paint dragged (by Auerbach) across the canvas having been replaced by a delicate rendering and subtle colored glazes; it is as if, in Brown's words, he has "ironed the wrinkles out of Auerbach's painting."[3] Not only does Brown drain the impastoed paint of its passion, he also refocuses the portrait; using shallow photographic space,[4] he seeks to make "paintings of *people made in paint*, rather than a portrait of a painting. . . . I play around with what would be the focal length, so the head is in focus and the background is not. Returning the subject to its original perspective, the head gets some depth."[5] Working against Auerbach's Modernist flattening of a dimensional figure into the picture plane, Brown produces instead a near-photographic likeness that carries a different kind of flatness. He seeks means that are fairly invisible, citing Dali's statement that his paintings are like handmade photographs of visions that could be captured in no other way.[6]

Brown eventually realized that the next step toward giving Auerbach's heads a new dimensionality was for them to move beyond both Auerbach's Modernist picture plane and his own quasi-photographic plane of focus by entering the viewer's space—as sculptures. The astonishing results are shocking in their violent beauty, whether lying on the floor literally, like a severed head,[7] or trapped in a vitrine like a biological specimen. We cannot help but circle, staring, seeking orientation or an image from the painterly mass.

The construction of the sculpture is quite simple: plaster is applied over a chicken-wire armature, then thickly and aggressively painted. While Auerbach painted the figure from only one angle, in Brown's sculptures we can continue around the full 360-degree head, much of which the artist must invent. Brown's work differs from other Expressionist sculpture, its closest parallel perhaps being painter Willem de Kooning's experiments with Expressionist figures. In those bronzes, however, especially in the intimate maquette scale, we sense the fingers of de Kooning the sculptor making mass, while Brown's forms are based on the way a brushstroke defines a surface. As with his paintings, Brown makes his sculptures by looking at reproductions in books, "with the paint colors mimicking bad color printing"[8]—yet another step away from the original. "Looking at pictures of artworks in books requires the brain to reconstitute the original from the meta-state of the reproductions; I want the viewer to again reconstitute the painting from this meta-state. It should not be like looking at a real sculpture."[9]

By painting or sculpting second-generation photographic reproductions of paintings, Brown's exploration of Modernism's Expressionist phase forces us to reconsider the ways we read and understand original works of art and their re-presentation in reproductions once, twice, and three times removed from the original subject. Brown's compelling but contradictory paintings and sculptures interrogate the methods and meanings of Modernist art, a key practice defining the Postmodern era.

1. Glenn Brown, telephone conversation with the author, July 4, 1998.
2. Glenn Brown, interview with Marcelo Spinelli, in *Glenn Brown* (Hexham: Northumberland County Library, and London: Karsten Schubert, 1996), pp. 5–6.
3. Glenn Brown, telephone conversation with the author, July 4, 1998.
4. In this context, it is interesting to compare Brown's backgrounds with Uta Barth's Ground series photographs, included in this exhibition (pp. 46–7).
5. Glenn Brown, telephone conversation with the author, July 4, 1998.
6. Ibid.
7. The artist said he likes that they can be read as props from a horror film, and to one he's even added a bloody neck.
8. Glenn Brown, telephone conversation with the author, July 4, 1998.
9. Ibid.

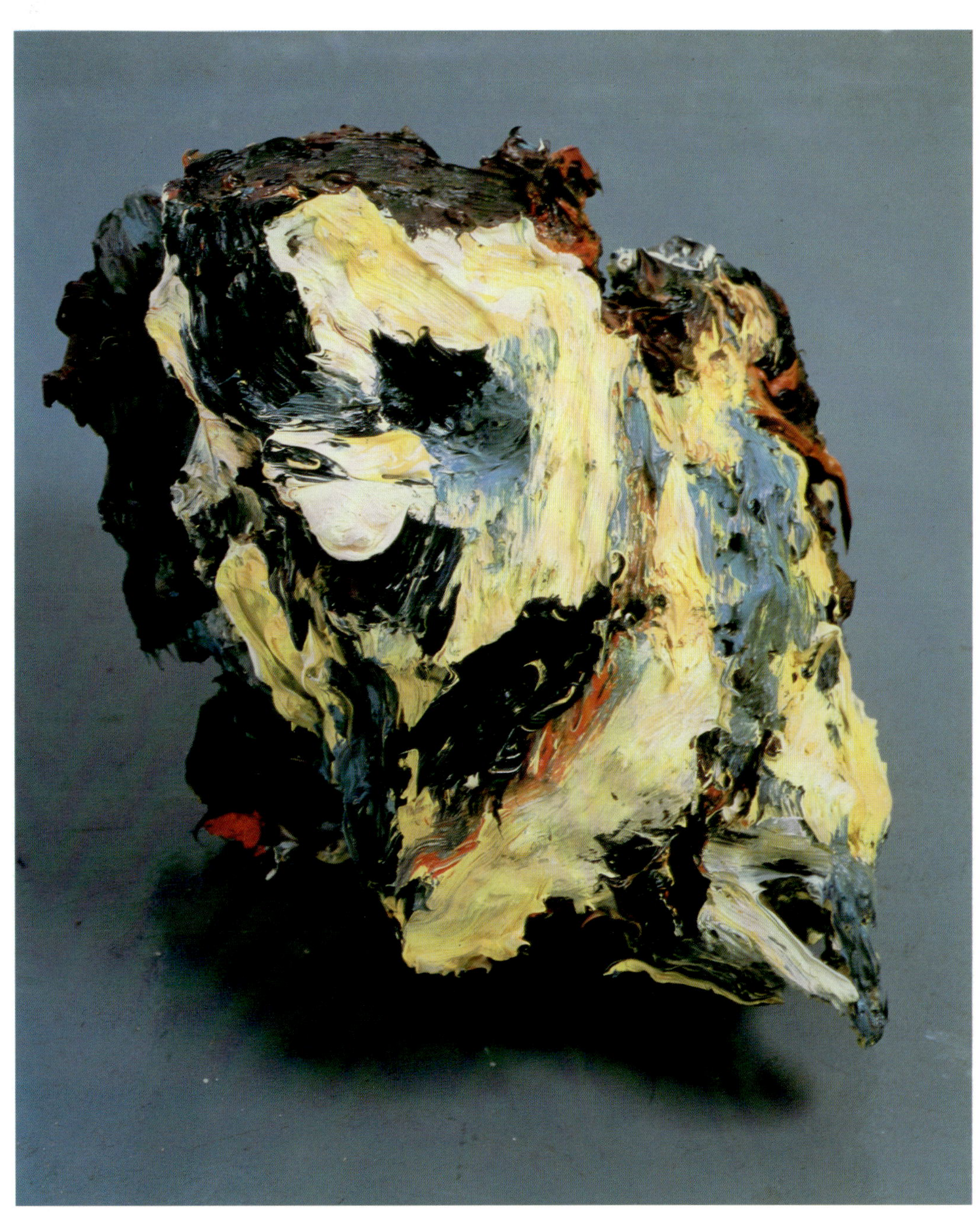

Ingrid Calame

Born 1965, The Bronx, New York
Lives and works in Los Angeles

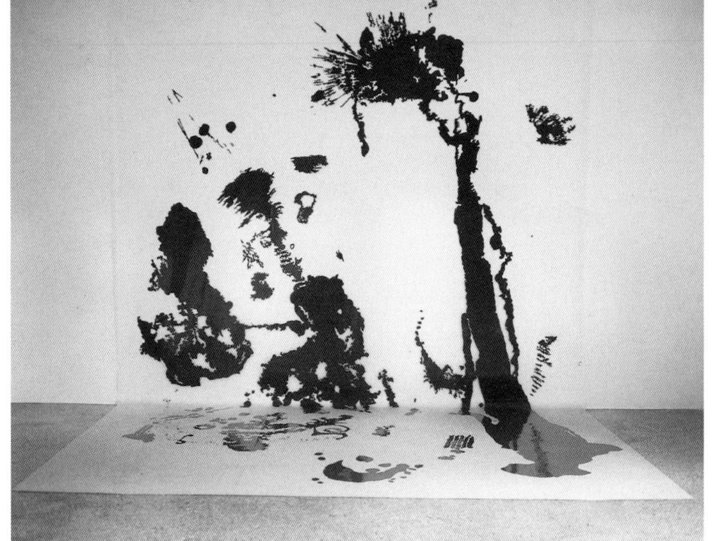

left:
***spalunk*, 1997**
Enamel on trace mylar
228 x 162 inches
Collection Rachel Lehmann

opposite:
***p-CHEEW-chtu-chtu*, 1998**
Enamel on aluminum
48 x 48 inches
Collection David Reed, New York

Ingrid Calame builds her explosive compositions by scavenging dried contours of spilled or scattered liquids from the streets of Los Angeles, tracing their silhouettes, and back in her studio, painting them on paper or aluminum panels. Calame began this documentary archiving process in 1994 using the shapes of dried paint accumulations on her studio floor, but she now limits her vocabulary to various functional and waste fluids found in public areas. She identifies transmission fluid, motor oil, dog urine, blood, spilled juices, fence paint, and bubble gum as sources for the shapes that have since evaporated but still left their mark.[1] In the studio, she composes arrangements on translucent mylar tracing paper to form what she calls "constellations." Once the contours are drawn, in a procedure the artist compares to children's coloring books or "paint by numbers," Calame fills in the forms with high-gloss sign painters' enamels.

Calame's strategy weaves together key chapters of twentieth-century art. Her amorphous found forms plumb the unconscious and recall the early Surrealists' use of frottage and automatic writing. Most images come from random, probably accidental spills, an incorporation of chance as a compositional strategy that traces an important lineage from Hans Arp and Marcel Duchamp, through Abstract Expressionism, to John Cage and Robert Rauschenberg.

Calame's practice also parallels aspects of 1960s and 1970s Documentary, Conceptual, and Process Art. Her habit of walking the streets in search of incidents echoes Vito Acconci's tactic of following strangers in public settings (and presenting photographic evidence as art), while her careful registering of the time, date, and location of every stain documented recalls On Kawara's obsessive notebook entries of his daily activities. Calame's curiosity about, and openness to, the way natural forces dictate her lexicon of shapes also has roots in the open-ended experimentation with entropy and natural forces of artists such as Robert Smithson (*Asphalt Rundown* and *Glue Pour*, 1969) or Hans Haake (*Water Boxes*, 1963).

Of course, Calame's lexicon has its strongest visual affinity with the drips of Jackson Pollock, who elevated splattered paint to existential levels by linking the artist's psychologically charged gesture with the depths of the artist's psyche. Calame's drips are ironic, however, derived from anonymous donors (even automobiles), and despite all visual cues, they have no psychological content whatsoever.

Calame currently paints on two different types of surfaces: long sheets of mylar tracing paper, abutted to form a large field mounted on the wall and extending across the floor, and aluminum panels two- or four-feet square. The aluminum pieces, such as *p-CHEEW-chtu-chtu*, 1998, hang on the wall as most paintings do, their compositions a concentrated compendium of drips from Calame's larger "constellations" of shapes on paper. Still scaling them one-to-one in relation to the original street stain, Calame subjectively arranges her silhouettes to build a growing pattern that pushes forward to catch the eye.

The monumental paper pieces, such as *spalunk*, 1997, have a quite different effect. Installed nearly to the top of the wall and flowing onto the floor to a length almost equal to the wall height, they bridge the horizontal and vertical planes. The matte paper surface is semi-transparent, allowing the wall and floor to faintly show through. The reflective paint forces the forms to pop off this surface when viewed from afar, so the shapes seem to float in space like a virtual reality or sci-fi version of an Expressionist painting. On closer inspection, the mirrorlike puddles of paint on the floor pick up in their reflection the outlines of the wall-mounted patterns, creating unusual visual resonances as layers of positive and negative space echo back and forth.

Calame's paintings have an aggressive visual authority recalling the epic nature of Abstract Expressionism, but her process calls into question long-held assumptions about the dynamic action and heroic content of this type of abstraction. We have learned to "read" a drip or splash as the result of an artist's psychically energized, purposefully directed gesture, but Calame's carefully traced and painted (organic, accidental, and mechanical) stains are much closer to Roy Lichtenstein's ironic Brushstroke paintings or Andy Warhol's flat-footed "paint by number" works than the angst of Abstract Expressionism, which they seem to want to replicate. Calame's paintings filter through a very different kind of artistic process that is more about *thinking* than about *expressing*, more about the streets *outside* the studio than the world *inside* the artist. This is the Postmodern point about which Calame's work pivots.

1. Ingrid Calame, unpublished artist statement, February 5, 1998.

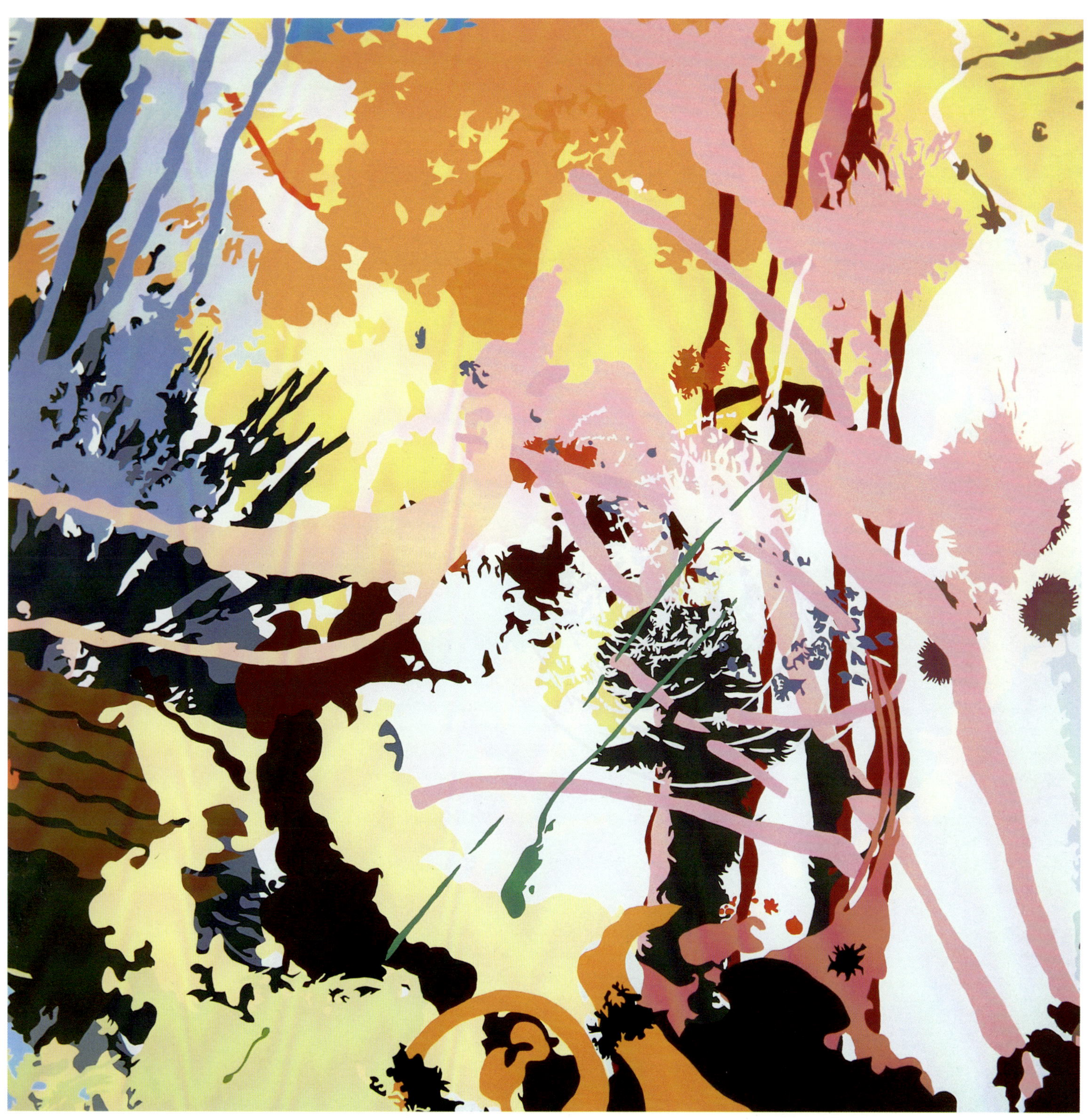

Fandra Chang

Born 1964, Taipei, Taiwan, Republic of China
Lives and works in Venice, California

left:
***Bit Fall #2*, 1994**
Ink on screen, paper, fabric, and plywood
31¼ x 33 x 2½ inches
Collection Cindy and Tony Canzoneri, Malibu, California

opposite:
***Between Map and Territory 8.2 (rectangular canvas)*, 1998**
Ink on canvas, film-laminated Plexiglas, and anodized aluminum
Seven panels: 39 x 60 inches (overall)
Courtesy Shoshana Wayne Gallery, Santa Monica, California

Fandra Chang confesses to a "very ambivalent relation to painting,"[1] yet her smart and seductive work addresses some of the key theoretical issues that painters are pondering today: the relation of the real to the abstract, of the surface to the image, of the original to the duplicate, and of the handmade to the technologically produced. Critics have described Chang's work as having a "mesmerizing . . . surreptitious glow and hyperatrophied color,"[2] and it is hard to deny the beguiling pleasure it offers the eye. Soon, however, the mind takes over, driven by curiosity about the source and process of her work's magic, and our initial observation shifts into another gear to analyze and decipher what we are looking at and how it was made. Chang has written:

> What interests me most in making these works is not necessarily in questions of photographic representation, or productions of the artificial, but in contemplating art's capacity/attempt to investigate the space between the object of art and the "thing" it purports to represent.[3]

In the early 1990s, plywood, its grain emphasized by sandblasting, served as both the material and the imagery for a series of works by Chang exploring mirroring and layering. Superimposing woodblock and silkscreen materials and processes in a series of overlapping and symmetrical pairings, she explored what she describes as "the co-presence of the real and the reproduced," a practice "infused with questions of origination and dissemination."[4]

Six upright stripes (or, more accurately, three sets of pairs) comprise *Bit Fall #2*, 1994, which mixes different surfaces, textures, and treatments. The artist began this work by loosely rolling paint onto a coarse silkscreen, depositing a pixillated grid pattern on the screen and on the paper below. The screen was then photographed and printed, in positive and negative, onto both paper and sheer fabric, with the more transparent elements (printed fabrics and the original silkscreen) stretched over a recessed box so we look through the semitransparent pattern to its opaque (photographic) twin below. Despite this complicated process, the work possesses an essential, systematic logic that, once recognized, provides an antidote to the seemingly random patterns pulsing through these works like the computer information bits to which the title refers.

In Chang's more recent paintings, she moves away from the earlier materials and procedures of woodblock and silkscreen printing. The painted canvas, presented as itself as well as reproduced in positive and negative photographic films, is now mounted onto Plexiglas and anodized aluminum to form works such as *Between Map and Territory 8.2 (rectangular canvas)*, 1998. With this shift has come a change in imagery and reference as well, away from the earlier landscape allusions of the wood grain works—with their horizontal format and their resemblance to Chinese brush painting—and toward the Modernist monochrome paintings of Kasimir Malevich, Josef Albers, and Ad Reinhardt. For these later works, Chang begins with an inexpensive factory-made, store-bought stretched canvas. She lightly rolls paint onto its surface, bringing attention to the detail of the canvas weave and the structure of the stretcher beneath. This "original painting" is then photographed and reproduced onto film—both in the actual size of the original canvas and enlarged to double its size—in positive and negative, using various colors selected by the artist. Sandwiching a sheet of clear Plexiglas between two transparent films, she mounts each set over anodized aluminum, except for one, which she places on top of the "original" painted canvas, the source for the imagery of the six other panels. Because we look *into* and *through* these objects, viewing Chang's *Between Map and Territory 8.2* feels as if we are watching a thin video screen embedded in the wall.[5] The panels quietly hum and shimmer as light modulated through the layers of film creates interference patterns that confuse our eyes, producing a visual fallout with the sensation of motion.

Although her hands touch paint and canvas only once—briefly—during the exacting production process, Chang's pixillated panels hang on the wall like traditional paintings, arranged in balanced units or in odd-numbered, asymmetrical groupings. By integrating careful handwork, an eye for visual effect, and mechanical reproductive processes, Chang creates objects that carry not the traditional "aura" of a painting about which Walter Benjamin wrote, but instead a mediated, technological "aura." This hybrid phenomenon, with which many of today's artists are completely comfortable, just might provide a new paradigm for painting.

1. Fandra Chang, conversation with the author, Venice, California, February 6, 1998.
2. Regina Basha, "Manufacturing Revelations," *art/text* February–April 1998, p. 55.
3. Fandra Chang, unpublished artist statement, 1996.
4. Fandra Chang, conversation with the author, Venice, California, February 6, 1998.
5. For a discussion of video and painting, see Jeremy Gilbert-Rolfe, "Cabbages, Raspberries and Video's Thin Brightness," *Art & Design*, May/June 1996, pp. 14–23.

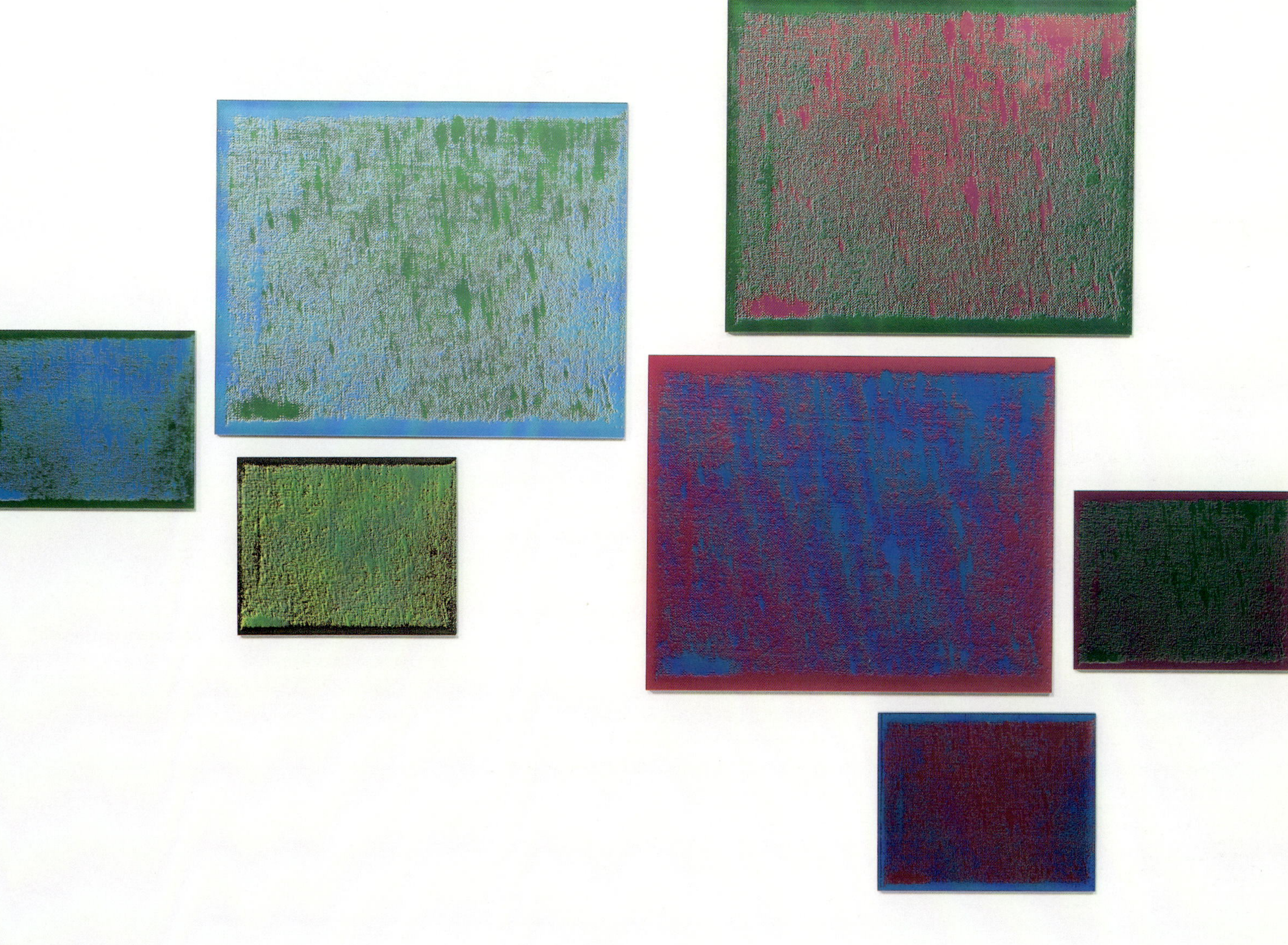

Mark D. Cole

Born 1965, Houston
Lives and works in Dallas

left:
***Cast Painting (Gray Diptych)*, 1997**
Polyurethane and pigment
26 x 32 x 1¾ inches
Collection Victoria Montelongo and Bob Sullivan, Dallas

opposite:
***Cast Painting (American Romantic)*, 1998**
Polyurethane and pigment
79 x 60 x 1¾ inches
Courtesy the artist

On a first encounter with Mark D. Cole's work, the tone, colors, and proportions recall the 1960s Color Field paintings of Mark Rothko and Brice Marden. Cole has clearly adopted the language of this Modernist monochrome tradition, and his works initially register the somber spirituality associated with those artists' saturated panels of pristinely applied color. Closer examination, however, reveals that what Cole presents are not traditional paintings on canvas but rather polyurethane casts, their identical base structures fabricated from molds. The artist has made five rubber molds for paintings of different sizes and shapes—each taken from "original" stretched canvases that he himself painted—and from these he casts both single works and diptychs. For each work he mixes colored pigment (and sometimes thickeners) into liquid polyurethane, then casts the back and sides of the work (including stretcher bars, canvas, even the tacks along the side) in breathtaking verisimilitude. Although molds and casts suggest an assembly line approach, bringing to mind Andy Warhol's Factory-produced silkscreen paintings, Cole keeps only two or three Cast Paintings under production at any one time.

The artist resolutely locates his objects in the realm of painting, describing them as "an abstraction of abstract painting."[1] Yet he also stresses the physicality of these works as *objects* rather than *images* (which is what we generally seek first when looking at a canvas). His statement continues, "By the extreme position that these works take to 'objectify' painting, they equate paintings to everyday objects. This focuses on paintings as objects . . . instead of as blank objects used as a writing surface."[2] This approach links Cole's project to the Minimalist emphasis on the gestalt of the object, connecting with key precedents such as Frank Stella's Black Paintings, where thick stretcher bars pull the face of the painting from the wall, or with the work of Dan Flavin, Lee Bonticou, and Richard Artschwager, which Donald Judd wrote about in his important 1965 essay "Specific Objects" as "neither painting nor sculpture."[3]

Once the structural "ground" is formed, Cole completes the surface of a work, as the artist describes it, "like actually painting a painting."[4] After pouring several polyurethane layers to build up the front face, he finishes it in one of a variety of ways. For example, in *Cast Painting (Gray Diptych)*, 1997, he sanded the skin to a matte finish, while in *Cast Painting (American Romantic)*, 1998, he applied the polyurethane thickly then manipulated the object itself, producing the drippy, slowly seeping line. While he mimics the stylistic language of highly regarded Modernists such as Rothko and Marden, the picture plane is simply manipulated plastic, the most maligned of all commercial materials.[5]

Cole works in the wake of Conceptualism and Postmodern appropriation, which strives to eradicate traces of the hand of the artist. Duchamp's 1914 development of the readymade, László Moholy-Nagy's ordering a "painting" to be made by a fabricator (over the telephone, no less!), or the industrially produced works by Judd, Les Levine, and others culminated in Sherrie Levine's 1980s critique of the cult of "originality" when she rephotographed famous photographs and made a casting of Duchamp's 1917 *Fountain*.

The most complicated (and interesting) aspect of Cole's Cast Paintings is how they defy our expectations—rooted in Modernist painting's emphasis on the artist's hand—for originality, sincerity, and uniqueness. Cole's base structure is a copy made from a mold. While sculptors may cast multiples of their work in bronze and other materials (even plastic) without question, Cole "objectifies" the structural support for a painting, multiplying it like a sculpture edition before adding to each surface a generic, unemotional facade. Possible comparisons for Cole's processes might be applying a special patina to a sculpture, hand-coloring a print or a photograph, or simply painting on a factory-made pre-stretched canvas rather than a support one has made oneself (except that Cole makes his own and then "paints" on it).

Cole's Cast Paintings inhabit a hybrid territory. Issued from a mold, they are multiples, but each is also finished differently by hand, so in this way they are unique. Cole has written, "I consciously try to promote paradoxes in the work such as high art vs. kitsch, handmade vs. mechanically produced, and original vs. fake."[6] In the end, he has moved far beyond Rothko's glowing fields and Marden's waxy distilled colors so conducive to contemplation; Cole provides a different answer to the questions of uniqueness, materiality, and the handmade mark of an artist in oil that still haunt us at the end of the century.

1. Mark Cole, unpublished "Artist Statement," 1998.
2. Ibid.
3. Donald Judd, "Specific Objects," *Arts Yearbook 8* (1965), reprinted in *Donald Judd: Complete Writings: 1959–1975* (Halifax: The Press of the Nova Scotia College of Art and Design, and New York: New York University Press,1975), p. 181.
4. Mark Cole, telephone conversation with the author, June 30, 1998.
5. While Cole's chosen materials are not found in the average painter's studio, there are strong precedents for making art from plastic. The 1960s "Fetish Finish School" of Southern California, including Larry Bell, Billy Al Bengston, Craig Kauffman, John McCracken, and DeWain Valentine, among others, worked with modern industrial materials such as fiberglass, sprayed automotive lacquer, or cast resin, but they added a handmade finish that inspired critics (and fans) to compare them with surfboard fanatics or car customizers rather than with artists, past or present.
6. Mark Cole, unpublished "Artist Statement," 1998.

Sally Elesby

Born 1942, Abilene, Kansas
Lives and works in Los Angeles

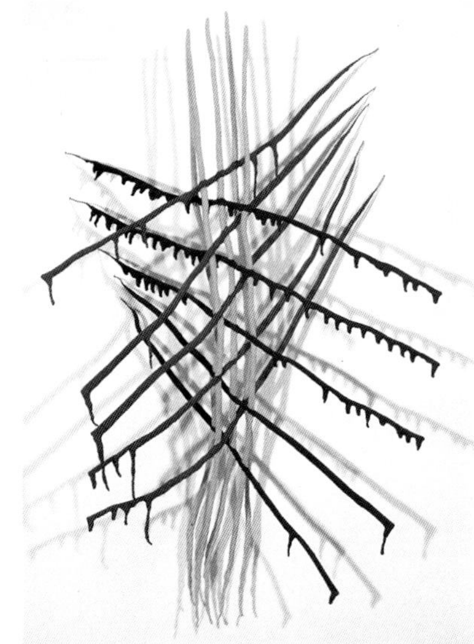

left:
***Motive Painting #3*, 1997**
Wire, colored glue, and oils
34 x 20 x 16 inches
Courtesy the artist

opposite:
***Interactive Monochrome Yellow-green/Lavender-blue*, 1997**
Wire, colored glue, and oils
43 x 46 x 15 inches
Courtesy the artist

Sally Elesby crafts her richly hued, wall-bound skeletons from wire, acrylic-colored glue, and oil paint. Though she began working with wire over ten years ago, it wasn't until 1995 that she started creating the wall-based works that relate most directly to abstract painting. At first, these works were woven mats of wire coated with color, as to depict a microscope's close-up view of painted canvas. In the more recent works exhibited here, it seems like the canvas has been eaten away by acid to reveal the warped structural outlines of a frame or grid, two key elements of the painter's vocabulary. Their shallow forms protrude only slightly from the wall, their flattened structure defying any reference to illusionism. It is the shadows projected onto the wall behind each work that provide an increased sense of depth, and the multiple cast images, along with the varied silhouettes provided by side views, complicate our perception and comprehension of the work.

Elesby begins each work with a wire armature, as if she were building a bridge, and bends each filament to attach around another. She coats each strand, first with tinted glues, then paint—often up to fifty coats in all—achieving a physical density and visual intensity while still maintaining a sense of fluidity. Unlike the liquid drips of the Abstract Expressionists, Elesby's drips are slow, accumulated, and solidified, suggesting icicles, stalagmites, or hand-dipped candles. They freeze time. Parallels to Elesby's work are also found in 1970s Process Art, such as Lynda Benglis' polyurethane foam works and the eccentric hanging forms of Eva Hesse.

Blue Painting Opened Up, 1996, is one of Elesby's quasi-rectangular works that speak in the vocabulary of painting. Its tripartite structure, rather than suggesting a stable triptych, recalls instead an almost violent surgery, with the painting slit down the center and its skin folded back, *opened up* to a void, a hollow center. The intense blue is a nice nod to that unmistakable International Klein Blue, the registered hue of French iconoclast Yves Klein. Like Klein, who "painted paintings" with fire, wind, rain, gold leaf, women's bodies, and sponges, Elesby seeks to stretch the limits of painting, but rather than altering the surfaces, she bends its very structure.

Motive Painting #3, 1997, pivots around the intersection of three distinct sets of parallel axes (or force fields, perhaps?), producing a multidimensional grid. Grids were an essential part of Piet Mondrian's Neo-Platonic view, and in the 1960s, of Sol LeWitt's stable, rational art of systems and Agnes Martin's horizons. But Elesby is not interested in such stability. More pertinent, perhaps, is the simultaneous emergence of Cubism and Einstein's special theory of relativity; both paradigms addressed the description of multiple events existing simultaneously in time and space. The shifting faceted planes of Analytic Cubism sought to show several views of an object within one frame. Ninety years later, Elesby's frameless, skewed webs, dyed in punk colors and dripping with energy, extend out in all directions.

Interactive Monochrome Yellow-green/Lavender-blue, 1997 is a spiderlike tracery that seems to slowly creep across the wall. Two branching systems of pathways extend out from a central spine and give a sense of movement, change, and transformation. The artist further increases the tension by bringing the two entities so close they almost touch.

Elesby locates her practice between that of Jackson Pollock and the virtual networks of cyberspace. She explains:

> I'm thinking about new ways to define and describe contemporary space. I am continuing an exploration of space that opened up when Pollock made his drip paintings with their seemingly limitless void, but he was trapped in Existentialism.[1]

Elesby's new models come not from art but from science and electronics where, for example, a computer can accomplish several tasks or a network can connect several people at the same moment. Elesby's works send their fingerlike extensions and their repeated shadows out across the wall, repeatedly replicating themselves. She has opened up the rectangle, painted on its skeletal support, and then unraveled its infrastructure to build roving, tentaclelike networks in an attempt to explore both the technical and the cultural structures of our world.

1. Sally Elesby, telephone conversation with the author, April 14, 1998.

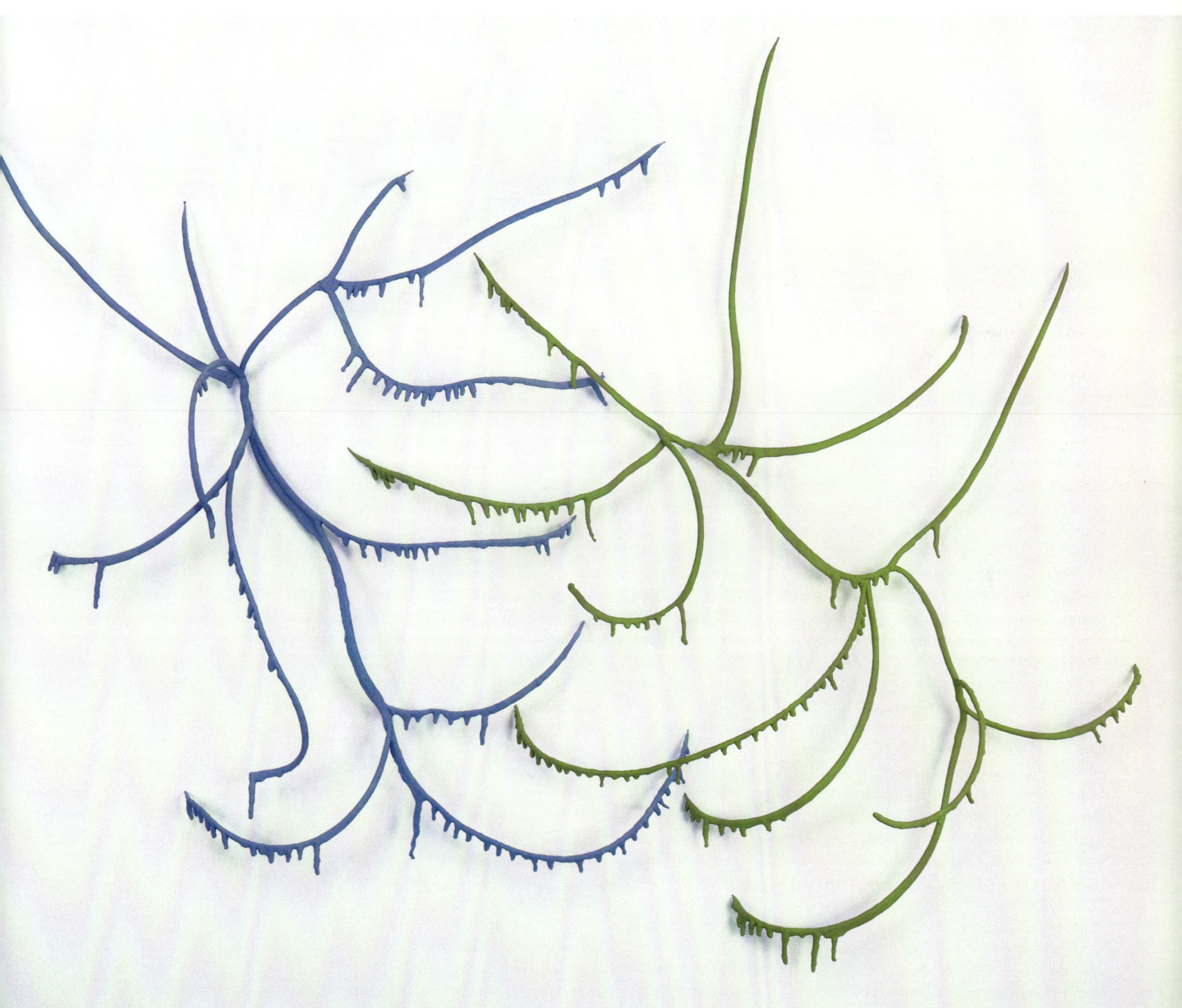

Jeff Elrod

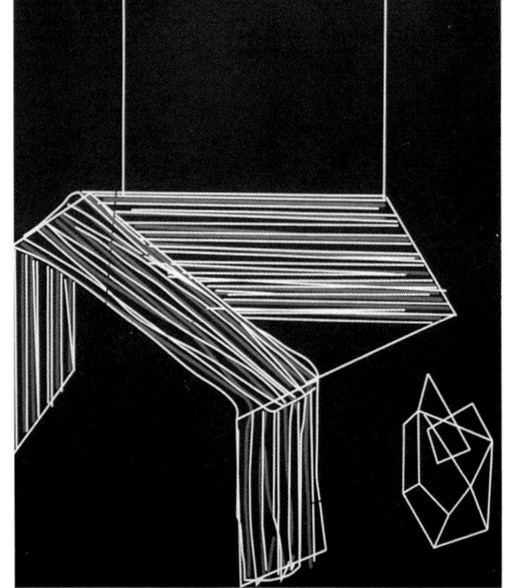

left:
***Still-Life*, 1998**
Acrylic on canvas
84 x 72 inches
Courtesy the artist and Texas Gallery, Houston

opposite:
***Turning Japanese*, 1998**
Acrylic on canvas
92⅛ x 83⅜ x 2 inches
Collection The Museum of Fine Arts, Houston; Museum purchase with funds provided by Mr. and Mrs. Andrew E. Schneck

Born 1966, Irving, Texas
Lives and works in Houston

Jeff Elrod paints large acrylic paintings on canvas or directly on the wall, courting a hybrid of 1990s digital technology and the careful, labor-intensive process of hard-edge painting as practiced in the 1960s and 1970s. "I have no interest in being painterly—I am an imagist and seek the super-flatness of an Andy Warhol painting, so that the viewer gets interested in what it is, not how it is painted."[1]

Warhol once declared, "The reason I am painting this way is that I want to be a machine."[2] Elrod, aligning himself with technology for the efficiency, speed, and uninhibited openness it offers, has different aspirations. But he has nonetheless followed the trajectory of Modernist painting by relying on technology, specifically a computer and a low-end drawing software program, and a color printer, to produce his images. "This machine has freed my repressed nature. It liberates my drawing in a way I have never been able to achieve with pen on paper. It's smooth, it's clean, there's no friction." Elrod's computer also provides lines and forms with an unmistakably technological "touch," an effect that Warhol's work could never achieve through silkscreened photographs.

Elrod's "drawings," which are actually color print-outs of his on-screen scribblings, are the starting point for his paintings and wall works, which often can expand to ten feet tall. Usually working late at night, Elrod starts at the computer with a loose idea, selects a color for the background, and begins to lay down lines and shapes. Dragging a mouse across the screen produces a line like no other: it can be started and stopped with precision while retaining its streamlined shape at varying widths, and it can feel tight or loose depending on software, settings, and user. Elrod begins with some arbitrary keystrokes or graphic commands, combined with quick moves of the mouse. He then responds to the results with specific additions to bring the image out further. Sometimes he drops the mouse on the floor or blindly hits random keys ten or so times to create exaggerations, repetitions, and unplanned incidents that he can either retain or remove electronically with just a few keystrokes. This improvisational, anarchical process gives his images a haptic, crazed energy.

"I love what sometimes happens with accidents. Though you cannot fake a good one," he admits, "sometimes I have to tweak it until it is perfectly screwed up."

As Elrod develops the images, he uses the printer to continually issue updated versions of the design, documenting the screen image every few minutes. His next step is to study the pile of print-outs, a process he compares to a photographer's careful study of negatives, then he chooses which image to paint. "I spend a lot of time looking, choosing, before I make a painting."

The shift from an 11 x 14-inch color print-out to a large canvas is a substantial step, considering the differences in process, scale, color, and texture between the "drawings" and the finished canvases. "I project an image onto primed canvas, carefully mask off the lines with tape, then roll on several layers of acrylic to get a broad, solid color with a flat surface." The taut lines of white that zip though the color are usually the negative space, unpainted areas of the ground.

Though painted this year, *Turning Japanese*,[3] 1998, was one of the first images Elrod produced when he developed this approach several years ago. Its hovering quasi-mechanical form (one of Duchamp's Bachelors, perhaps?), enmeshed in a tangle of straight, angled, and loopy lines, is accompanied by hints of letters (J-A-P-A-N) and awkward arabesques repeated like clones. *Still-Life*, 1998, also one of the artist's most recent canvases, is dominated by sets of parallel white lines that form a furniturelike structure (perhaps to hold that strange complicated polygon in the lower right corner?) guaranteeing the painting's composition and imparting some sense of depth. Lines of darkish red and blue cut over, under, and through the dark background, and the white lines, less available to the eye than the graphics, extend through to the white ground.

Considering Elrod's computer process of composition, one is forced to wonder why the artist didn't choose a means more compatible than painting to present his images. Elrod is quite resolute on the subject. "I suppose that the project of Modernist painting ended with [Frank] Stella's Black Paintings, and that abstract painting along that line may be boring and defunct. But I am thinking about the future, and though it may seem warped, I just want to make a very good painting."

1. Jeff Elrod, conversation with the author, Houston, June 30, 1998. All quotes are from this discussion.
2. Andy Warhol, quoted in "Andy Warhol," *ARTnews*, November 1963, p. 26.
3. The artist has said that the title came after the work was finished, a reference not only to one of his favorite New Wave songs from the 1980s, but also about the politics and sociology of computer technology. "By choosing that title, I wanted to reflect the paranoia about the Japanese dominance of high tech at that time, but also to champion their influence on our society; many of us have become computer people, and they had all the advancements before us."

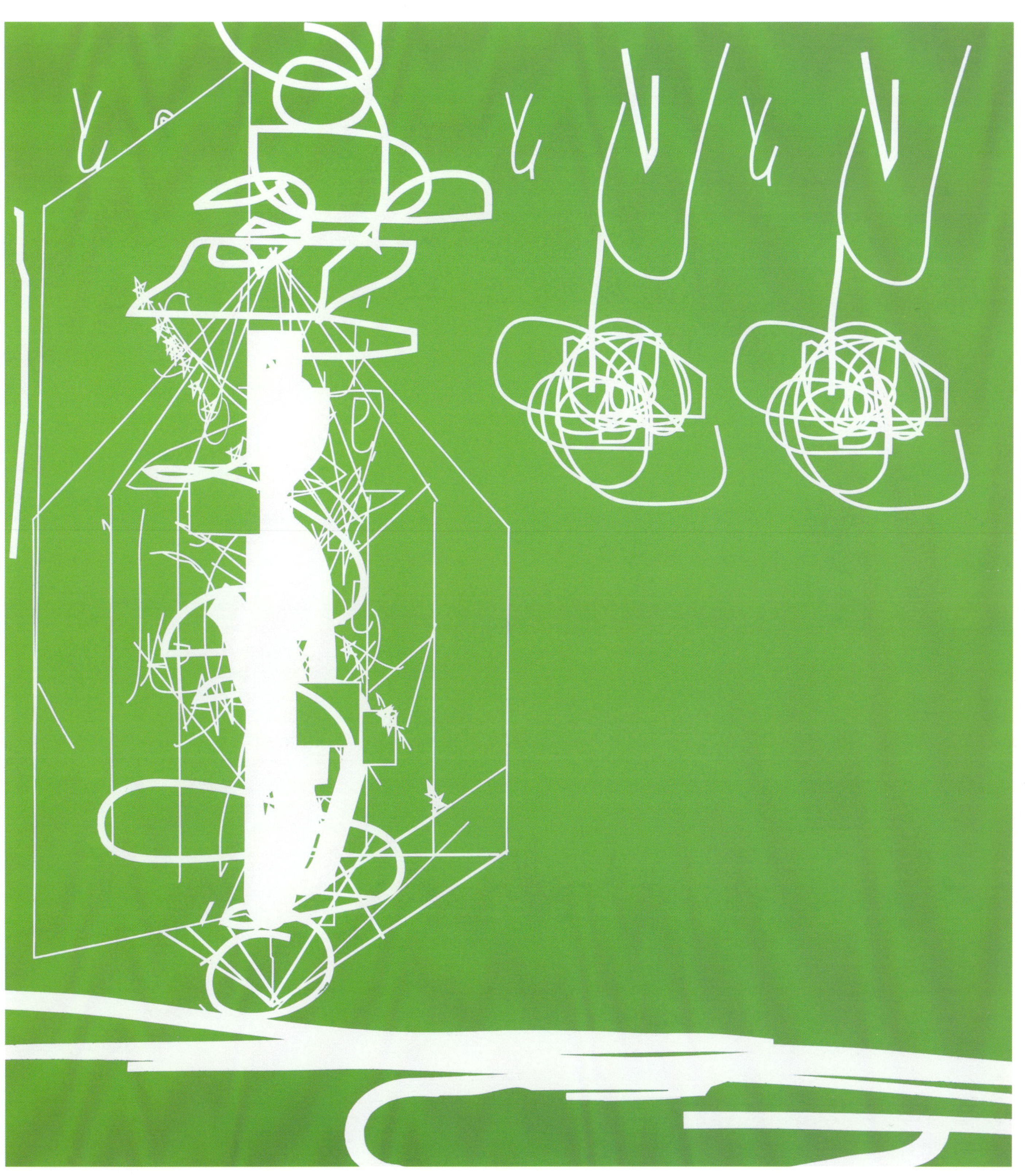

Tad Griffin

Born 1966, Houston
Lives and works in Houston

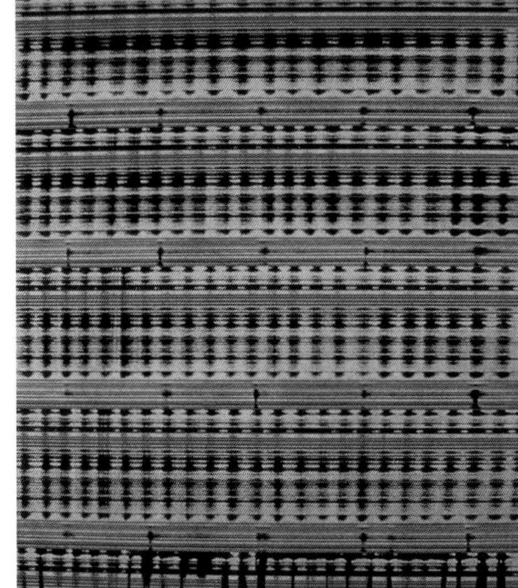

left:
***Echolate 1*, 1994**
Oil on canvas
82 x 72 inches
Courtesy the artist and Texas Gallery, Houston

opposite:
***Echolate 5*, 1994**
Oil on canvas
82 x 72 inches
Courtesy the artist and Texas Gallery, Houston

Like abstract painters of previous generations, Tad Griffin seeks to distill a primal zeitgeist into an art that speaks on a universal level. His imagery finds a close analogue in the output from high technology, which has become such an essential part of the fabric of our cultural communication, whether it be bar coding for computer price scanning, magnetic medical imaging, optical soundtracks for the movies, or the stuttering visual staccato of a fax machine misfeed. Griffin has written, "My aim is to create images that convey a sense of the abstract reality in which we live—a world of data, speed, and simulation."[1]

The works in this exhibition are drawn from a series of eight paintings that Griffin now calls Hyper Touch Transfer Process, a personalization of "Hypertext Transfer Protocol" or http, the code exchange that occurs when two computers communicate via the Internet. Originally, the title of each work included the artist's complicated formula actually based on musical notation,

$$\frac{41}{6(^{-}2 \cdot 12)} + \frac{40}{2 \cdot {}^{-}2} \dashv B(8)$$

but for simplicity in speaking and writing Griffin uses the shorthand title *Echolate 1–8*. This hybrid term coined by the artist is derived from the words *echo* and *locate,* recalling the use of sonic waves to determine one's position. This reference finds visual parallels in the repeating oscillations that fill the surfaces or fields of Griffin's work.

Through his work, the artist seeks "to connect to our time, our culture, and to each other"[2] using an essential, direct visual language. Griffin's stated quest recalls an important 1947 text by Barnett Newman about the totemic works of the Kwakiutl tribe of the Pacific Northwest. In examining the paradox of relating pure idea and the aesthetic act, Newman wrote:

> The abstract shape [the Kwakiutl] used, his entire plastic language, was directed by a ritualistic will towards metaphysical understanding. . . . To him a shape was a living thing, a vehicle for an abstract thought-complex . . . real rather than a formal "abstraction" of a visual fact, with its overtone of its already-known nature.[3]

Fifty years later, Griffin is working to make visible the sensations of the technological paradigm that shapes the abstract thought-complex of *our* time and community. Griffin finds inspiration in the conceptual distance and visual texture of technological data, a mediated language that describes an object or phenomena impossible for human senses to perceive. For example, the elementary particles and "fundamental forces" of quantum physics act on a level far below the range of our highest power microscopes. We *visualize* their existence through data. Musing about the digital data that helps us cross phenomenal, perceptual, and conceptual distances, Griffin has observed that by "extending our senses beyond wonder, into the realm of understanding, our awe at the workings of nature is renewed," thus echoing the sentiments of artists such as Newman, Mark Rothko, and others who sought to reconnect with the primal forces of nature.

Despite the immediate technological sensation offered by these paintings, Griffin aspires toward "high tech with high touch."[4] These works were not created by sophisticated electronics, but by the artist's hand. For the Echolate series, the artist crafted two different, carefully carved vinyl templates, much like a squeegee, with which he carefully dragged black oil paint across a white gessoed canvas surface, leaving the jagged trail of marks.

Griffin's methods—his customized tools, his rigidly choreographed polyrhythms—are far different from the romantically free-spirited, improvisational encounters with paint and canvas of earlier generations. Those painters sought to reveal internal or eternal truths directly in paint on canvas, but Griffin courts the implicit distance between the paint and the painter through the rigid, calibrated tool he uses to scrape through the paint—very unlike the responsive, flexible brush with which, for example, Willem de Kooning swept colors on, across, and around. Dismissive of the need for artists to express themselves personally, Griffin instead prefers to be "a sensitive listener, a delicate seismograph in tune to the subtle rumblings of our culture."[5]

The fact remains, however, that Griffin's canvases are *not* high-tech paintings at all, but carefully handcrafted works. He freely admits enjoying the process, making paintings out of "the pure calligraphy that could only come from my hand." He adds, "I like it that each painting has subtle and unique variations—that's why I do so many."[6] Griffin's low-tech technique for producing high-tech imagery allows us the pleasure of reconsidering both the look and the process of a painting made for—and about—a world bombarded with technology.

1. Tad Griffin, "Artist's Statement," in *Tad Griffin, Tom Moody, John Pomara, David Szafranski* (Dallas: Eugene Binder Gallery, 1994), p. 4.
2. Tad Griffin, telephone conversation with the author, August 5, 1998.
3. Barnett Newman, *The Ideographic Picture* (New York: Betty Parsons Gallery, 1947), reprinted in Maurice Tuchman, *New York School, The First Generation* (Greenwich, Conn.: New York Graphic Society Ltd., 1965), p. 105.
4. Tad Griffin, telephone conversation with the author, August 5, 1998.
5. Tad Griffin, notes prepared for the author, July 1998, n.p.
6. Tad Griffin, telephone conversation with the author, August 5, 1998.

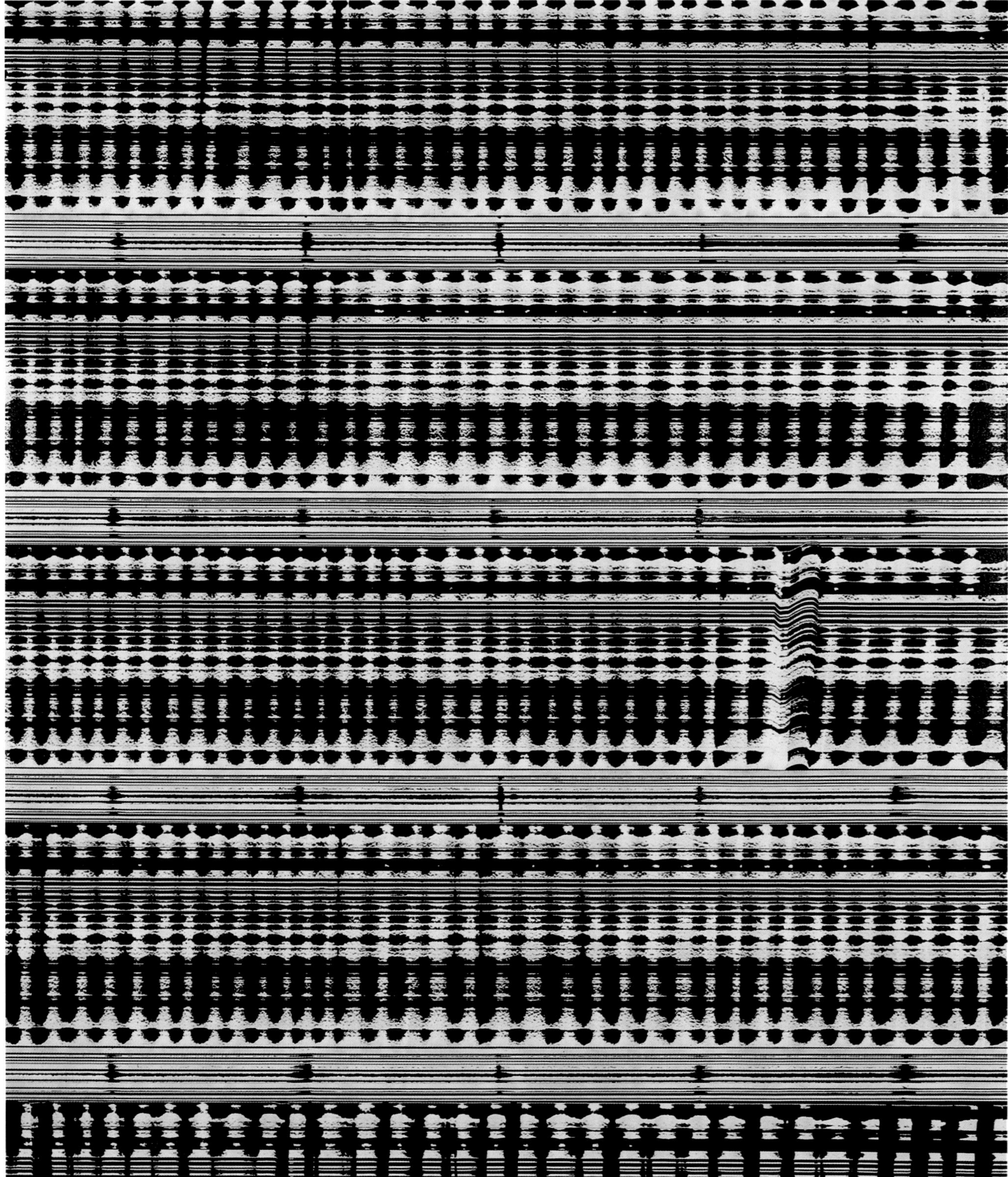

Jim Hodges

Born 1957, Spokane, Washington
Lives and works in New York

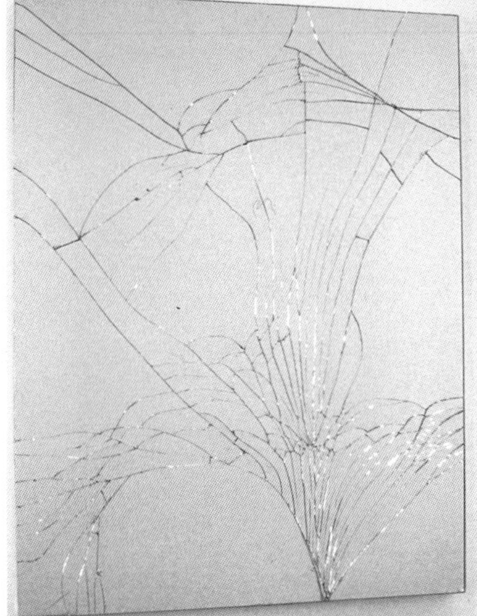

left:
***No Dust*, 1996**
Mirror on canvas
28 x 22 inches
Collection Dean Valentine, Beverly Hills, California

opposite:
***Nearing*, 1998**
Plastic, fabric, wire, and pins in 270 parts
50 x 79 inches
Courtesy the artist and CRG Gallery, New York

Although Jim Hodges creates art from coffee shop napkins, jewelry chains, paint swatches, color ink samples, silk flowers, and broken mirrors, his training is as a painter. But after receiving his BFA and MFA in painting, he confessed to an artist friend, "I just can't find myself in that material."[1] And yet, as demonstrated by the wall-mounted silk flowers and mirror-on-canvas works in this exhibition, he has transferred his evident affection for and clear knowledge of the formal aspects of painting to the mixed-media objects he creates today.

Hodges works with decorative silk flowers in several different formats, including sewing together blossoms and leaves into large curtains that drop from the ceiling to the floor, and gently pinning carefully arranged fragments to a wall. From a distance, Hodges' pinned flower work *Nearing*, 1998, looks like splashed color, as if each petal were a dab of paint on a large, expansive field. He describes his procedure:

> I start with one flower, pull apart the bits that make it up, and start attaching them to a wall, progressing like animation, making a suspended cartoon. . . . I work from the center out, "drawing" without any borders. I think of the artwork moving into the blankness, and the blankness moving into the artwork, with a lightness like air.[2]

As the viewer deciphers the medium and process in play, the arrangement seems almost clinical, but it is also poignant, as if each shred were pinned down like a butterfly wing. The work suggests loss, the fragile quality of life, the fleeting beauty of nature, and our vain attempts to preserve that beauty through artificial means. "When you see fireworks explode, there's always that instantaneous thrill, but then they always disappear—I want to freeze that emotion,"[3] Hodges has remarked. To do so, he deconstructs cheap, mass-produced decorations to make a gesture toward and about beauty. Content is carried here by his choice of materials and the process of their presentation.

Mirrors are a more recent addition to Hodges' repertoire. The artist was drawn to this material because it "provides a constant state of being present; a mirror is always awake, it is permanently in a state of non-permanence."[4] In addition to the superstition connecting broken mirrors to seven years of bad luck, Hodges considers smashing the mirror as making a break from the past, from history, as well as an attack on the mirror's constant, watchful immediacy. In cracked mirror works such as *No Dust*, 1996, he glues a pristine mirror to unprimed canvas, turns it face down onto a table, then strikes it through the back of the canvas with a hammer until he is sure he has broken it. This blind, violent gesture overturns the thrust of "action painting." More pertinent parallels are found in the radical approaches of European artists such as Lucio Fontana, who sliced and punctured canvases, and Yves Klein, who torched them. Hodges' cracked mirror works distill the violence that occurred to make them; rather than reflect a pristine parallel world, these mirrors present reality through a cracked cage that freezes time, a "live" version of Pablo Picasso's Analytical Cubism.

Hodges' mirror mosaics, such as *On Earth*, 1998, have a completely different character from the violent veining in the cracked works. In *On Earth* the artist has carefully broken a mirror into roughly square fragments that he then applied sequentially to the canvas in a grid, each abutting the previous piece. The viewer's attention focuses first on the tesserated surface and then on the thousands of reflections that it produces—as opposed to the dramatic lines which cut across the cracked mirror works. One might think about earlier artists who have used the grid for its systematic or stable properties, but unlike them, Hodges builds his grids fragment by fragment, following a system without any pre-drawn schematic. "The mosaic pieces are more like standing on a flattened disco ball; it pulls you deeper in, like a thousand reflective eyes open as wide as they can be,"[5] he explains. Taken together, the effect is irregular—the view is unstable—or as Hodges observes, "Mirrors offer more questions than answers."[6]

Of course, mirrors and flowers carry myriad associations on their own. The magic of Hodges' work comes from his ability to build upon those powerful connotations. Much of Modernist painting stressed the formal qualities of paint, and the resulting work often felt closed off, ungenerous, and elitist. By working with common materials that already have deeply embedded symbolisms, then transforming them into configurations that approximate abstract paintings, Hodges has opened up newly expressive possibilities to make eloquent statements in a fresh language.

1. Jim Hodges, conversation with the author, New York, December 3, 1997.
2. Jim Hodges, telephone conversation with the author, July 7, 1998.
3. Ibid.
4. Jim Hodges, conversation with the author, New York, December 3, 1997, and by telephone, July 7, 1998.
5. Jim Hodges, telephone conversation with the author, July 7, 1998.
6. Jim Hodges, quoted by Dana Self in *Jim Hodges* (Kansas City, Missouri: Kemper Museum of Contemporary Art, 1998), n.p.

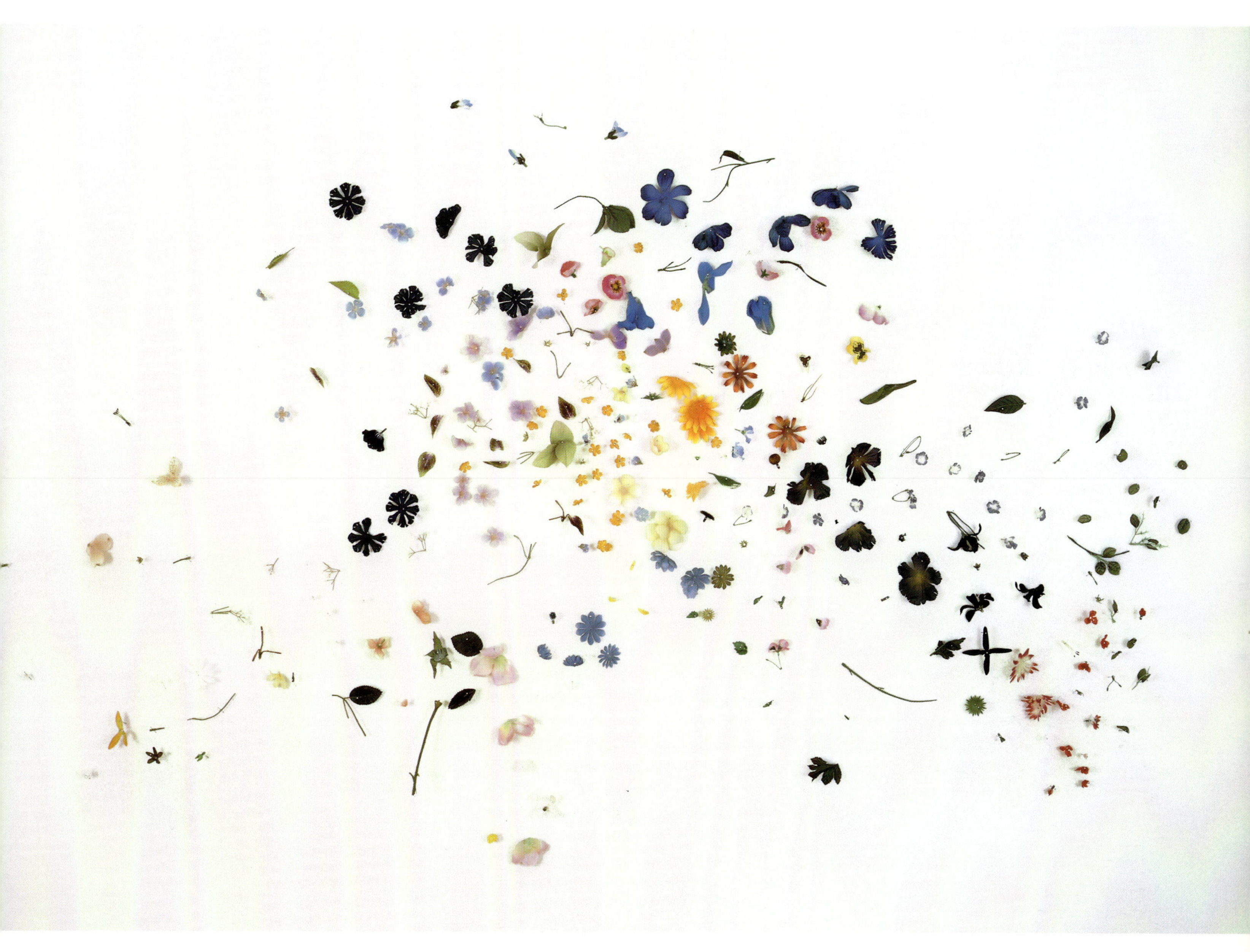

Callum Innes

Born 1962, Edinburgh
Lives and works in Edinburgh

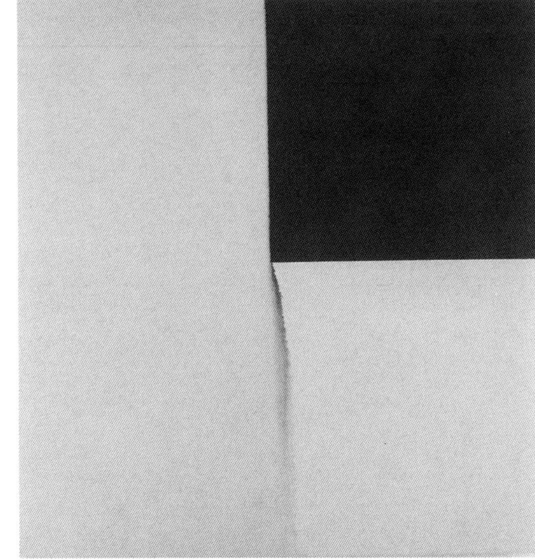

left:
***Exposed Painting, Charcoal Grey*, 1996**
Oil on canvas
39¼ x 38 inches
Collection John Robertshaw, New York

opposite:
Untitled, 1996
Oil and shellac on canvas
88½ x 87¼ inches
Collection Howard E. Rachofsky, Dallas

Callum Innes makes paintings that are literally "once removed" as he harnesses the alchemy of the spirits (as in solvents, such as turpentine) and paints then *un-paints* his delicately ethereal abstractions. His geometries are judged and proportioned by eye, not ruler, their edge lines painted by a steady hand with neither masking tape nor straight edge. All is freehand, the artist explains, "so there is still a frailty in the process I choose."[1]

Innes raises process to ritual, and faith in art is what inspires him to explore both the sureties and the capricious shifts of making a painting. One British art historian has observed, "Innes does not look for something in painting, but instead hopes that something is found there."[2] Each step, from the preparation of the stretcher bars and the canvas including its sizing with rabbitskin glue or gesso, to the application *and subtraction* of paint, is carefully orchestrated. While some procedures are necessarily standardized—repeatable—others involve more risk and a quiet daring.

To create shellac paintings such as Untitled, 1996, Innes pours pools of shellac onto the surface of a prepared canvas and, as the solvent itself finds its own level, slowly places dabs of oil paint onto the surface of the alcohol-based liquid. Like the proverbial oil and water, the paint floats atop the shellac, the result of a chemical incompatibility: the oil paint seems to skate unpredictably like mercury droplets about the surface. Innes carefully manipulates each dab of paint, dragging, swirling, and stirring it with the brush so that the two liquids hesitantly merge and bond. With only a few hours to work, he builds fields of speculative marks that fuse into the hardening lacquer shell, explaining, "This process is the exact opposite of the splattering of painting which it so much resembles."[3] The shellac itself develops broad, soft areas of gold with rippling outlines as the alcohol evaporates and deposits its residue, offering a sensuous fluidity to the composition. Innes works the isolated paint marks or specks into the shellac, interrupting, even frustrating, the traditional use of paint and the act of painting. The result is paint caught like a fly in amber.

In his series of Exposed Paintings, such as *Exposed Painting, Charcoal Grey,* 1996, the removal of the paint is as critical as its application. Again, a ground is carefully prepared onto which Innes lays a flat, pristine monochrome plane of paint (usually cadmium red, dark purple, deep olive, dark grey, or white), covering all or often only a portion of the canvas. Before this paint begins to dry, Innes reverses the process, removing a part of the pigment by repeatedly dragging a turpentine-laden brush across some part of the painted area, wiping away all but the faintest traces. Innes creates an imperfect geometry, making our eye struggle to adjust to the balance between what is and what was. The artist confides, "This sets up a multiplicity of centers. The relations between the sections are always shifting and moving, keyed by the part that runs down, which appears to both recede and come towards you."[4] The removed section becomes the most compelling, a middle ground with only the slightest of modulations, delineated by the faint trail marking the edge between the painted and the exposed ground. The result is as delicate and evocative as a waterfall in a Chinese ink-brush painting.

Formed White Painting, 1995, is built from hundreds of dots in the sublime non-color white. After the application of a dab, Innes would thin it to a whisper with a wash of turpentine. One critic wrote about his processes:

> To use a monochrome painting as the point of departure for something else—a different pictorial undertaking—is to work against its structure.
> A monochrome abstract embodies the very principle of reduction, both of pure geometric form and of a specific colour; Innes responds with a technique of further reduction. . . .[5]

The effect—both conceptually and visually—is heightened further when the color in question is white.

Innes may seem to be a traitor to the tradition of painting, obsessed as he is with undoing what has been carefully painted or with trying to pair materials such as paint and shellac, doomed to repel each another. Yet, with a startling shift in logic and philosophy, he engages both the positive and the negative means to paint (i.e., paint and its thinner) to create works that tease the eye and poke at the imagination. Suspending a drop of paint in time and space, or peeling a layer back to reveal the story of the work's own particular production, Innes' abstract canvases interrogate the Modernist painting approach.

1. Callum Innes, telephone conversation with the author, July 4, 1998.
2. Andrew Wilson, "Callum Innes: A Quality of Detachment," *Forum International,* March/April 1993, p. 87.
3. Callum Innes, telephone conversation with the author, August 13, 1998.
4. Callum Innes, telephone conversation with the author, July 4, 1998.
5. Friedrich Meschede, "The Reduction of Reduction," translated by David Britt, in *Callum Innes* (Zurich: Galerie Bob van Orsouw, 1995), p. 18.

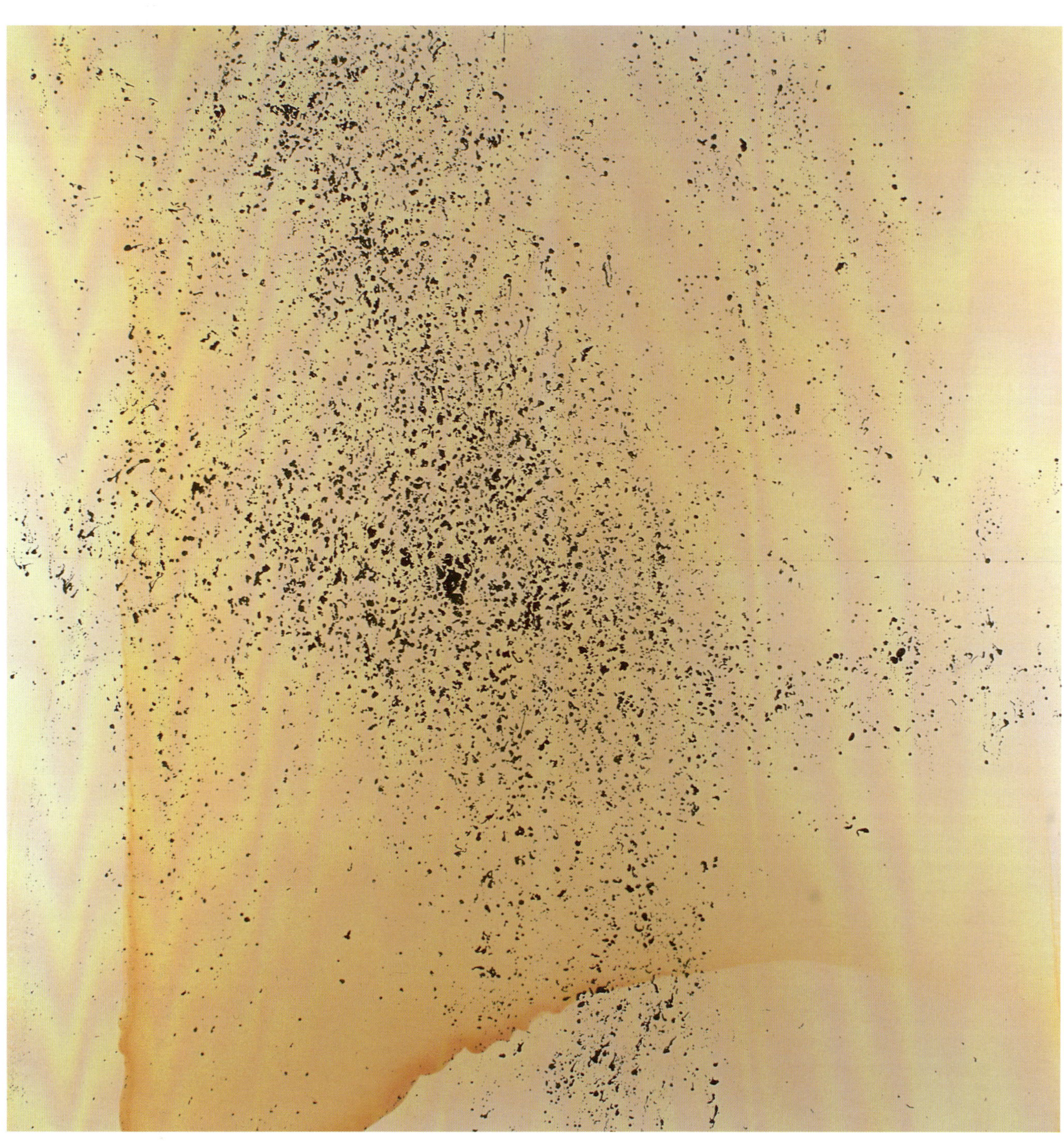

Emil Lukas

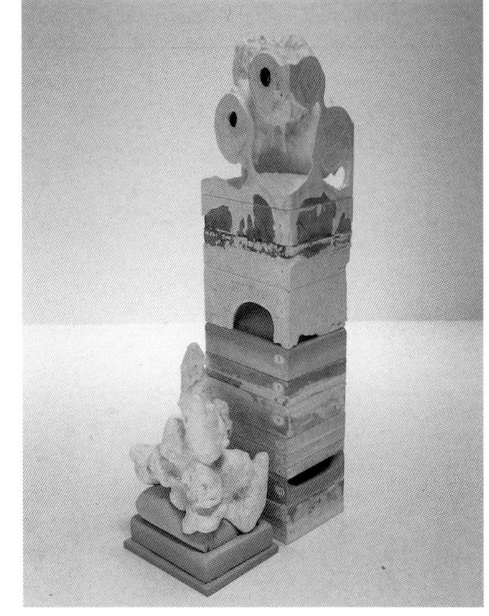

left and opposite:
***Paint Bulge*, 1998**
Plaster, paint, wood, fabric, foam, paper, rubber, and plastic in sixteen sections
Dimensions variable; 57¼ x 9½ x 12 inches (overall)
Courtesy the artist and Haines Gallery, San Francisco, and Gorney Bravin & Lee, New York

Born 1964, Pittsburgh
Lives and works in Stockertown, Pennsylvania

Emil Lukas extends the long legacy of serial Modernist painting in which each work in a group has a visual and/or conceptual relation to the next, a strategy that goes back as far as Claude Monet's light studies of grain stacks in the late nineteenth century. Lukas is interested not only in correspondences between each panel but also in the relation of a part to the whole, front to back, and one to the next. Although his work has its sculptural aspects, he begins each piece like a painter on a flat plane. But to Lukas it is not just a surface to carry images: it is a membrane, a physical plane to be viewed from both sides and, in his words, "to be stained, punctured, sewn through, and saturated, when sometimes it gives way. At that point it is no longer a surface, but jumps into the realm of sculpture."[1]

Process is key to the genesis of these works. Each one evolves through a series of actions and reactions within Lukas' laboratory-studio, a site for inquiry and improvisation with an assortment of materials and procedures. The artist sees them as a series of experiments:

> I make systems. These systems utilize a wide range of experiments, both traditional and non-traditional; cultured fly larvae, fresco painting, plaster casting from nature, stains made with sap, ink, body fluid, seed germination, double-sided stitched drawings, collaborative drawings with my children, recycled waste, by-products from past experiments. These experiments form a language.[2]

This "language" is used to create a narrative—the artist uses the analogy of scripting or storyboarding—a trail of visual and physical events, which open up as we move through the work. Movement, transition, and change are central to the unconventional format and presentation of Lukas' work; a viewer often has to stroll along a row, weave between individual sections, or turn over by hand each component of these strange sandwiches.[3] By requiring such physical activity to view his work, Lukas effectively highlights the relationships and transitions embedded between the layers of each work.

Paint Bulge, 1998—sixteen components cast of such truly mixed media as plaster, paint, wood, fabric, foam, paper, rubber, and plastic—stands nearly five feet high. As with other Painting Stack pieces, its presentation can take diverse configurations: as a single stack, split into two shorter stacks, or with each tablet standing upright in a row on the floor (like a line of dominoes). One moves through Lukas' Painting Stacks as if one were reading a book, turning over each "page" to "read" one side, then the other, building one pile higher the further one goes into its "story," stopping where one wishes, though the artist does not allow the parts to be rearranged out of sequence.

Paint Bulge, which takes its title from the tendency of a paint drop to swell with surface tension as it dries, was created specifically for this exhibition. The work contains flatter sections with drips, drizzles, and bleeds of paint as well as passages that explode into bulbous masses, which conceal (then reveal when the next "page" is turned) smooth domelike voids, all topped off (or bottomed out) with the base of a plastic paint bucket.

Buffer, 1998, represents a recent development: five large upright panels that stand (mounted to the floor) in a row about three feet apart, starting (or ending) with a dark, brooding red-stained plaster field punctuated with sky-blue orbs. As with all of Lukas' work, each surface of *Buffer* relates to the next through visual repetition and through physical hints of its production, whether casting, staining, drawing, etc. With a height of eighty inches, these works create an ambiguous kinesthetic relationship between object and viewer that is far from the intimacy of reading a book; its two-sided freestanding format undermines any clear connection with how we usually encounter paintings this size. Like the 1960s Minimalist and Postminimalist sculptors who engaged particularly unconventional installation strategies, Lukas locates this work in a hybrid area between painting and sculpture and architecture.

Lukas' work, with its anarchic experiments and democratic logic, undermines our commonly held assumptions about the structure, process, and presentation of painting. In this way, he not only offers quietly radical objects and images that tell the story of their own production, but stretches our understanding and expectation of what a painting can be.

1. Emil Lukas, telephone conversation with the author, July 3, 1998.
2. Emil Lukas, unpublished artist statement, 1997.
3. During this exhibition, the "leaves" of the stack piece *Paint Bulge*, 1998, will be turned a few times each day by the Museum staff, revealing a new pair of surfaces as the work cycles and recycles back and forth through its sequence.

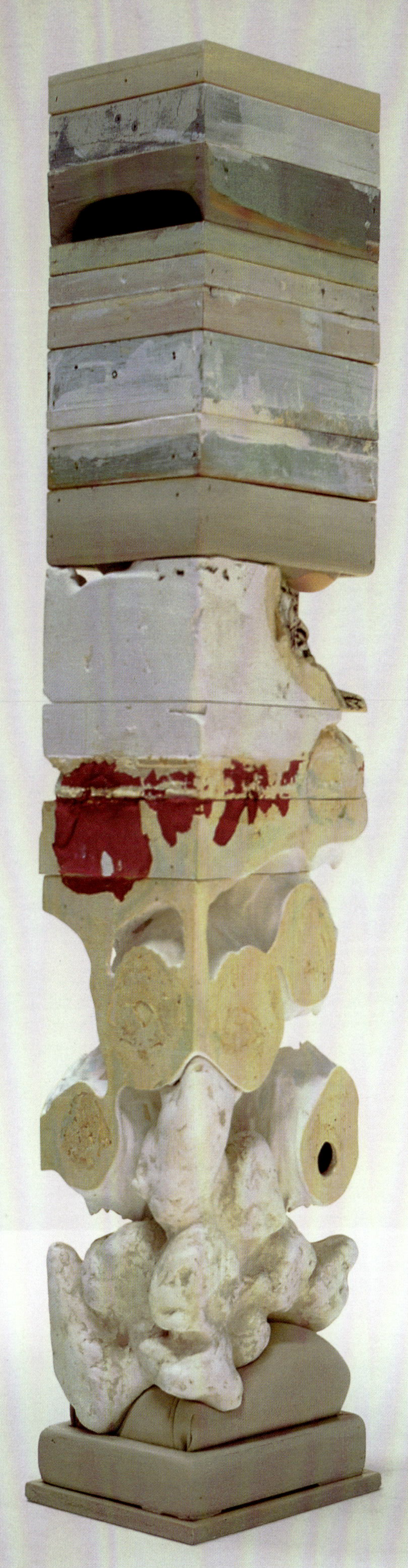

Fabian Marcaccio

Born 1963, Rosario de Santa Fe, Argentina
Lives and works in New York

left
***560 Conjectures For a New Paint Management*, 1996** (detail)
Artist-published booklet
[not in exhibition]

opposite:
***Idiotic Model for Several Types of Realness*, 1991**
Collograph on fabric, burlap, oil, silicon, plaster cast, and wall drawing
84 x 144 inches
Courtesy Gorney Bravin & Lee, New York

Deconstructing, stripping, and otherwise bastardizing abstract painting, Fabian Marcaccio produces reconfigurations that are so audacious one might genuinely laugh aloud or cry in despair. But these are serious artworks by a committed painter who has taken as his goal "to make abstraction extroverted."[1]

Marcaccio extends Modernism's own isolation of its elements of production and presentation—stretcher, canvas, brushstroke, and wall—although by 1992, the artist had concluded that Modernism's exploration of its language had devolved into "a geography of clichés and corruption."[2] He determined instead to apply current theories about society, technology, and the body to "work within the idea of [painting's] code in a condition of metastasis."[3] His subsequent painting "turned in on (against) itself . . . the pictorial elements crash[ing] into one another."[4]

Marcaccio has a voracious appetite for strategies to "multiply the viewer's relationships with the piece."[5] In recent works he has stretched canvas over contorted frames of copper plumbing pipe, while colorful bungee cords try to tack them to the wall. Last year one painting successfully sprang away from the gallery wall, spiraling into the space to form a freestanding environment.

"Abstract Painting, Once Removed" features Marcaccio's *Idiotic Model for Several Types of Realness*, 1991, a major earlier work that is in some ways more restrained than his other creations. One of the artist's Drag Painting series, the painting's scope is enlarged and further animated by a painted plaster cast fragment that has been pulled loose from the canvas and dragged across the wall a good five feet where it would seemingly exist on its own but for the trail of paint it has left in its wake.

The stretcher for *Idiotic Model* started as a seven-foot square. In its ruptured form, with a giant notch pried from one corner, the mangled wooden stretcher bar, bereft of its canvas cover, becomes a misshapen baroque curl, while the top edge of the painting is rippled from the impact. In this horizontally bisected canvas, the bottom section is colored in strong pink with some blue areas onto fine cotton, while the top half is raw, loosely woven burlap, allowing the oil from the strokes of thickly applied paint to seep into the fabric. The resulting stain around the paint feels as much like an aura or a glowing halo as it does an unsightly chemical residue. In the pink and blue section of this work, brushstrokes connect with and flow upstream against a flat underlayer comprising a geometric pattern of stripes, a sardonic nod to the 1960s work of Frank Stella. In the large arc of red and black stripes in the top section, Marcaccio has cut a squarish notch, and from there a single red stroke leads out and across the painting. As the red traverses the territory, it splits to disgorge a stream of orange paint (an effect the artist refers to as "metastasization"), then intersects a zone of black stripes before taking a curve that sends the black lines into centrifugal disarray. Another set of lines appears to regroup in a grid in the upper right corner.

For Marcaccio, canvas is both a support and an image. Many of his works are overprinted with photographically enlarged pictures of canvas weaves, calling close attention to the textured matrix of threads. In the lower right corner of *Idiotic Model*, "threads" from the (overprinted) patch seem to come loose and get pulled into the magisterial sweep of his painted brushstrokes.

Marcaccio's imagery works on multiple layers, but the liquidity of brushed paint is his primary icon. *560 Conjectures For a New Paint Management*[6] is an ongoing lexicon of sketchy schematic line drawings showing plots in which paint and brush and canvas and wall encounter each other in hundreds of different positions and relationships. For example, the bottom ridge of a horizontal swipe of paint might start leaking a row of drips, or another line of paint might bisect and its two ends turn back to reconnect to its own tail. These playful scenarios are writ large in Marcaccio's paintings, painted thin or thick, though they sometimes appear just as a printed image. He also likes clear silicone gel, a medium that holds the textural character of a brushstroke and adds another layer to his sandwich of strategies without obscuring prior painting underneath.

Marcaccio's playing with paint is fully serious. He has explained:

> I am not producing a cartoonish version of the brushstroke; I am using this as a new ground for painting. Instead of looking at Lichtenstein's cartoon brushstroke and being content with the cliché, or denying it, or reaching back for some kind of transcendence, I think we can find transcendence through the rubble of the cliché. I hate postmodern eclecticism. I'm a total believer.[7]

In the end, Marcaccio's pounding against painting's components becomes not constructive criticism of the medium's weaknesses, but an exercising of its strengths.

1. Fabian Marcaccio, conversation with the author, New York, December 5, 1997.
2. "Fabian Marcaccio," interview with Patricia Collins and Richard Milazzo, *Tema Celeste*, Fall 1992, p. 93.
3. Ibid.
4. Ibid.
5. Fabian Marcaccio, conversation with the author, New York, December 5, 1997.
6. These are compiled in periodically updated self-published booklets issued by the artist, although they have been reproduced in exhibition catalogues such as *With-JecT Spain* (Madrid: Galeria Salvador Diaz, and Barcelona: Galeria Joan Prats, 1998).
7. Fabian Marcaccio, quoted in Raphael Rubinstein, "Abstraction in a Changing Environment," *Art in America*, October 1994, p. 108.

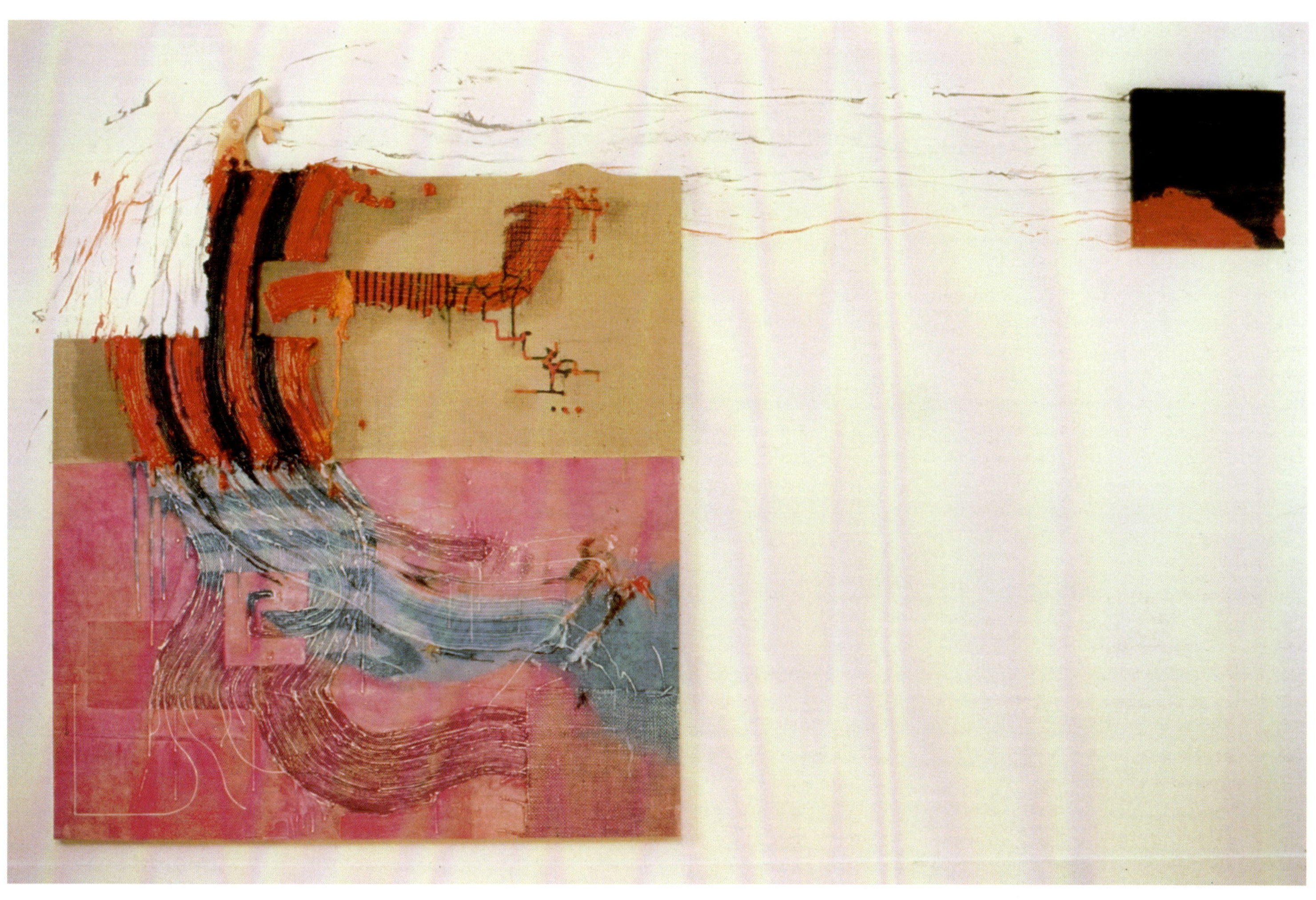

Beatriz Milhazes

Born 1960, Rio de Janeiro
Lives and works in Rio de Janeiro

left:
***As Quatro Estações [The Four Seasons],* 1997**
Acrylic on canvas
101½ x 112 inches
Collection The Bohen Foundation

opposite:
***Fleur de la Passion: Maracujá [Passion Flower: Passion Fruit],* 1995–96**
Acrylic on canvas
48 x 78 inches
Collection Stephen D. Susman, Houston

The boldly baroque abstract fields of Beatriz Milhazes' paintings draw deeply from the multicultural streams of Brazil, yet also exude a quirky, independent personal character. She explains, "My painting is a kind of sewing; I start with a white space and fill it with a world," then adds, "But I love the illusionism possible through painting."[1] Milhazes' work is inventive and experimental but also approaches the documentary. She appropriates and adapts everyday and celebratory motifs from Rio de Janeiro as well as from the different regions and peoples of Brazil. For example, her visual vocabulary includes roses, beads, circles, waves, carnival lights, arabesques, frills, embroidery, the cashew nut, the lily, the eye, and the compass flower.[2] As one New York critic aptly observed, "[These paintings] show an artist looking deep into herself and her cultural roots and figuring what to give painting that it hasn't quite had before."[3]

The artist stresses the order behind her work, expressing admiration for Constructivism and for Piet Mondrian, as well as the uncanny sense of structure found in certain outsider artists. We see this in the bottom layer of geometric forms in white, black, gray, and pink in *Fleur de la Passion: Maracujá [Passion Flower: Passion Fruit]*, 1995–96. Yet we also get a sense of the *horror vacuui* of the European Baroque, imported by Portuguese colonizers and made manifest in dramatic cathedral architecture and decorative arts. Brazilian critic Stella Teizeira de Barros comments about this tension in Milhazes' paintings:

> For Beatriz, the Baroque is maintained as a cultural given, but only as archetypal memory. As emotion, it is displaced and misleads nostalgic motivations. It has doubtless been extracted by her from the deep roots gathered from our historical time, yet it has been transformed into mirror images, a simulacrum which enters and reinforces the vortex of the work's constructive structures.[4]

One feels this sense of distance, of what Teizeira de Barros calls "conceptual rigor and constructive discipline,"[5] because Milhazes does not so much *paint* her paintings as *build* them. The density of layers found in *As Quatro Estações [The Four Seasons]*, 1997, shows how Milhazes creates depth by coming forward with a series of overlapping forms. Onto a prepared background she has layered prefabricated patterns and ornaments as if they were individual marks, events, and images, a process that recalls arranging an installation as much as laying down marks on a canvas. For many of the motifs, she actually used a reversal process, painting them in acrylic onto transparent plastic sheets, positioning them onto the canvas in progress, and peeling them off their backing. This procedure requires a certain amount of previsualization, given that the images are created in reverse—a method found in artistic monoprinting, folk art's reverse glass painting, and other forms of mirror-image appliqué that have counterparts in Pre-Columbian, Colonial, and contemporary craft traditions in Brazil.[6]

With their roots in carnival celebration, symbols of love, ceremony, and decoration, one would expect to find an exuberance, delight, and flourish in the brushwork of Milhazes' ornamental elements, but instead we find a muted, flattened, even-handed gloss, the result of their transfer from a sheet of plastic, rather than originating on the surface of the painting. The real feeling of their function in life and in ceremony thus seems severed, suffocated.

Milhazes' goal is not to evoke a faraway festival or to make decorative art. Instead, she taps into familiar cultural motifs and opens them wide for their universal visual appeal, building abstract paintings that explore the kinds of space that Frank Stella discussed in the lectures published as *Working Space*. He presents the problem:

> Our contemporary painterliness cannot seem to produce anything like the fullness of Delacroix, Turner, or Monet; it is as though pigment, light, and surface have disappeared into Mondrian's black grid. We are left to worry about pictorial space almost by default.[7]

And the solution he finds in Caravaggio:

> the Renaissance artist began to direct himself away from decoration and illustration, away from altarpieces and fresco cycles, toward his newfound responsibility: the creation of his own space. This is the task to which Caravaggio addressed himself with amazing success.[8]

Milhazes *creates her own space* by combining the flattened geometry of Mondrian with decorative motifs from her own culture. She offers us a deep, activated abstract space full of the flair and flavor of a contemporary Brazilian woman.

1. Beatriz Milhazes, conversation with the author, Rio de Janeiro, October 14, 1996.
2. For a fascinating examination of many of Milhazes' motifs, see Adriano Pedrosa, "Gloss," in *Beatriz Milhazes* (São Paulo: Galeria Camargo Vilaça, 1996), pp. 2–12.
3. Roberta Smith, "Beatriz Milhazes at Edward Thorp Gallery," *The New York Times*, March 22, 1996, p. C27.
4. Stella Teizeira de Barros, in *Beatriz Milhazes* (Caracas: Sala Alternativa Artes Visuales, and São Paulo: Galeria Camargo Vilaça, 1993), n.p.
5. Ibid.
6. Holland Cotter, "Beatriz Milhazes at Edward Thorp Gallery," *The New York Times*, December 5, 1997, p. E33.
7. Frank Stella, *Working Space* (Cambridge, Massachusetts and London, England: Harvard University Press, 1986), p. 5.
8. Ibid.

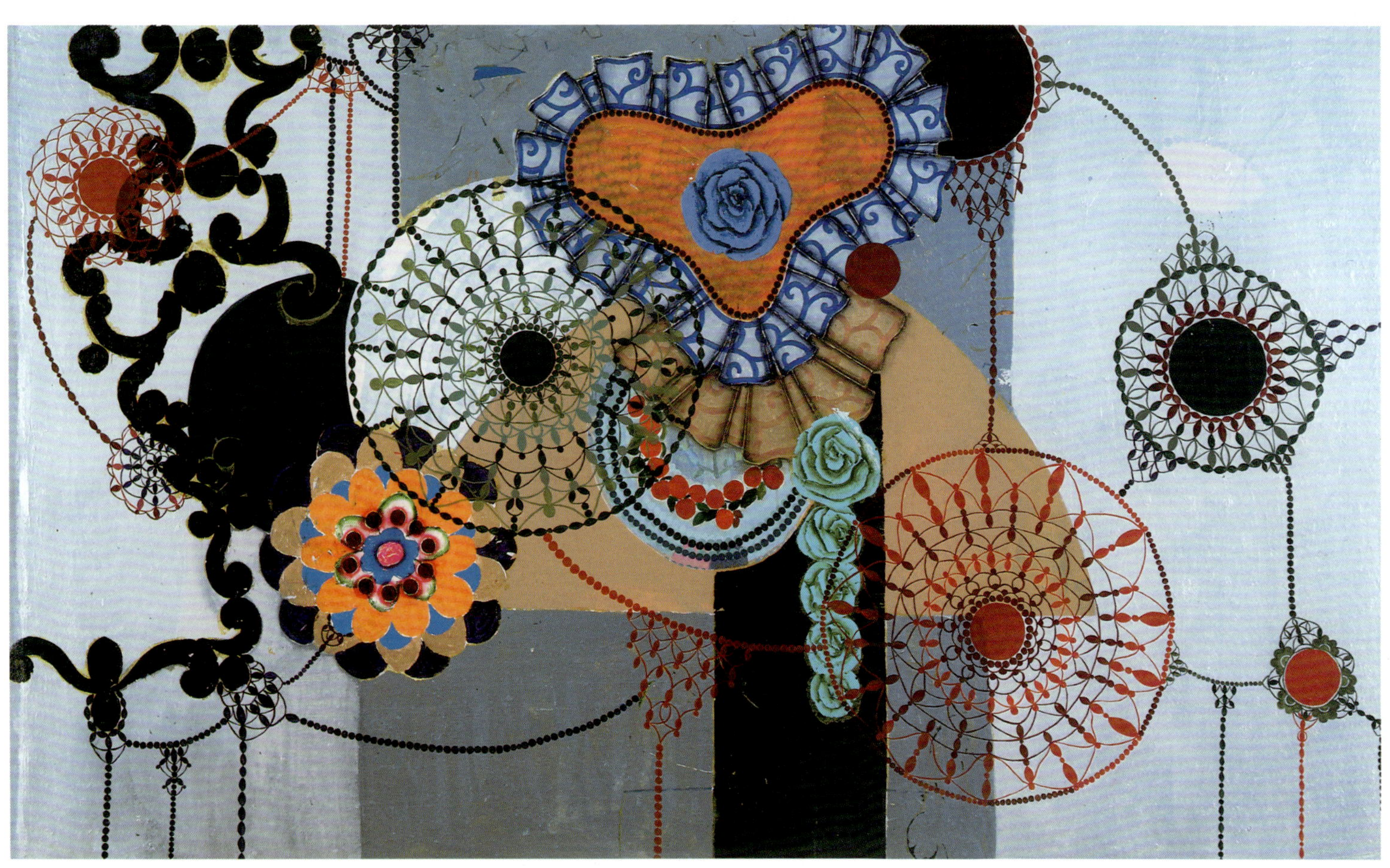

Takashi Murakami

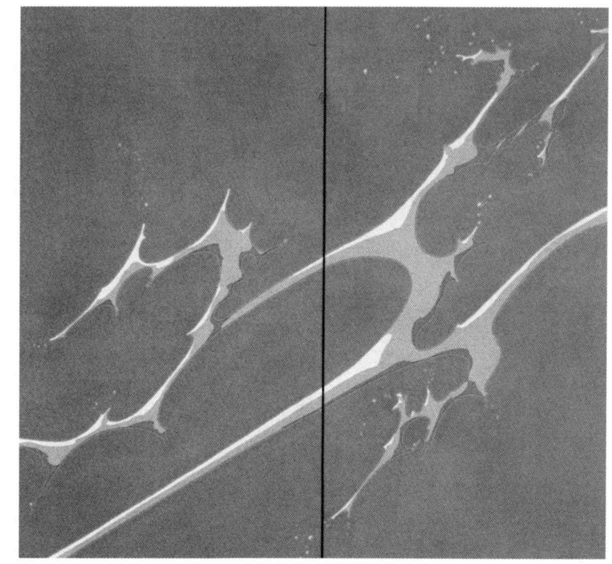

left (detail) *and opposite:*
***Cream*, 1998**
Acrylic on canvas on wood panel
96 x 192 inches
Collection Eileen and Peter Norton, Santa Monica, California

Born 1962, Tokyo
Lives and works in Tokyo and New York

Many people find it ironic that Takashi Murakami, born and raised in Japan's "post-recovery" era of abundant goods and information, received the equivalent of a Ph.D. specializing in *Nihon-ga*—the Japanese national traditional painting style using natural pigments on paper.[1] For nearly a decade he has drawn his imagery both from his own childhood and from today's youth culture in Japan. By conceptually (and sometimes literally) recasting plastic toy models, cartoon animation (*anime*), and comic books (*manga*), Murakami offers a sly critique of Japan's sense of its own commodity culture and its place within the international sphere in the shadow of Western, especially American, influence. His dramatic projects have included paintings, lightboxes, installations, and monumental inflatable balloons. He has recently created human-scale hand-painted, fiberglass and resin figurines based on his own invented cartoon characters, *Hiropon*, 1997, and *My Lonesome Cowboy*, 1997. In the first, an athletic, assertive young woman jumps a rope formed by streams of milk flowing from her breasts, while her companion, equally self-sufficient, spins a lasso from his own ejaculate.

In *Cream*, 1998, from his Splash Painting series, Murakami mixes metaphors and motifs from Japan's pop culture and its traditional art with American Abstract Expressionism and Pop Art. This series is linked to the concurrently produced *Hiropon* and *My Lonesome Cowboy* works by its iconographic invocation of fertile fluids suggesting (pro)creativity and sustenance. In addition to juggling issues of gender, identity, and pop culture, however, Murakami has embedded specific art historical references into this work. Within the Japanese landscape painting tradition, he is interested in the artist Sansera Kano, whose mannered, floating "naturescapes" hang organic elements in vast empty fields. *Cream's* four-panel structure suggests a Japanese folding screen, traditionally ornamented with a landscape (often rendered as sparsely as a few isolated cloudlike forms.) The fluidity of Murakami's "splashes" recalls the dramatic wave imagery in Hokusai's famous woodblock prints, but *Cream's* jagged forms can also be read as lightning flashes, which in *Ukiyo-e* Kabuki prints symbolize ghosts or spirits. The sweeping, thrusting strokes Murakami employs also suggest calligraphy.

Westerners are likely to respond first to the scale of *Cream*, reading a reference to Abstract Expressionism, the style that inspired art historian Irving Sandler's book title *The Triumph of American Painting*—a political posturing not overlooked by this Japanese artist. Murakami surely mocks the heroic stance of Abstract Expressionism, with its current popular image as a macho, paint-flinging men's club, and the gestural paint drip as a primal representation of the existential self. The surface of this painting, despite its painterly allusions, is flat and dry, and more like Andy Warhol's or Ed Ruscha's uninflected renderings of everyday Pop icons than the brushy gestures of a Willem de Kooning that it might appear to replicate.

Another painting in this series, *Milk*, 1998, not included in this exhibition, has its splashes sprayed across a pink field, providing a feminine alternative as dramatic as *Cream*, obviously a boy's version. In earlier series, Murakami addressed the representation of gender and sexuality in *manga* comic books; in light of that fact, and his full-size sexually heroic action figures, male and female Splash Paintings make perfect sense. Feminist theorists such as Hélène Cixous have discussed the importance of women inscribing themselves into history and culture as *l'ecriture féminine*, speaking metaphorically of the "white ink" of breast milk to describe a pure female expression.[2] Murakami, perhaps unknowingly, has opened the door to a new form of feminist abstraction.

The graphic outlines and simple highlights of the splashes in *Cream* and *Milk* remind us that these works are, after all, cartoons—probably a nod to Roy Lichtenstein's famous flattening of the angst-laden brushstroke and also to the way that Japanese *manga* artists get around the censor's ban on explicit sex by depicting the by-products of pleasure rather than the thing itself.

The Japanese art critic Noi Sawaragi has addressed Murakami's position between Japan and the United States:

> Murakami recognizes that the symbols that identify "Japan" have been formed not by the accretion of ancient traditions but by gathering various elements artificially in the process of modernization, and he is able to draw, in his criticisms, on his thorough training within the tradition of *Nihon-ga*.[3]

With *Cream*, as with his other work, Murakami skates across cultural constructs to harness the possibilities of a hybrid culture created from global modernization and mass communication. The results are multilayered and often contradictory, but they offer new points to consider regarding the place of painting (and comic characters and national identity) in culture at the close of the century. Pundits say the twentieth century is "The American Century" and that the next will be Asia's. If this is so, then Murakami is perfectly poised to paint our future.

1. For an insightful examination of the political role of the development of *Nihon-ga* painting and Murakami's critique of it, see Noi Sawaragi, "Takashi Murakami," *World Art*, Summer 1997, p. 76.
2. Lisa Tickner, "Nancy Spero: Images of Women and *la pienture féminine*," in *Nancy Spero* (London: ICA, Derry, Ireland: Orchard Gallery and Foyle Arts Project, and Edinburgh: Fruitmarket Gallery, 1987), p. 7.
3. Noi Sawaragi, "Takashi Murakami," p. 76.

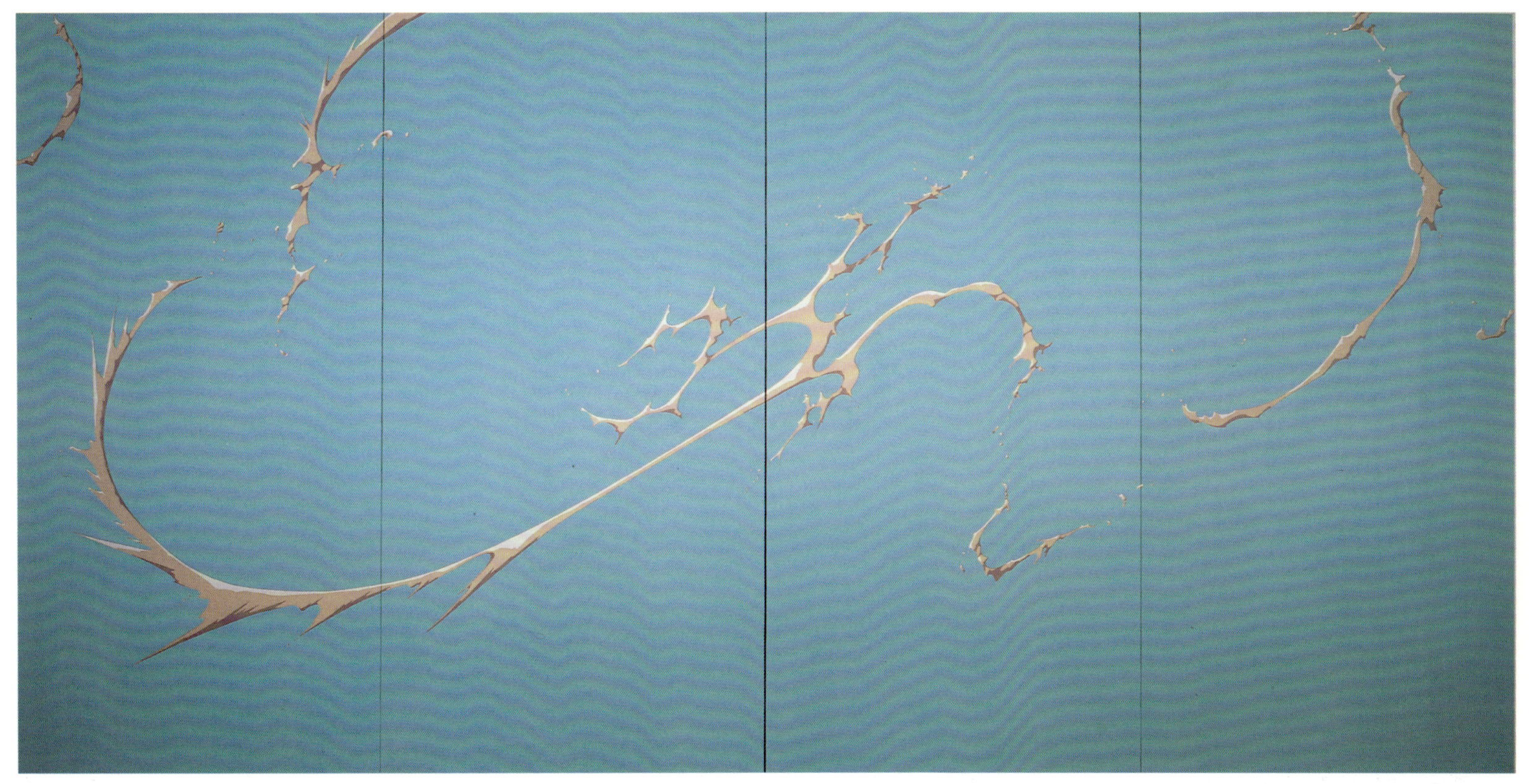

Aaron Parazette

Born 1960, Ventura, California
Lives and works in Houston

left:
***Beggar's Joys*, 1996**
Oil enamel on canvas
75 x 75 inches
Collection Stephen D. Susman, Houston

opposite:
***Tournament*, 1998**
Oil enamel on canvas
96 x 72 inches
Collection J. Scott Caruthers, Houston

Though he currently creates expansive paintings of animated splashes from clip-art books made for graphic designers, Aaron Parazette once confessed "sincere doubts regarding the significance of the [painting] activity and its residual objects."[1] Like many of his generation, Parazette reveals a knowledgeable wariness of Modernist painting and the claims made on its behalf that have produced a self-consciousness that interferes with the ability of today's artists to pursue painting with full sincerity. This caution shapes Parazette's process and strategy. "I paint signs for paintings,"[2] he explains, relishing the irony.

Parazette's exploration of generic imagery began in 1991 with a series of ten-inch-square canvases. Entitled *Empty Abstractions*, the ten works were covered with geometric patterns painted in saturated colors using artists' oils. Another work, *Decorative Painting Painted in the Style of The Old Masters*, 1991, was based on his own bathroom floor and shower curtain, predicting his later Wallpaper Paintings. That 1994–95 series, which furthered his appropriation of banal repetitions of kitschy domestic decoration, was rendered with a dedicated deadpan intensity. The first of the Wallpaper Paintings were intimate oil panels, twenty inches square, but a move to a larger scale brought on a crisis, then an important solution. The artist has recalled:

> When I tried painting large paintings in oil paint, I couldn't stomach it. I couldn't avoid the trail of the brush. My anxiety came from the standard art education, which teaches that the mark-making left as evidence is what makes or breaks a painting; I felt as though my professors were still looking over my shoulder. When I switched to sign painters' enamel, which cannot hold the trace or marks of a particular artist's hand—the authorial identity—I felt I was finally making my own paintings.[3]

Clearly engaged by the flat, hard-edged, carefully applied coatings, Parazette soon sought wallpaper designs "so banal that the viewer's interest would focus on the way they were painted."[4] Avoiding the pressure of perfect brushstrokes, he produced a flatness favored by the earlier Pop artists.

Parazette's current Splash Painting series began in 1995, when the artist happened onto "clip-art books" of graphic images of splashes and bursts while looking for motifs he might use to build his own patterns:

> I couldn't ignore the issue of image entirely, so making a painting which references "Painting" seemed right. Robert Ryman once said, "I paint the paint." I am doing that in a contemporary way.[5]

To compose most of the series, the artist photocopied these found "designer splashes" from the sourcebook in an array of sizes, arranged them on a tracing table to build a composition, and made an ink drawing. He scanned the drawing into a computer and assigned colors so he could test basic hue and value relationships to find a starting point for the painting. Further along in the series, he became less dependent on the clip-art books, and more free with the invention of his splashy shapes. After the projecting and tracing of the drawing on the canvas came the carefully anonymous application of paint.

Until *Tournament*, 1998, Parazette's Splash Paintings followed a square format, filled with superimposed splashes and exploding drips. His compositions vary greatly and include concentric whorls and centrifugal spins, as well as drips in lines from above and random splashes from all four edges. *Beggar's Joys*, 1996, pivots around a slightly off-center circular blue splash that steps forward like a medal of honor, while less well-behaved splatters (roughly in increasing order of size) fall in behind until the canvas is filled. The large, vertical *Tournament*, on the other hand, is a vibrant melee of spattering, its energy dissipated into drips large and small, left and right, top and bottom, over and under, skimming off the top layer of Jackson Pollock's misty veils, then clarifying the silhouettes against a black background.

Each work in the Splash Painting series appropriates its title from a work in The Museum of Modern Art's important Abstract Expressionist exhibition *The New American Painting* that was circulated by the U.S. Information Agency across Europe in 1958–59. While Parazette admits that this homage is made in nostalgic reverence for the sincere poetry of those mythic paintings,[6] their namesakes leave behind the intense passion once invested in those works. Parazette distills the fluid energy of action painting into pure Pop pattern, distancing himself from the ethos of the earlier generations for whom the liberation of paint—through drips, strokes, or splashes—paralleled their own liberation. Parazette explains:

> I *want* to make sincere paintings, but at this point in time you cannot do that without a certain sense of self-consciousness about where paintings are made, exhibited, distributed, and considered today.[7]

1. Aaron Parazette, from an unpublished 1994 artist statement, quoted by Al Harris F. "Faith in Doubt," in *Forging Ahead* (Arlington: University of Texas at Arlington, Center for Research in Contemporary Art, 1994), p. 17.
2. Aaron Parazette, conversation with the author, Houston, July 6, 1998.
3. Ibid.
4. Ibid.
5. Ibid.
6. Aaron Parazette, telephone conversation with the author, August 5, 1998.
7. Ibid.

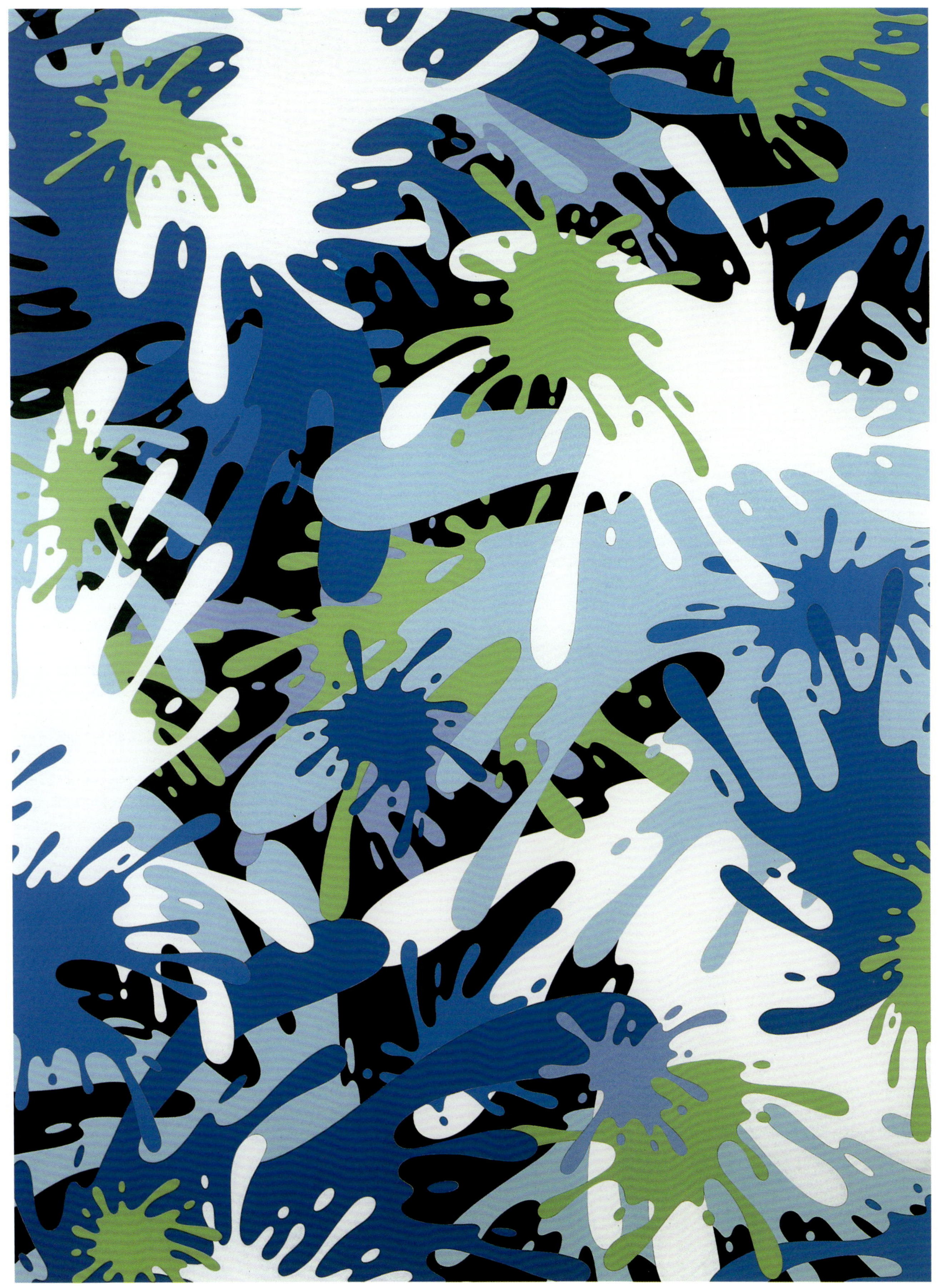

Richard Patterson

Born 1963, Leatherhead, Surrey, England
Lives and works in London

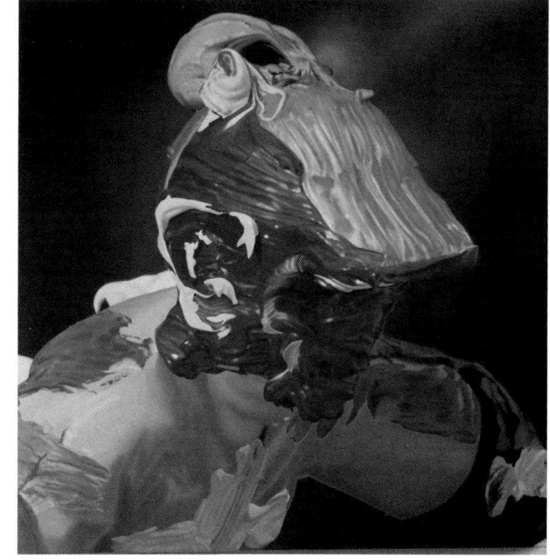

left:
***Head,* 1998**
Oil on canvas
26 x 26 inches
Collection The British Council

opposite:
***Painted Minotaur,* 1996–97**
Oil on canvas
82 x 62¼ inches
Tate Gallery, London; Purchased from Evelyn, Lady Downshire's Trust Fund, 1997

In the late 1980s and early 1990s, Richard Patterson explored many styles of painting, but he ended up destroying all he created. "Between [Gerhard] Richter and [Sigmar] Polke, it seemed like they had all of painting sewn up," he recalls. "There were no gaps left." He found some freedom when he realized that "maybe I could do an unabashedly figurative painting."[1]

Patterson's breakthrough came in 1995 when he smeared paint from his palette onto a small toy motocross rider given to him by a friend, then photographed it from different angles in various settings. The resulting photograph was finally rendered in oil on canvas as tightly and meticulously as a 1960s Photorealist painting.

The macho, sporty, pop culture subject of motocross racing drew much of the initial public attention to this work (Patterson is an enthusiast). But it also provided an important distance from the painted photographs of Richter. Looking back, the artist observes, "Painting a photograph relates to Richter, but the subject was from a very different culture and time. As you see in his pictures of burning candles, he is sentimental in a Germanic way."[2]

Head, 1998, extends the Motocrosser series, isolating a detail from the artist's first painted toy, illustrating clearly how the viscous paint has transformed the head and helmet, and how the paint itself has conformed to the surface on which it had been brushed. In an interview, Patterson recalled Frank Stella's observation that in order to make a painting, it is necessary to construct an object (traditionally a stretched canvas, but for Stella's Exotic Bird series, it was wood panels, and later aluminum shapes), then paint onto it.[3] Taking a Duchampian approach popular with his peers in London, Patterson uses a readymade surface (which carries its own connotations) on which to sweep his strokes of pure paint.

Patterson's Minotaur series, which consists of five works, is based on a pencil eraser. The Minotaur, a monster from Greek mythology, lived in the circular labyrinth in Crete and fed on the bodies of youths and maidens until he was slain by Theseus.[4] The mythical creature appealed to Modern artists such as Pablo Picasso because of its psychological implications. As one historian has observed, "Surrealist artists and writers adopted the myth of the Minotaur as their own, and the Minotaur came to symbolize man's bodily desires (the body of a man) and his irrationality (the head of a bull)."[5] Patterson says, "The possibility of some mythical figure that had somehow been dragged into the twentieth century seemed quite interesting to me."[6] In this series, he has positioned his Minotaur model standing on the crossbar of the artist's easel, as if looking out to distant shores when in reality it is looking across the studio at various finished works. "Using my easel to create this frame made it a doorway, but a doorway the Minotaur is unable to pass through, because its feet are attached to the easel with the paint."[7] Rather than confined in the labyrinth of Crete, Patterson's Minotaur is trapped in the studio, stuck in paint, sealed into the painting.

Young Minotaur, 1997, pairs the figure with a colorful vertical brushstroke of identical height, a curious mating of animal and the artist's expressionistic signal of human existence. Actually, the brushstroke is Patterson's own, painted onto acetate (in the same way Roy Lichtenstein did), then enlarged. The picture carries a curious composition: the Minotaur stands on the easel frame, which sets up a diagonal plane, while the brushstroke seems to float on the surface of the picture plane, more in the viewer's space—or rather on the painting's flat surface—than in the illusionistic space that the toy inhabits.

Painted Minotaur, 1996–97, also plays with this tension between illusion and painterly paint, emphasizing the photographic flattening, the shallow depth of field that occurs with objects too near and too far from the camera's lens. In this tour-de-force of painterly flourishes, the forlorn Minotaur is enmeshed in a floating field of (seemingly) wet paint.

Patterson deftly positions himself between painted objects of two and three dimensions, between photography and painting, between realism and abstraction, between high cultural subjects like Greek mythical figures and the low kitsch of sports toys. Whatever he is painting, we are drawn to his brushstrokes, both the careful, tiny applications of paint that make up his crystalline images and the broad, wet, activated thick ones he creates as illusions. He has spoken of a common understanding that "if you can't see good brushstrokes, it is not a good painting," adding slyly (and avoiding the fact that they are often the subject of his pictures), "but in defiance of that, I try to completely eradicate any trace."[8]

1. Richard Patterson, telephone conversation with the author, July 2, 1998.
2. Ibid.
3. Stuart Morgan, "Tonite We Improvise," in *Richard Patterson* (London: Anthony d'Offay Gallery, 1997), p. 10.
4. James Hall, "Theseus," in *Dictionary of Subjects and Symbols in Art* (New York: Harper & Row, Publishers, 1979), p. 300.
5. Michael Govan, *The Minotaur & the Light: Sources for Picasso c. 1935* (Williamstown, Massachusetts: Williams College Museum of Art, 1985), p. 9.
6. Richard Patterson, quoted in Morgan, p. 20.
7. Ibid., p. 28.
8. Richard Patterson, telephone conversation with the author, July 2, 1998.

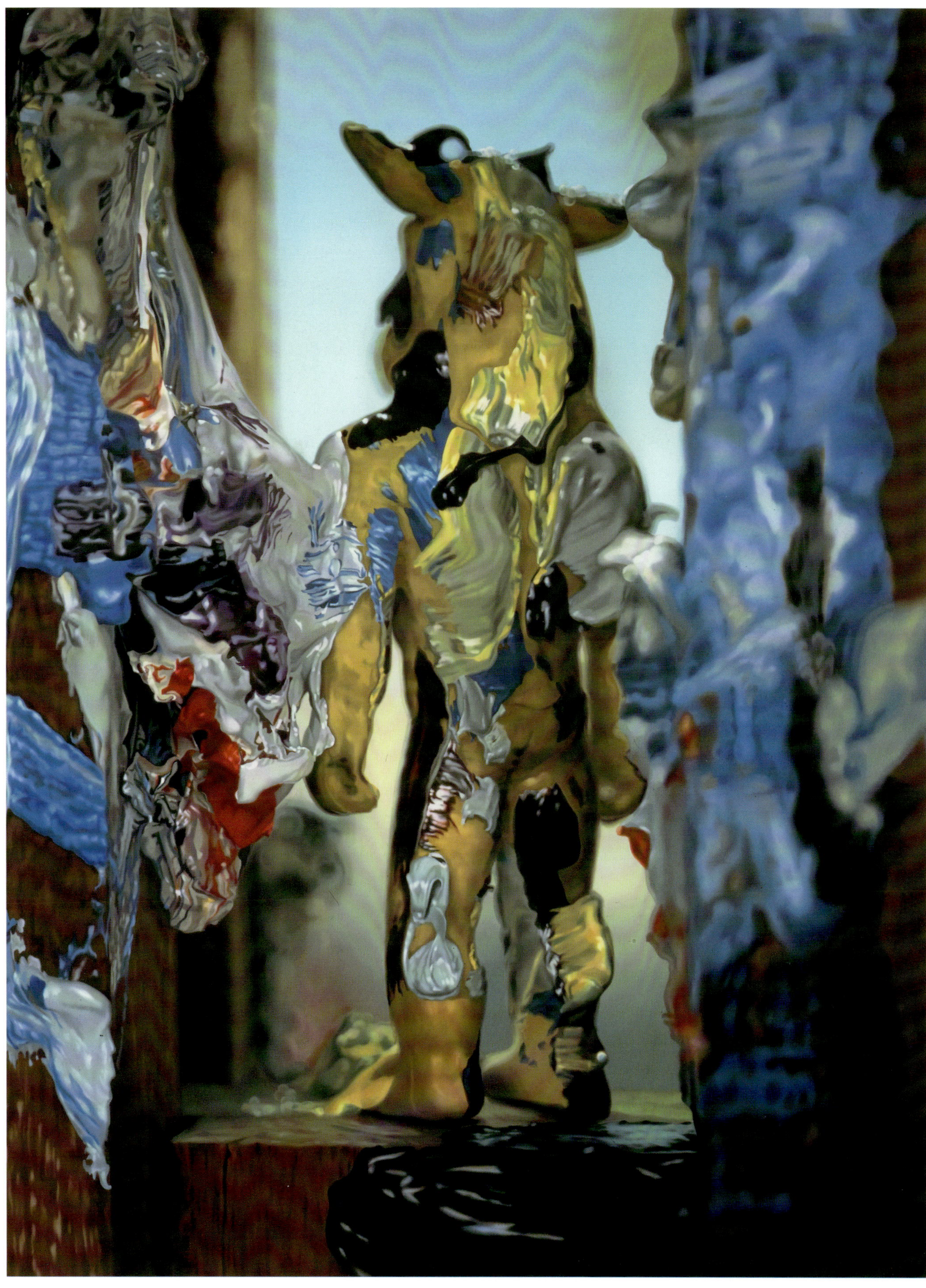

Monique Prieto

Born 1962, Los Angeles
Lives and works in Los Angeles

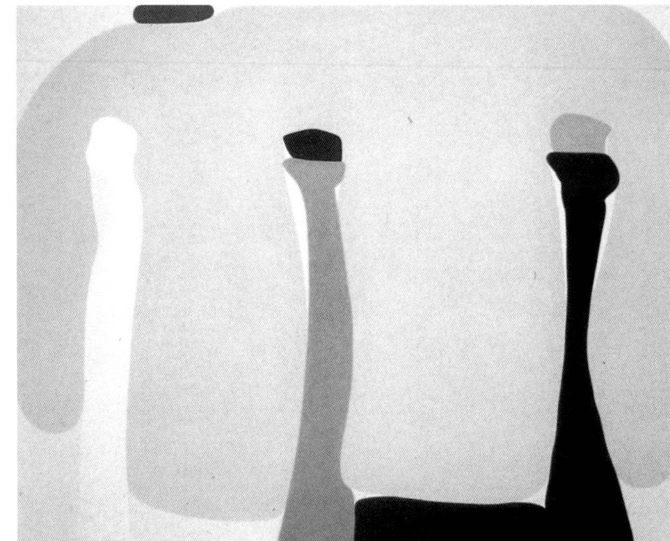

left:
***Chronicle*, 1996**
Acrylic on canvas
36 x 48 inches
Collection of the artist
Courtesy ACME., Los Angeles

opposite:
***Jet Stream*, 1996**
Acrylic on canvas
84½ x 54 inches
Collection Dean Valentine,
Beverly Hills, California

With their playful, lumpy, candy-colored shapes arranged topsy-turvy like stuffed animals or bean bags, Monique Prieto's paintings have been described as "frivolous . . . and silly as a cartoon"[1] and as having a "quirky visual humor all their own,"[2] which suggests "ice cream sundaes built by an unusually ambitious, acrobatically inclined soda jerk."[3] Despite their organic shapes and broad fields of flat color on natural canvas, which recall Lyrical Abstraction and Color Field painting, their rollicking, glib imagery is antithetical to the seriousness with which mid century Modernism, and especially its proponents led by Clement Greenberg, was revered.

In the 1990s, abstract painting does not command wide respect. When Prieto discusses her development and education as a painter (which includes a BFA from UCLA in 1987, a few years in New York, and a BFA in 1992 and MFA in 1994 from Cal Arts), she underscores the debased position that painting held when she started:

> When I was at UCLA, rather than the painting courses, where there was nothing really good going on, Paul McCarthy's "New Forms and Concepts" was important to me. When I went to Cal Arts (in 1992) and started making paintings, almost everyone said, "You're still painting?!?" Although some responded, "Great! You can paint and you are doing something different."[4]

Acknowledging a critical resistance to her chosen medium, she entered gingerly at the time, making paintings of shadowy silhouettes or monochrome nets in oil, covering a large canvas in one sitting, perhaps as if it were a performance. Referring to these as "ghost paintings," she sought to "get rid of everything, to empty out the canvas to start somewhere else."[5] These were followed by paintings of colored grids. The improvisational looseness and buoyancy that now characterize Prieto's work came as she embraced drips, one well-known signifier of the freewheeling personal drama of Abstract Expressionist paintings—an arena Prieto did not want to enter. She explains:

> Accepting the drips was a way to break out of the grid. Drips are a representation of the subjective self. By controlling—choreographing—them, I keep whatever is being expressed in check. But rather than rely on the paint, I would configure the ooze myself, to control the "angst factor" without getting back to the Conceptual.[6]

Ironically, it was working on a computer that ultimately opened the creative doors to her current paintings, which show no trace of the grid. The stable areas of color and the flat, clean shapes offered by first the stylus pen and tablet and now the touch pad don't compare to the ink washes or oil pastels she used for earlier studies. She predetermines the size of a painting, then draws shapes with her finger on a pressure sensitive touch pad—a kind of electronic fingerpainting—assigning their colors, "erasing" portions of shapes, or deleting a mark in an improvisational way through the program, pointer, and keyboard. When working on-screen, she follows a particular narrative in her head (which she never reveals), simply letting that story drive the additive progression of the individual elements in the composition. Forms are shaped, details are added, and every drip is put in place before the composition is printed out. None of the usual give and take, experimentation, or testing of ideas or images occurs while this artist is working on the canvas because it has all taken place beforehand electronically.

The paintings' genesis in a computer dictates aspects of their form. Sometimes, especially in horizontally oriented works such as *Chronicle*, 1996, these forms seem figurative or like objects with particular relationships to one another. Critic Raphael Rubinstein has observed that Prieto's compositions have a procedural relationship with 1960s sculpture, such as the "one-thing-after-another" serial, Minimal sculpture or the Postminimalist and Process artists whose works "squeeze and flatten" each other.[7] Like theirs, her forms interact with one another as unique objects against the unmodulated, flat "space" of the natural canvas. Yet, Prieto also points to another narrative reference from earlier Modernist painting. When she was a child in the 1960s and 1970s, Prieto's father would take her to art museums, and together they would play games by inventing stories about forms within the abstract paintings; today, as a mother with two small children, such storytelling is again a part of her life and has become part of making her paintings.

Prieto mixes the personal and the formal in ways that relate to, but are completely separate from, precedents in Abstract Expressionism and Color Field painting, which her paintings resemble only on the surface. Though she mimics the vocabularies of Modernist painting, her own works with their implied but elusive narrative, their exuberant playfulness, and their genesis in electronic media make them unique 1990s paintings—and Prieto's own.

1. David Pagel, "Adding a Splash of Fun to Abstraction," *Los Angeles Times*, December 5, 1997.
2. Raphael Rubinstein, "Monique Prieto at Bravin Post Lee," *Art in America*, December 1996, p. 100.
3. Roberta Smith, "Monique Prieto," *The New York Times*, May 10, 1996.
4. Monique Prieto, conversation with the author, Los Angeles, February 2, 1998.
5. Ibid.
6. Monique Prieto, telephone conversation with the author, July 1, 1998.
7. Rubinstein, p. 100.

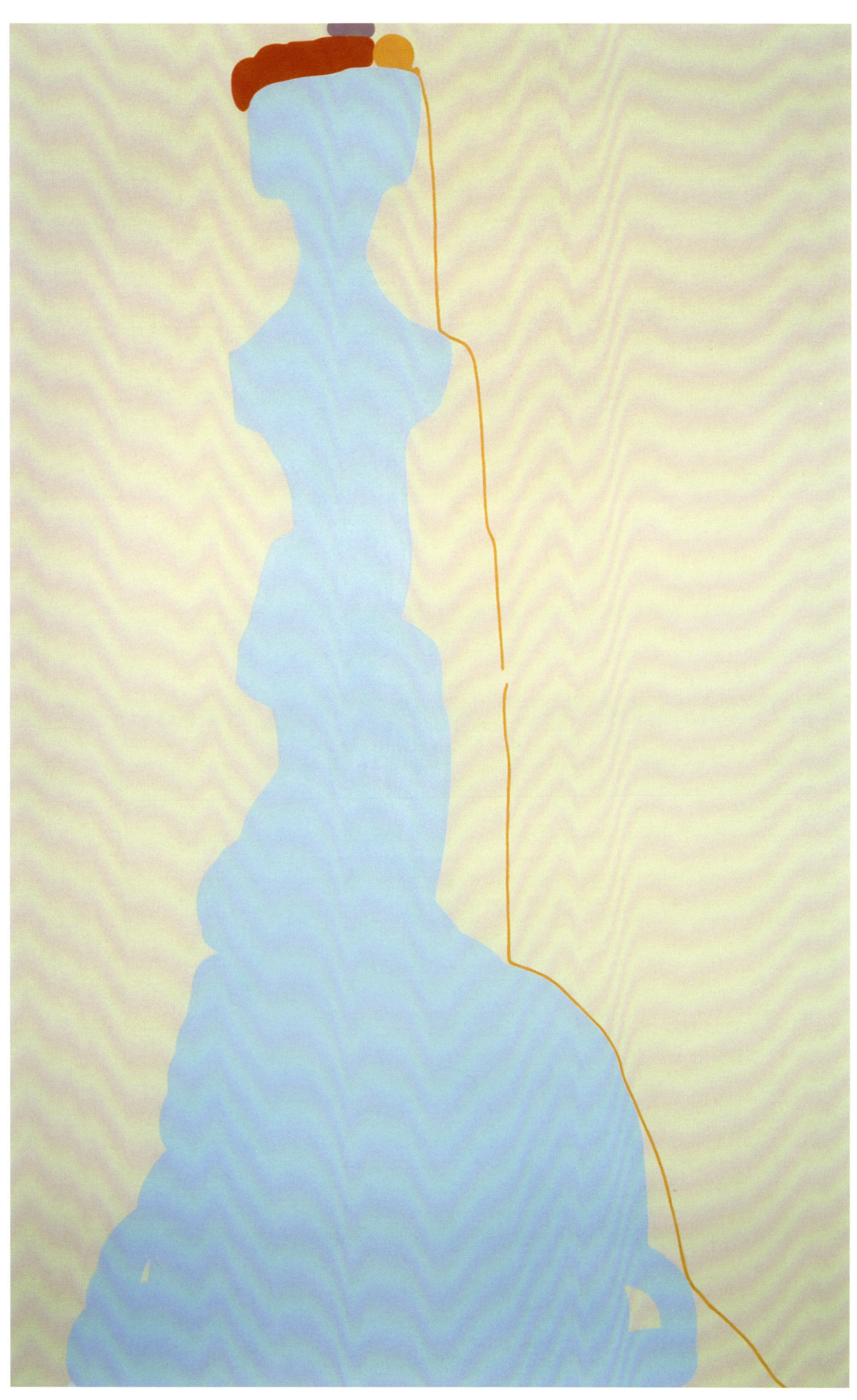

Scott Richter

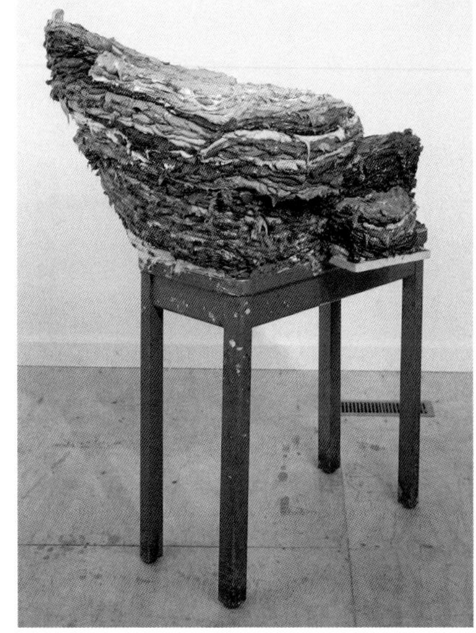

left:
Untitled, 1994
Oil paint, medium, and steel palette table
35 x 33 x 50 inches
Courtesy Pamela Auchincloss Arts Management, New York

opposite:
***Who's Afraid of Red, Yellow and Blue (for Barnett)*, 1994**
Oil paint, medium, and steel table
64 x 33 x 49 inches
Courtesy Pamela Auchincloss Arts Management, New York

Born 1943, Atlanta
Lives and works in Weston, Connecticut

Scott Richter can't get his paintings off the ground—or onto one. His table-bound piles of paint might be seen as a statement about the challenge of making an original contribution to painting at this point in its daunting history. "Painting is a square that has been very well stepped on,"[1] the artist admits, but he has developed a simple, yet radical response to the problem of engaging the color, texture, and viscosity of paint in a new way: "I would go into the studio, mix paint . . . and leave."[2]

Richter speaks with a wary enthusiasm about the heavy history of thick painting, citing the use of impasto in Claude Monet's water lilies and Chaim Soutine's intense blood-and-guts images as springboards for his own project. In a succession of works that would eventually lead to this exhibition's Palette Table Paintings, he experimented with layers of paint one or two inches thick into which he would embed cultural icons such as Barbie dolls, a telephone, and even the Paris phone book in an attempt to activate the surface. "Excess was a key issue, and thinking about Richard Serra, I realized that I needed to avoid style and content, and get involved with the process. I decided *not* to paint—to just stop at the palette."[3] In these works, layers of paint mixed with a custom silicone medium (to make it dry permanently) are built up on steel tables to create dynamic masses of pure painterliness.

One of the earliest works in this series, Untitled, 1994, is a precariously balanced pile of slathered paint layers propped on a small steel table and traversed with a modest wooden board, as if to provide stability. We look down upon its sloping topography, a chaotic churning of light grays, greens, and yellows, as if into a stormy J.M.W. Turner seascape. Viewing the work from the sides makes us more aware of the arrangement of the variously shaped masses that animate the overall volume. The sedimentation suggests the passage of time, and the artist makes a direct connection to time by describing his works as "diaries, records of the work."[4]

Who's Afraid of Red, Yellow and Blue (For Barnett), 1994, is a homage to Barnett Newman's famous question and his painting series of the same name. In 1969 Newman wrote a statement describing the genesis of his series of daring paintings limited to the three primary colors. According to art critic Thomas B. Hess, he intended to confront:

> The Neo-Plasticism [of Piet Mondrian and his followers] by using its basic color units in a way that totally contradicts the older style's emphasis on equivalences, nicely wrought balances, pictorial architectonics. The painting is laid open—flat to the surface—as if by three chops of a sword.[5]

On a sturdy, workmanlike steel conference table, Richter seems at first to have segregated the three hues laid out by Newman in smooth, flat planes, but in fact he has fearlessly undermined the purity of Newman's color fields; not only using high piles of thick paint, Richter at numerous points in the process has sacrilegiously embedded crossover colors into the "wrong" pile, flaunting his subversion of Newman's—and Mondrian's—sacred color categories by slathering red on top of the yellow layer. "I like to be free to 'change channels' every once in a while; when my moods change, the colors change."[6]

The top-view topography of Richter's multidimensional "paintings" challenges our expectations and viewing habits. Created on, and viewed primarily as, horizontal surfaces, they nonetheless bear little relation to Jackson Pollock's horizontal process—drips applied to canvases on the floor—or to Leo Steinberg's model for Robert Rauschenberg's "flatbed" mode of production. Curiously, Richter's Palette Table Paintings are related more to the human-scale easel paintings of Mondrian's era, which Newman, Pollock, and their generation rejected with the majestic scale and epic content of their works, and the dynamic action required to make them.

Richter stresses an immediate, intimate relationship with paint rather than large fields or heroic imagery. The rectangular surfaces of Richter's paint piles have the proportions of an easel painting, not a large canvas tacked to the wall or laid on the floor. They are further aligned with human scale by their support, which instead of a frame or stretcher bars is real furniture, something we respond to kinesthetically, a familiarity felt with our body more than our eyes. Although never reaching a canvas, Richter's piled palettes nevertheless bring us closer to painting.

1. Scott Richter, telephone conversation with the author, June 30, 1998.
2. Ibid.
3. Scott Richter, telephone conversation with the author, April 1998.
4. Scott Richter, telephone conversation with the author, June 30, 1998.
5. Thomas B. Hess, *Barnett Newman* (New York: The Museum of Modern Art, 1971), p. 132.
6. Scott Richter, telephone conversation with the author, June 30, 1998.

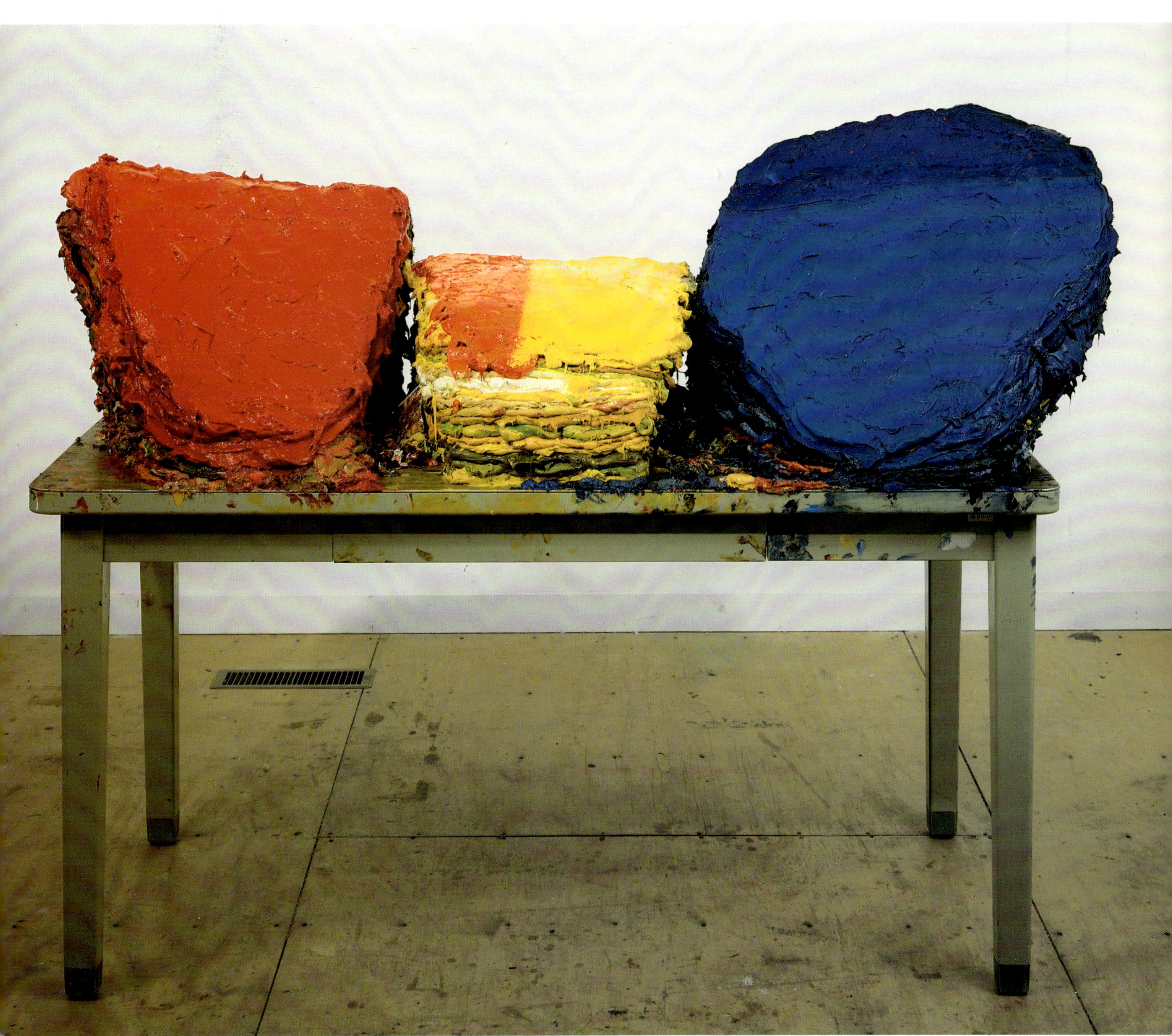

Pae White

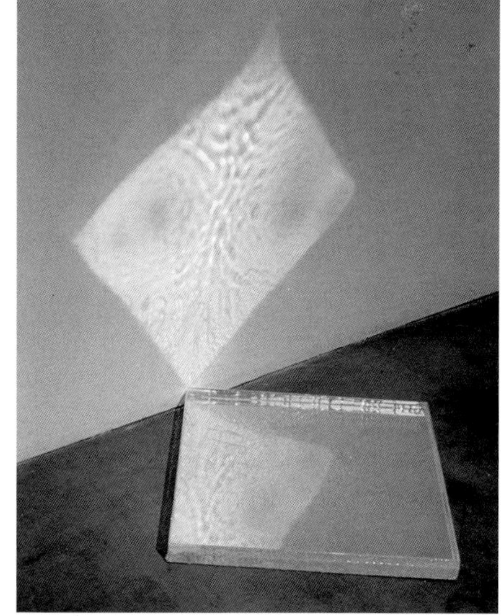

left:
***The Inconsolable Wailing of the Damned*, 1994** [Yellow]
Plexiglas and resin
18 x 18 x 1¼ inches
Private Collection
[not in exhibition]

opposite:
***Vera© Retrospective Series*, 1994** [Paris]
Chair, silk scarves, and glass
Dimensions variable
Collection of the artist
[not in exhibition]

Born 1963, Pasadena, California
Lives and works in Pasadena, California

In Pae White's art objects, installations, graphic designs, and theatrical sets, she matches a seductive allure with a formal or physical approach that carries deep Conceptual roots. This exhibition features examples from two bodies of work that relate to the practice and presentation of Modernist painting in everyday life.

The Inconsolable Wailing of the Damned, 1994, is a series of Plexiglas floor works the artist has produced in a variety of colors, shapes, and proportions. For works in this series, she bonds three layers of Plexiglas with industrial laminating solvent, which works to dissolve the plate surfaces and bind them solidly together. Since she lacks the factory equipment to properly clamp and squeeze the layers tight, patterns of bubbles are produced as a by-product at each layer, sealing in a sense of the block's temporary liquid life. Her original aim was to create a pristine tablet, but, as she explains, "the bubbles arranged themselves across the surface by chance, and what I originally saw as a flaw in the production became the most interesting thing about these works."[1] The floor works' floating, organic shapes recall Jackson Pollock's dripping of thinned paint onto a canvas spread across the floor, as well as the Surrealists' use of chance operations such as charcoal rubbings against the floorboards to coax images from their imaginations. But White's bubbles are largely playful, plastic, and Pop.

In this exhibition, *The Inconsolable Wailing of the Damned,* 1994 [Red] is a sandwich with one sheet of mirrored Plexiglas on the bottom layer, a one-inch-thick clear panel at its core, and a top layer tinted red. This combination, along with the trapped bubbles, interacts with the gallery lighting to produce a range of optical effects, unconfined to the object itself, that spill out into the space it inhabits. We look down at and *through* the red tint and the bubbles to the mirrored bottom, which then reflects our gaze, doubling the bubbles and distorting our image in that bright red liquid pool, not unlike a psychedelic Narcissus. When lights shine obliquely onto the surface, they splash a tinted reflection up onto nearby walls and the ceiling, insinuating the work's color, light, and patterns throughout the environment.

In spite of its transparency and reflective luminosity (qualities that usually dematerialize form), this plastic slab has an emphatic physicality—due to its scale (the size of a piece of plywood), its thickness (nearly two inches), and the artist's special treatment of the edges, which calls attention to its boundaries. On one side, a ruffle or wave has been carved from a formerly even edge, a Mannerist flourish that flirts with the viewer. On other sides, the melted plastic was allowed to ooze beyond the border during production, and White has chosen to leave this liquid residue as a trace reminder of the process.

For each installment of White's Vera© Retrospective Series, an ongoing project begun in 1994, the artist arranges laminated wood chairs by Scandinavian designer Arne Jacobsen and a retro-styled ceramic ashtray or two around an array of scarves designed by Vera© that have been sandwiched between glass and placed directly on the floor.

In the early 1990s, White began collecting design objects by Vera Neumann (1910–96), the textile and home furnishings designer whose colorful, upbeat designs were popular during the 1960s and 1970s, when White was growing up. To date, White has collected nearly 1,500 scarves, from which she selects an ensemble for each presentation the way a curator selects an exhibition. White explains:

> Vera seemed to be working with a sort of Bauhaus model by taking elements of contemporary art, reducing them to design motifs, and then implementing them into bed sheets, place mats, curtains, scarves, and so on. You have a very different relationship to a Frank Stella when you are sleeping on it every night, and then you see it in a museum—perhaps this relationship with the art becomes richer.[2]

In her "fabric retrospectives," White brings Vera's versions back to the museum, sealed between plates of tempered glass, which not only protect them as important relics but also flatten them into images, as if to deny their original fashionable function as accessories. When installed outdoors, the glass also reflects changing light and cloud patterns of the sky, another way the work incorporates its site.

White's inventive, eclectic approach not only stretches the boundaries of art's influence on the world, and the world's influence on art, but it causes an important shift in the way we previously interacted with abstract painting.

1. Pae White, telephone conversation with the author, July 2, 1998.
2. Jan Tumlir, "A Conversation with Pae White, artist," *Artweek*, November 17, 1994, p. 11.

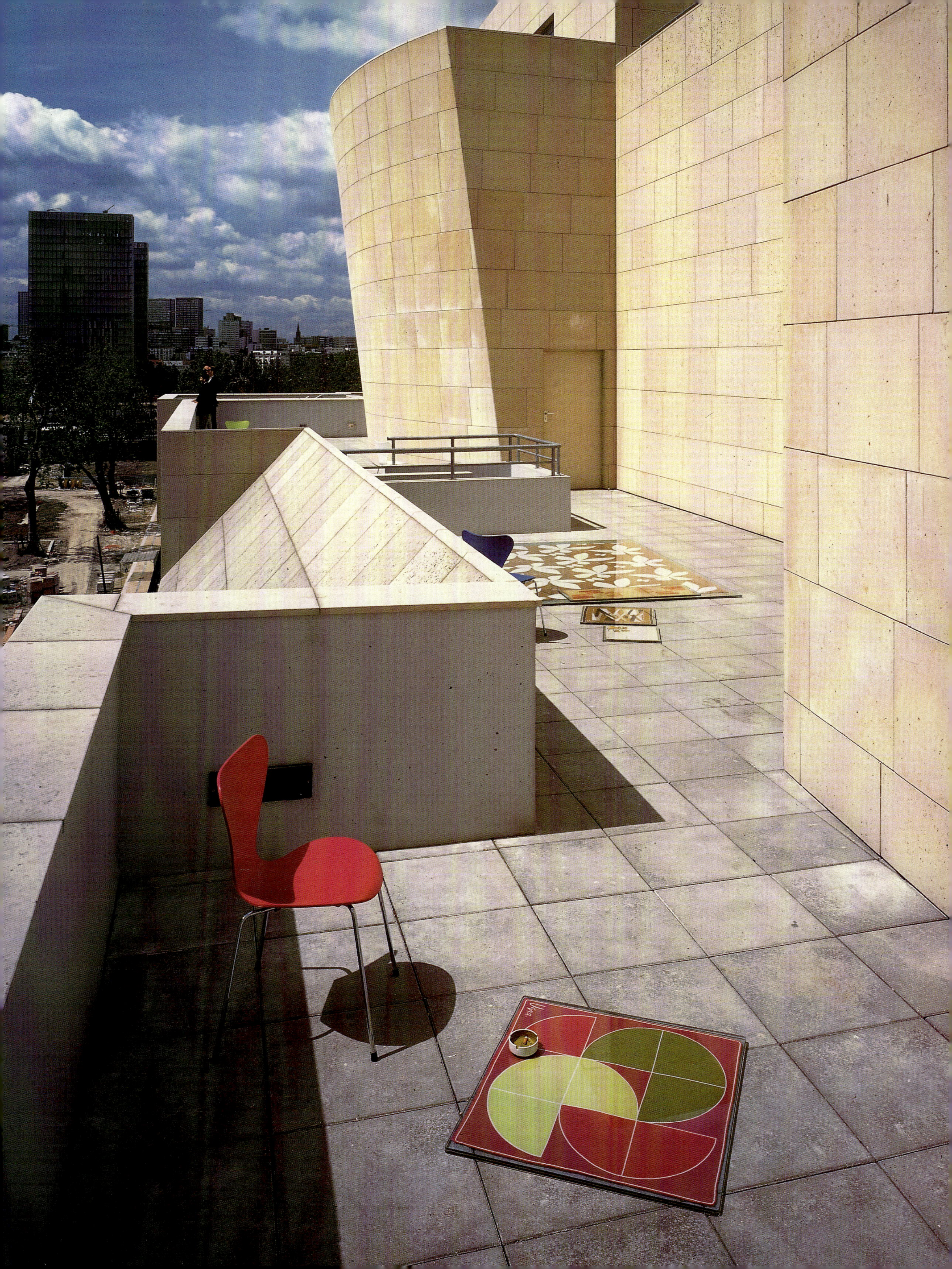

Artist Biographies

Compiled by **Alexandra Irvine**

Exhibition histories are listed chronologically, and bibliographies are listed alphabetically, within each each year.

Polly Apfelbaum

Born 1955, Abington, Pennsylvania
1974–75, State University of New York, Purchase
1978, Tyler School of Art, Elkins Park, Pennsylvania, BFA
Lives and works in New York

Selected One-Person Exhibitions

1992
Polly Apfelbaum, Amy Lipton Gallery, New York, March 14–April 11.

1993
Polly Apfelbaum, Galerie Etienne Ficheroulle, Brussels, Belgium, March 5–April 3.

1994
Polly Apfelbaum, Postmasters Gallery, New York, January 7–February 27.
Polly Apfelbaum, Residence Secondaire, Paris, May 21–June 26.
Polly Apfelbaum, Neuberger Museum of Art, Purchase College, State University of New York, September 11–January 15, 1995. Brochure, text by Cornelia H. Butler.

1995
Polly Apfelbaum, Hirschl & Adler Modern, New York, March 11–April 22.

1996
Polly Apfelbaum, Boesky & Callery Fine Arts, New York, September 3–October 5.

1997
Polly Apfelbaum, Realismusstudio der NGBK, Künstlerhaus Am Acker, Berlin, February 15–March 23. Brochure, text by Libby Lumpkin.
Polly Apfelbaum, Walter/McBean Gallery, San Francisco Art Institute, July 24–September 7. Brochure.

1998
Polly Apfelbaum: Ice, D'Amelio Terras Gallery, New York, April 25–June 6.
Polly Apfelbaum, Kiasma, Museum of Contemporary Art, Helsinki, May 30–August 30. Catalogue, text by Libby Lumpkin.

Selected Group Exhibitions

1986
Artists in the Marketplace, The Bronx Museum of Art, New York, July 12–31. Catalogue.
Selections from the Artists File, Artists Space, New York, September 18–October 18. Catalogue, text by Valerie Smith.
New Uses, White Columns, New York, October 8–November 1.

1987
The Double Bind, Loughelton Gallery, New York, June 6–July 3.
Fabricated, Not Found, Loughelton Gallery, New York, November 8–December 8.

1988
Polly Apfelbaum/Tom Radloff/Carol Szymanski, Loughelton Gallery, New York, February 21–March 15.
Palestra, Castello di Rivara, Italy, September 24–November 15. Catalogue, text by Vera Vita Gioa.

1989
Containers, Shoshana Wayne Gallery, Santa Monica, California, May 12–June 13.
The Milky Way, Shoshana Wayne Gallery, Santa Monica, California, July 22–September 16. Catalogue, text by Stephen Westfall.
Filling in the Gap, Feigen Gallery, Chicago, September 8–October 7. Catalogue, text by Saul Ostrow.

1990
Fragments, Parts, Wholes: The Body and Culture, White Columns, New York, February 16–March 11.
Je Viens de Chez le Charcutier. . . , Galerie Ghislaine Hussenot, Paris, June 7–July 14.
Corporealities, Sue Spaid Fine Art, Los Angeles, July 28–August 26. Brochure, text by Sue Spaid.
Reconciling the Unverified: New Metaphysical Art, Amy Lipton Gallery, New York, September 15–October 13.

1992
There is a Light that Never Goes Out, Amy Lipton Gallery, New York, January 4–February 1. Brochure, text by Terry R. Myers.
Detour, International House, Columbia University, New York, April 24–May 27. Catalogue, text by Alisa Tayel.
An Esemplastic Shift, A/C Project Room, New York, June 5–July 1.
Selected Passages, Galerie Jousse Seguin, Paris, June 30–July 31.
Anti-Masculine, Kim Light Gallery, Los Angeles, December 5–January 16, 1993.

1993
Yours, Wooster Gardens, New York, January 9–February 13.
Just to name a few. . . , Barbara Weiss Gallery, Berlin, January 26–February 27.
Future Perfect, Heiligenkreuuzerhof, Vienna, April 7–May 15. Catalogue, text by Dan Cameron.
Empty Dress: Clothing as Surrogate in Recent Art, organized by Independent Curators, Inc., New York. Traveled to Neuberger Museum of Art, Purchase College, State University of New York, October 3–January 2, 1994; Virginia Beach Center for the Arts, Virginia, January 9–February 20; University of North Texas Art Gallery, Denton, March 1–April 25; Sir Wilfred Grenfell College, University of Newfoundland, Corner Brook, Canada, May 20–July 3; Mackenzie Art Gallery, Regina, Saskatchewan, Canada, August 19–October 30; The Gallery, Stratford, Ontario, Canada, April 14–May 14, 1995; Selby Gallery, Ringling School of Art and Design, Sarasota, Florida, August 14–September 23. Catalogue, text by Nina Felshin.
Legend in My Living Room, Rhona Hoffman Gallery, Chicago, October 22–December 24. Brochure, text by Terry R. Myers.

1994
Sense and Sensibility: Women and Minimalism in the '90s, The Museum of Modern Art, New York, June 16–September 11. Catalogue, text by Lynn Zelevansky.
Revisioning the Familiar, Zilkha Gallery, Wesleyan University, Middletown, Connecticut, August 30–October 2. Catalogue, text by Ayako Nezu and Elizabeth Toohey.
D.I.Y., White Columns, New York, November 11–December 18.
The Social Fabric, Beaver College Art Gallery, Glenside, Pennsylvania, November 9–December 20. Catalogue, text by Paula Marincola.

1995
Pittura-Immedia, Neue Galerie am Landesmuseum Joanneum, Graz, Austria, March 11–April 18. Catalogue, text by Peter Weibel.
Art at the Edge: Tampering, High Museum of Art, Atlanta, October 10–January 7, 1996. Brochure, text by Susan Krane.
Re:Fab Painting Abstracted, Fabricated and Revised, Contemporary Art Museum, University of South Florida, Tampa, October 30–December 22. Traveled to Wolfson Galleries, Miami-Dade Community College, Miami, Florida, November 6–December 20, 1996; Robert Hull Fleming Museum, University of Vermont, Burlington, January 21–April 20, 1997. Catalogue, text by Rochelle Feinstein, Shirley Kaneda, Margaret A. Miller, W.J.T. Mitchell, and Christine Van Schoonbeck.
Painting Outside Painting: 44th Biennial Exhibition of Contemporary American Painting, The Corcoran Gallery of Art, Washington, D.C., December 16–February 19, 1996. Catalogue, text by Terrie Sultan, and David Pagel on Apfelbaum.

1996
The Kingdom of Flora, Shoshana Wayne Gallery, Santa Monica, California, February 3–March 30.
Der Fleck, Galerie Im Kornerpark, Berlin, March 9–April 14.
Installations, St. Mark's Positions, New York, September 20–October 26.
Painting—The Extended Field, Magasin 3 Stockholm Konsthall, October 13–December 19 and February 2–April 20, 1997; and Rooseum Center for Contemporary Art, Malmö, Sweden, October 5–December 15, and January 25–February 6, 1997. Catalogue, text by Sven-Olov Wallenstein.
Getting Physical, Johnson County Community College, Kansas City, Missouri, October 17–December 8. Brochure, text by David Pagel.

1997
After the Fall: Aspects of Abstract Painting since 1970, Newhouse Center for Contemporary Art, Snug Harbor Cultural Center, Staten Island, New York, March 27–September 7. Catalogue, text by Lilly Wei.
Vraiment: Feminisme et art, Le Magasin, Grenoble, France, April 5–May 25. Catalogue, text by Laura Cottingham.
Fashion Moda, Cleveland Center for Contemporary Art, May 2–August 10. Brochure, text by Lisa Marie Marks.
Onomatopoeia, Studio la Cittá, Verona, Italy, July 5–September 27. Brochure, text by Anthony Iannacci.

Hanging By A Thread, Hudson River Museum of Westchester, Yonkers, New York, October 3–February 17, 1998. Catalogue, text by Ellen J. Keiter.
Simple Form, Henry Art Gallery, University of Washington, Seattle, November 13–February 1, 1998.
Other, 4th biennale d'art contemporain de Lyon, France. Catalogue, text by Harald Szeemann.
Polly Apfelbaum, Mary Beyt and Fandra Chang, Galerie Ludwig, Krefeld, Germany.

1998
Homemade Champagne, The Claremont Graduate University, California, January 12–February 13. Catalogue, text by David Pagel.
Chromaform: Color in Sculpture, University of Texas at San Antonio Art Gallery, September 3–October 16. Catalogue, text by Frances Colpitt.
Everyday, 11th Biennale of Sydney, Australia, September 17–November 8. Catalogue, text by Jonathan Watkins.

Selected Bibliography

1986
Harris, Patty. "Loughelton Show." *108 Review*, March/April 1986.
Pincus, Robert L. "New York's Newest Artists." *San Diego Union*, August 1986.
Westfall, Stephen. "Polly Apfelbaum at Paulo Salvador Gallery." *Arts Magazine*, September 1986, p. 121.

1988
Phillips, Patricia C. "Polly Apfelbaum at Loughelton Gallery." *Artforum*, September 1988, p. 142.
Rubinstein, Raphael, and Daniel Weiner. "Polly Apfelbaum at Loughelton Gallery." *Flash Art*, Summer 1988, pp. 137–38.
Westfall, Stephen. "Polly Apfelbaum at Loughelton Gallery." *Art in America*, December 1988, pp. 156–57.

1989
Levin, Kim. "Choices." *The Village Voice*, December 12, 1989.
Westfall, Stephen. "Three Interviews." *BOMB*, Spring 1989.

1990
Grundberg, Andy. "A Force of Repetition." *The New York Times*, August 24, 1990, p. 22.
Hixson, Kathryn. "Joe Smith, Polly Apfelbaum and Richard Rezac." *Arts Magazine*, March 1990, pp. 123–24.
Mahoney, Robert. "Polly Apfelbaum at Loughelton Gallery." *Arts Magazine*, February 1990, p. 102.
Smith, Roberta. "Suggestive Objects." *The New York Times*, April 27, 1990, p. 22.
Zimmer, William. "Repetition as a Theme." *The New York Times*, September 9, 1990, p. 18.

1991
Mahoney, Robert. "Polly Apfelbaum at Amy Lipton Gallery." *Flash Art*, March/April 1991, pp. 140–41.
Pagel, David. "Fortune's Orbit: Polly Apfelbaum's Evocative Arrangements." *Arts Magazine*, January 1991, pp. 39–43.
Phillips, Patricia C. "Polly Apfelbaum at Amy Lipton Gallery." *Artforum*, February 1991, pp. 127–28.
Raynor, Vivien. "Sculpture with Canaries." *The New York Times*, August 11, 1991, p. 10.
Smith, Roberta. "Plastic Fantastic Lover." *The New York Times*, November 1, 1991, p. C16.

1992
Avgikos, Jan. "Polly Apfelbaum at Amy Lipton Gallery." *Artforum*, Summer 1992.
Cameron, Dan. "(Critical Edge) The Changing Tide." *Art & Auction*, January 1992.
Levin, Kim. "Choices." *The Village Voice*, April 7, 1992.
Mahoney, Robert. "There is a light . . . " *Arts Magazine*, April 1992.
Scott, Andrea K. "An Eloquent Silence." *Tema Celeste*, Fall 1992, pp. 37–38.
Smith, Roberta. "Abstraction: A Trend That May Be Coming Back." *The New York Times*, January 10, 1992, p. C28.
——. "Polly Apfelbaum." *The New York Times*, April 3, 1992, p. C30.
——. "An Esemplastic Shift." *The New York Times*, June 26, 1992, p. C24.

1993
Braff, Phyliss. "Hybrid Sculpture." *The New York Times*, June 13, 1993, p. 22.
Smith, Roberta. "Things of Beauty." *The New York Times*, January 15, 1993, p. C30.

1994
Avgikos, Jan. "Sense and Sensibility." *Artforum*, October 1994, pp. 98–99.
Hess, Elizabeth. "Minimal Women." *The Village Voice*, July 15, 1994.
Smith, Roberta. "Postmasters." *The New York Times*, February 25, 1994, p. C22.
——. "Space is Spare for Women's Work at the Modern." *The New York Times*, June 24, 1994, p. C26.
Zimmer, William. "Avery May Echo Matisse But His Humor Is All His Own." *The New York Times*, October 30, 1994, p. 22.

1995
Apfelbaum, Polly. "A Partial Taxonomy." *Journal of Art and Philosophy*, no. 5, 1995.
Karmel, Pepe. "Color, Sign, System, Sensibility." *The New York Times*, July 21, 1995, p. C23.
Pagel, David. "Polly Apfelbaum: Constelaciones de color." *Lapiz*, Summer 1995.
Schaffner, Ingrid. "Polly Apfelbaum at Hirschl & Adler Modern." *Artforum*, Summer 1995, p. 107.

1996
Bell, Tiffany. "Polly Apfelbaum's Medley of Signs." *Art in America*, February 1996, pp. 78–81.
Edelman, Robert G. "Polly Apfelbaum." *Art Press*, October 1996, pp. 70–71.
Landi, Anne. "Polly Apfelbaum." *ARTnews*, October 1996, pp. 136–37.
Moreau, Patric. "Vardagen blir konst pa golvet." *Goteborgs-Posten*, November 10, 1996.
Pagel, David. "Polly Apfelbaum: Ring-A-Ring-A-Roses." *art/text*, January 1996, pp. 48–53.
Schwendener, Martha. "Polly Apfelbaum." *Time Out New York*, September 4–11, 1996.
Smith, Roberta. "Testing Limits at the Corcoran." *The New York Times*, January 6, 1996, p. 11.
——. "Polly Apfelbaum." *The New York Times*, September 6, 1996, p. C19.
Thurson, Alice. "Polly Apfelbaum." *The Kansas City Star*, October 27, 1996, p. J3.

1997
Baker, Kenneth. "Polly Apfelbaum's Suggestive Scatterings." *San Francisco Chronicle*, July 31, 1997, p. C1.
Bonetti, David. "Gallery Watch." *San Francisco Examiner*, August 1, 1997.
Clausnitzer, Von Beate. "Ein Lacheln aus Samt." *Berliner Zeitung*, February 26, 1997.
Conrads, Martin. "Popund Glam." *Zitty*, February 28, 1997.
Helfand, Glen. "Polly Apfelbaum." *San Francisco Bay Guardian*, July 30, 1997.
Kreis, Elfie. "Ein Toast auf den Samt." *Tagelspiegel*, February 18, 1997.
Porges, Maria. "Polly Apfelbaum, San Francisco Art Institute." *Artforum*, November 1997, pp. 120–21.
Rubinstein, Raphael. "Polly Apfelbaum." *Art in America*, January 1997, p. 93.
——. "Abstraction Out of Bounds." *Art in America*, November 1997, pp. 104–15.
Wachtmeister, Marika. "Kvinna med ratt att pyssla." *Femina*, June 1997, p. 6.

1998
Condon, Elizabeth. "Polly Apfelbaum/Lynn McCarty." *New Art Examiner*, March/April 1998, p. 44.
Olsson, Thomas. "Dalarnas Museum, Falum." *Svenska Dagbladet*, January 10, 1998, p. E1.

Kevin Appel

Born 1967, Los Angeles
1990, Parsons School of Design, New York, BFA
1995, University of California, Los Angeles, MFA
Lives and works in Los Angeles

Selected One-Person Exhibitions
1994
Kevin Appel, Food House, Santa Monica, California, February 2–19.

1996
Kevin Appel, Spanish Box, Santa Barbara, California, September 14–28.

1998
Kevin Appel, Angles Gallery, Santa Monica, California, February 6–March 7.

Selected Group Exhibitions
1991
Kevin Appel, Peter Kamberski, Opus Gallery, Los Angeles, April 28–May 25.
Paintings, Opus Gallery, Los Angeles, July 22–August 22.
Burning in Hell, Franklin Furnace, New York, September 27–December 14.

1992

Food House at Far Bazaar, Los Angeles, December 3–20.

1993

Paintings: Kevin Appel, Steve Hanson, Michael Pavoni, Food House, Santa Monica, California, January 7–23.

Germinal Notations, Food House, Santa Monica, California, November 10–27.

1994

Thanks Again, Food House, Santa Monica, California, June 8–25.

1995

Pretty, Food House, Santa Monica, California, January 6–February 4.

Sean Duffy's Chalk Truck, Lemoyne Kennels, Los Angeles, August 5–12.

1996

Interiors, Los Angeles Contemporary Exhibitions, April 11–May 26.

1997

Bastards of Modernity, Angles Gallery, Santa Monica, California, January 17–February 15.

Ten Los Angeles Artists, Stephen Wirtz Gallery, San Francisco, February 5–March 1.

Beau Geste, Angles Gallery, Santa Monica, California, September 5–October 4.

Quartzose: 20 Los Angeles Artists, Galleri Tommy Lund, Odense, Denmark, September 5–October 21.

Kevin Appel, Francis Cape, Jorge Pardo, Janice Guy, New York, October 8–November 22.

In Touch With . . ., Galerie + Edition Renate Schröder, Cologne, October 9–November 22.

Inhabited Spaces: Artists' Depictions, Long Beach Museum of Art, California, December 5–February 1, 1998.

1998

Paintings Interested in the Ideas of Architecture and Design, Post, Los Angeles, February 28–March 28.

Painting From Another Planet, Deitch Projects, New York, June 5–July 31.

Architecture and Inside, Paul Morris Gallery, New York, June 12–August 15.

Selected Bibliography

1993

Darling, Michael. "'Paintings' at Food House." *Picturebook*, January 1993.

1995

Darling, Michael. "Pretty at Food House." *Artweek*, March 1995, pp. 38–39.

1996

Wilson, William. "Wry and Witty Observations Decorate Images of 'Interiors.'" *Los Angeles Times*, May 1, 1996.

1997

Bonetti, David. "Gallery Watch." *San Francisco Examiner*, February 28, 1997.

DiMichele, David. "Bastards of Modernity at Angles Gallery." *Artweek*, April 1997, pp. 22–23.

Hainley, Bruce. "'Bastards of Modernity,' Angles Gallery." *Artforum*, March 1997, pp. 98–99.

Helfand, Glen. "Ten Los Angeles Artists." *San Francisco Bay Guardian*, February 19, 1997.

Kandel, Susan. "Modernism Montage." *Los Angeles Times*, February 7, 1997, pp. F16, 30.

Maslon, Laura Stevenson. "Art Chatter About Art Matters . . ." *Art-Talk*, October 1997, pp. 42, 44.

Tanner, Marcia. "'Ten Los Angeles Artists' at Stephen Wirtz Gallery." *Artweek*, April 1997, p. 22.

Young, Paul. "Bastards of Modernity." *Buzz Weekly*, February 14–20, 1997, p. 19.

1998

Darling, Michael. "Kevin Appel, Angles Gallery." *frieze*, June–August 1998, p. 88.

Joyce, Julie. "Kevin Appel." *Art issues.*, Summer 1998, p. 40.

Pagel, David. "Fresh Outlook." *Los Angeles Times*, February 13, 1998, p. F23.

——. "Visual Stimulation in L.A.: Paintings From Another Planet." *Flash Art*, Summer 1998, pp. 116–20.

Uta Barth

Born 1958, Berlin, Germany

1982, University of California, Davis, BA

1985, University of California, Los Angeles, MFA

Lives and works in Los Angeles

Selected One-Person Exhibitions

1990

Uta Barth, Howard Yezerski Gallery, Boston, January 6–February 7.

Uta Barth, Addison Gallery of American Art, Andover, Massachusetts, January 19–March 11. Catalogue, text by Jim Sheldon.

1993

Uta Barth, S.P.A.S. Gallery, Rochester Institute of Technology, New York, March 27–April 15.

1994

Uta Barth, Wooster Gardens, New York, December 4–January 29, 1995.

1995

Uta Barth, Tanya Bonakdar Gallery, New York, January 21–February 18.

Uta Barth, Rena Bransten Gallery, San Francisco, September 7–October 7.

Uta Barth, The Museum of Contemporary Art, Los Angeles, September 17–November 12. Catalogue, text by Elizabeth A.T. Smith.

Uta Barth, ACME., Santa Monica, California, October 6–November 4.

1996

Uta Barth, Rena Bransten Gallery, San Francisco, March 7–April 6.

Uta Barth, Tanya Bonakdar Gallery, New York, March 23–April 20.

Uta Barth, London Projects, London, June 14–July 27.

Uta Barth, S.L. Simpson Gallery, Toronto, October 10–November 5.

1997

Uta Barth, Presentation House Gallery, North Vancouver, Canada, April 5–May 11.

The Wall Project, Museum of Contemporary Art, Chicago, April 17–September 21.

. . . . in passing, ACME., Santa Monica, California, June 7–July 5.

Uta Barth, Rena Bransten Gallery, San Francisco, October 9–November 15.

Uta Barth, Andéhn-Schiptjenko, Stockholm, October 30–November 30.

Uta Barth, Institute of Contemporary Art at Maine College of Art, Portland, November.

1998

Uta Barth, ACME., Santa Monica, California, January 31–March 7.

Uta Barth, Lawing Gallery, Houston, February 27–April 12.

Uta Barth, Bonakdar Jancou Gallery, New York, March 20–April 25.

Uta Barth, London Projects, London, September.

Selected Group Exhibitions

1986

Proof and Perjury, Los Angeles Institute of Contemporary Art, September 18–October 19.

1989

Uta Barth, Jeff Beall, Paul Boettcher, Eric Magnuson, Roy Boyd Gallery, Santa Monica, California, June 3–July 1.

Deliberate Investigations: Recent Works by Four Los Angeles Artists: Uta Barth, Dede Bazayk, David Bunn, Connie Hatch, Los Angeles County Museum of Art, September 7–November 12. Catalogue, text by Sheryl Conkelton and Kathleen Gauss.

Thick and Thin: Photographically Inspired Paintings, Fahey/Klein Gallery, Los Angeles, September 8–October 14.

Logical Conclusions, Jan Kesner Gallery, Los Angeles, December 2–January 6, 1990.

1990

The Conceptual Impulse, Security Pacific Gallery, Costa Mesa, California, June 17–August 12. Catalogue, text by Benjamin Weissman and Mark Johnstone.

Spirit of Our Time, Contemporary Arts Forum, Santa Barbara, California, November 6–December 27.

1991

LA TIMES, Boise Art Museum, Idaho, August 31–October 27. Traveled to Western Gallery, Western Washington University, Bellingham, November 11–December 14. Catalogue, text by Jacqueline S. Crist.

1992

Abstraction in the '90s, Jan Kesner Gallery, Los Angeles, January 18–February 22.

Voyeurism, Jayne Baum Gallery, New York, February 13–March 14.

1993

A Carafe, That is a Blind Glass . . ., Weingart Gallery, Los Angeles, January 29–March 12. Brochure, text by Amelia Jones.

Index in French, California Museum of Photography, Riverside, February 14–April 11. Catalogue, text by Marilu Knode.

1994

The World of Tomorrow, Tom Solomon's Garage, Los Angeles, February 12–March 12.

Love in the Ruins, Long Beach Museum of Art, California, March 4–May 22. Catalogue, text by Noriko Gamblin and Denise Spampinato.

New Acquisitions, Los Angeles County Museum of Art, April 26–July 10. Traveled to San Francisco Museum of Modern Art.

The Abstract Urge, Ansel Adams Center for Photography, San Francisco, April 27–June 12.

Breda Fotografica '94, De Beyerd Center of Contemporary Art, Breda, The Netherlands, July 19–September 11. Catalogue, text by Jean Reuiter.

Uta Barth and Vikky Alexander, Domestic Setting, Los Angeles, July 23–August 20.

Transtextualism, Mark Moore Gallery, Santa Monica, California, August 6–September 1.

Uta Barth, Chris Finley, Joyce Lightbody, Jennifer Steinkamp, ACME., Santa Monica, California, October 15–November 12.

Diverse Perspectives: Inland Empire Photographers, San Bernardino County Museum of Art, California.

1995

Between Breath and Air; Uta Barth, Karin Davie, Shirley Irons, Patrick Callery Gallery, New York, January 21–February 26.

Contemporary Collections, Los Angeles Center for Photographic Studies, March 30–May 27.

Human/Nature, The New Museum of Contemporary Art, New York, April 20–May 18.

P.L.A.N.: Photography in Los Angeles Now, Los Angeles County Museum of Art, July 6–September 17. Catalogue, text by Robert Sobieszek.

Presence: Recent Portraits, Angles Gallery, Santa Monica, California, September 8–23.

Neotoma, Otis College of Art and Design Gallery, Los Angeles, September 16–November 4.

New Photography 11: Uta Barth, Joseph Bartcherer, Ulrich Görlich, Eric Rondepierre, The Museum of Modern Art, New York, October 19–January 9, 1996.

Contemporary Photography from the Permanent Collection, Princeton Art Museum, New Jersey, November 28–January 7, 1996.

Content and Discontent in Today's Photography, The Bruce Museum, Greenwich, Connecticut, July 2–August 27. Traveled to Pritchard Art Gallery, Moscow, Idaho, December 8–January 27, 1996; Lowe Art Museum, Coral Gables, Florida, March 14–April 28; Art Museum, Tampa, Florida, August 26–September 20; Samuel P. Harn Museum of Art, Gainesville, Florida, October 10–December 1. Brochure, text by Andy Grundberg.

1996

Clarity, Art Gallery, Northern Illinois University, Chicago, March 1–April 13. Catalogue, text by Grant Samuelsen.

Paper or Plastic: On the Productivity of Absence, Guggenheim Gallery, Chapman University, Orange, California, March–April. Catalogue, text by D.H. Bailey.

Light, Time, Focus, Museum of Contemporary Photography, Chicago, April 8–June 1.

Chalk, Factory Place Gallery, Los Angeles, June 1–29.

. . . e la chiamano pittura . . . , Studio la Città, Verona, Italy, June 28–August 3. Catalogue, text by Mario Bertoni.

Portraits of Interiors, Studio la Città, Verona, Italy, September 5–October 6. Catalogue, text by Peter Weiermair.

Extended Minimal, Max Protetch Gallery, New York, September 7–28.

silence, Lawing Gallery, Houston, September 12–October 19.

Blind Spot: The First Four Years, Paolo Baldacci Gallery, New York, October 1–26.

Making Pictures: Women and Photography, 1975–Now, Nicole Klagsbrun, New York, November 1–December 7.

Painting—The Extended Field, Magasin 3 Stockholm Konsthall, October 13–December 19 and February 2–April 20, 1997; and Rooseum Center for Contemporary Art, Malmö, Sweden, October 5–December 15, and January 25–February 6, 1997. Catalogue, text by Sven-Olov Wallenstein.

1997

Twenty years . . . almost, Robert Miller Gallery, New York, January 8–February 8.

Evidence: Photography and Site, Wexner Center for the Arts, Columbus, Ohio, February 1–April 13. Traveled to Cranbrook Art Museum, Bloomfield Hills, Michigan, November 15–January 4, 1998; The Power Plant, Toronto, January 16–March 15. Catalogue, text by Sarah Rogers and Mark Robbins.

Coda: Photographs by Uta Barth, Günther Förg, Jack Pierson, and Carolien Stikker, Center for Curatorial Studies, Bard College, Annandale-on-Hudson, New York, March 16–April 13.

Uta Barth, Rineke Dijkstra, Tracey Moffatt, Inez van Lamsweerde, Matthew Marks Gallery, New York, Summer.

Blueprint, De Appel Foundation, Amsterdam, June 6–August 17. Catalogue, text by Pierre Bismuth, Saskia Bos, and Hans den Hartog Jager.

LA International Biennial: Portraits of Interiors, Patricia Faure Gallery, Santa Monica, California, July 12–August 17.

Portraits of Interiors, Gallery Blancpain Stepczynski, Geneva, Switzerland, July 12–August 18.

Pool, Rena Bransten Gallery, San Francisco, July 17–August 23.

Scene of the Crime, Armand Hammer Museum of Art and Cultural Center, University of California at Los Angeles, July 23–October 5. Catalogue, text by Ralph Rugoff, Anthony Vidler, and Peter Wollen.

Object and Abstraction: Contemporary Photography, The Museum of Modern Art, New York, July 24–October 7, 1998.

New Acquisitions: Works on Paper, Museum of Contemporary Art, Chicago, July 29–September 21.

Spheres of Influence, The Museum of Contemporary Art, Los Angeles, August 7–September 7.

Defining Eye: Women Photographers of the Twentieth Century, Saint Louis Art Museum, Missouri, September 23–January 11, 1998. Catalogue, text by Olivia Lahs-Gonzales and Lucy Lippard.

Light Catchers, Bennington College Art Gallery, Bennington, Vermont, September 24–October 24.

Elusive Paradise: Los Angeles Art from the Permanent Collection, The Museum of Contemporary Art, Los Angeles, October 5–May 17, 1998. Brochure, text by Kerry Brougher, Connie Butler, and Stacia Payne.

Uta Barth, Jean Baudrillard, Luigi Gherri, Parco Gallery, Tokyo, November 7–December 9.

Heart, Mind, Body, Soul: American Art in the 1990s, Whitney Museum of American Art, New York, November 26–January 4, 1998.

Developing a Collection: The Ralph M. Parsons Foundation and the Art of Photography, Los Angeles County Museum of Art, December 4–February 23, 1998.

Painting into Photography/Photography into Painting, Museum of Contemporary Art, North Miami, Florida, December 20–February 16, 1998. Catalogue, text by Bonnie Clearwater.

1998

Mysterious Voyages: Exploring the Subject of Photography, The Contemporary, Baltimore, February 7–May 2.

LA Cool, Rocket Gallery, London, April 4–May 30. Traveled to Bruning + Zwischke, Düsseldorf, July–August.

(Not Pictured) The Presence of Absence, The Light Factory, Charlotte, North Carolina, April 4–June 17.

Claustrophobia, Ikon Gallery, Birmingham, England, June 6–August 2. Traveling within Great Britain to Middlesboro Art Gallery, August–October 1998; Mapping Art Gallery, Sheffield, January–March 1999; Dundee Contemporary Arts, March–May; Cartwright Hall, Bradford, May–August; Aberystwyth Arts Centre, September–October; Centre for the Visual Arts, Cardiff, November–January 2000. Catalogue, text by Claire Doherty and Soo Jin Kim.

Picture Show, Weinstein Gallery, Minneapolis, July 15–August 5.

Under/Exposed, Public Art Project, Stockholm, Summer–Fall 1998.

Multiplicity, Vanderbilt University Fine Arts Gallery, Nashville, September 3–October 18.

The Sondra Gillman Photography Collection, Art Museum of South Texas, Corpus Christi, Texas.

Selected Bibliography

1989

Carlson, Lance. ". . . Or, Images of a Make-believe Reality?" *Artweek,* September 30, 1989, p. 1.

Curtis, Cathy. "Photography Lies And Tricks Are Focus of 'Investigations.'" *Los Angeles Times,* October 23, 1989, p. F3.

French, David. "Uta Barth." *Visions–Art Quarterly,* Spring 1989, pp. 2–3, 31.

Gardner, Colin. "Uta Barth at the Los Angeles County Museum of Art." *Artforum,* November 1989, p. 160.

Kandel, Susan. "LA in Review: Deliberate Investigations." *Arts Magazine,* December 1989, pp. 103–104.

Knight, Christopher. "Narrative Puzzle to Please Eye." *Los Angeles Herald Examiner,* June 23, 1989, p. 4.

——. "Finding the Point of 'Deliberate.'" *Los Angeles Herald Examiner,* September 15, 1989, p. 36.

Pagel, David. "Disposable Diagrams." *Artweek,* October 14, 1989, p. 4.

Rugoff, Ralph. "Remembering the Present: Advertisements Against Our Own Amnesia." *L.A. Weekly*, November 3–9, 1989, pp. 39–41.

1992

Haus, Mary. "Voyeurism." *ARTnews*, May 1992, p. 130.

1993

Anderson, Michael. "'A Carafe, That is a Blind Glass' and 'Sugar N' Spice.'" *Art issues.*, May/June 1993, p. 39.

Pagel, David. "Smart and Sensuous." *Los Angeles Times*, March 4, 1993, p. F5.

1994

Hagen, Charles. "Review: Wooster Gardens." *The New York Times*, January 28, 1994, p. 19.

Jones, Amelia. "Uta Barth at Domestic Setting." *Art issues.*, November/December 1994, p. 41.

Joyce, Julie. "Images of Anywhere." *Artweek*, August 18, 1994, inside back cover.

Knight, Christopher. "A Suggestion of Cultural Edginess." *Los Angeles Times*, March 10, 1994, pp. F1, 11.

Muchnic, Suzanne. "Uta Barth and Vikky Alexander." *ARTnews*, November 1994, p. 166.

Pagel, David. "Taking a Glimpse Into 'The World of Tomorrow.'" *Los Angeles Times*, February 24, 1994, p. F10.

1995

Aletti, Vince. "Choices." *The Village Voice*, February 14, 1995, p. 8.

Decter, Joshua. "Uta Barth at Tanya Bonakdar Gallery." *Artforum*, April 1995, p. 91.

Fiskin, Judy. "Trompe l'oeil for Our Time." *Art issues.*, November/December 1995, pp. 27–29.

Green, David A. "Warm and Fuzzy." *Los Angeles Reader*, November 3, 1995, pp. 14–16.

Hapgood, Susan. "Uta Barth at Tanya Bonakdar Gallery." *Art in America*, May 1995, p. 120.

Kandel, Susan. "Artist Projects: Uta Barth." *art/text*, September 1995, pp. 48–54.

Knight, Christopher. "Art in All the Right Spaces." *Los Angeles Times*, September 21, 1995, pp. F1, 11.

Knode, Marilu. "Uta Barth in Conversation with Marilu Knode." *Artlies*, June/July 1995, pp. 30–32.

Rugoff, Ralph. "Smear Tactics." *L.A. Weekly*, October 20–26, 1995, p. 39.

Schwendener, Martha. "Uta Barth at Tanya Bonakdar Gallery." *New Art Examiner*, April 1995, p. 41.

1996

Conkelton, Sheryl. "Uta Barth." *Journal of Contemporary Art*, www.thing.net/jca/barth.html, 1996.

Curtis, Cathy. "Filling The 'Absence.'" *Los Angeles Times*, April 4, 1996, pp. F1, 3.

Gilbert-Rolfe, Jeremy. "Cabbages, Raspberries and Video's Thin Brightness," *Art & Design*, May/June 1996, pp. 14–23.

Johnson, Patricia C. "Communication, or lack of it, is exhibit's theme." *Houston Chronicle*, September 20, 1996, p. 3.

Jordan, Betty Ann. "Uta Barth and Michael Snow at S.L. Simpson." *The Globe* (Toronto), November 2, 1996.

Pedrosa, Adriano. "Uta Barth—Museum of Contemporary Art, Los Angeles." *frieze*, May 1996, p. 47.

Thrift, Julia. "Uta Barth." *Time Out London*, July 15–24, 1996, p. 52.

Van de Walle, Mark. "Uta Barth at Tanya Bonakdar." *Artforum*, September 1996, p. 109.

1997

Aletti, Vince. "Uta Barth/Rineke Dijkstra/Tracey Moffatt/Inez van Lamsweerde." *The Village Voice*, July 25, 1997.

Folland, Tom. "Uta Barth: S.L. Simpson Gallery." *Parachute Contemporary Art Magazine*, Spring 1997, pp. 44–45.

Kandel, Susan. "Pointed Images." *Los Angeles Times*, June 27, 1997, p. F22.

Meneghelli, Luigi. "Portraits of Interiors." *Flash Art*, February/March 1997, p. 122.

Pagel, David. "Inside Jobs: Portraits of Interiors." *Los Angeles Times*, August 1, 1997, p. F1.

Rugoff, Ralph. "L.A.'s Female Art Explosion." *Harper's Bazaar*, April 1997, pp. 204–205, 246.

Scott, Michael. "Background Comes to the Fore." *Vancouver Sun*, April 19, 1997, p. B5.

Stament, Bill. "Uta Barth, 'Field #20,' and 'Field #21.'" *The Chicago Sun Times*, June 25, 1997, p. 41.

Willette, Jeanne S.M. "Reinventing Photography: Photography as commentary: The camera (obscura) and post-philosophical systems." *Artweek*, July 1997, pp. 16–17.

1998

Grabner, Michelle. "Fuzzy Logic." *Cakewalk* (Los Angeles), Spring/Summer 1998, pp. 19–22.

Hedberg, Hans. "The Photograph as Cannibal." *Index*, January 1998, pp. 48–55.

Hicks, Robert. "Blurred Images Used to Highlight the Subject." *The Villager*, April 15–21, 1998.

Pagel, David. "Diptych World." *Los Angeles Times*, February 13, 1998, p. F23.

Pederson, Victoria. "Uta Barth." *Paper*, March 1998, p. 132.

Tumlir, Jan. "Uta Barth at ACME." *art/text*, August–October, pp. 90–91.

Glenn Brown

Born 1966, Hexham, Northumberland, England

1984–85, Norwich School of Art, Foundation Course
1988, Bath College of Higher Education, BA (Fine Art)
1992, Goldsmiths' College, London, MA (Fine Art)
Lives and works in London

Selected One-Person Exhibitions

1995

Glenn Brown, Karsten Schubert, London, July.

1996

Glenn Brown, Queen's Hall Arts Centre, Hexham, Northumberland, England, June. Catalogue, text by Phil King and Marcelo Spinelli.

1997

Glenn Brown, Galerie Ghislaine Hussenot, Paris, April.

1998

Glenn Brown, Patrick Painter Inc., Los Angeles, May 2–30.

Selected Group Exhibitions

1989

Christie's New Contemporaries, Royal College of Art, London, March.

B. T. New Contemporaries 1989, organized by The New Contemporaries, Ltd. Traveled within Great Britain to the Institute of Contemporary Arts, London; Cornerhouse Gallery, Manchester; South Hill Park, Bracknell; Dean Clough, Halifax; and Brewery Arts Centre, Kendal. Catalogue, text by Sacha Craddock.

1990

B. T. New Contemporaries 1990, organized by The New Contemporaries, Ltd. Traveled within Great Britain to Arnolfini Gallery, Bristol; John Hansard Gallery, Southampton; Dean Clough, Halifax; Ikon Gallery, Birmingham; Arts Council Gallery, Belfast; Third Eye Centre, Glasgow; and Institute of Contemporary Arts, London. Catalogue.

1991

Group Show, Todd Gallery, London, December–February 1992.

1992

Surface Values, Kettle's Yard, Cambridge, February–March.

How Did These Children Come To Be Like That, Goldsmiths' Gallery, London, May. Catalogue.

With Attitude, Galerie Guy Ledune, Brussels, Belgium, May. Catalogue.

And What Do You Represent?, Anthony Reynolds Gallery, London, December–January 1993.

1993

Barclay's Young Artist Award, Serpentine Gallery, London, January–February. Catalogue, text by Sarah Kent.

Re-Present, Todd Gallery, London, March–April.

Launch, Curtain Road Arts, London, May.

Painting Invitational, Barbara Gladstone Gallery, New York, June 22–July 30.

Mandy Loves Declan 100%, Mark Boote Gallery, New York, September–October. Catalogue, text by Stuart Morgan.

1994

Every Now and Then, Rear Window at Richard Salmon Ltd., London, May–June.

Here and Now, Serpentine Gallery, London, June–July. Catalogue.

Summer Group Show: Gallery Artists, Karsten Schubert, London.

1995

Painter's Opinion, Bloom Gallery, Amsterdam, January.

From Here, Waddington Galleries, and Karsten Schubert, London, March–April. Catalogue, text by Andrew Wilson.

That's Not The Way To Do It, Project Space, University of Northumbria at Newcastle, England, March–April.

Young British Artists V: Glenn Brown, Keith Coventry, Hadrian Pigott and Kerry Stewart, Saatchi Collection, London, September–November. Catalogue, text by Sarah Kent.

Brilliant! New Art from London, Walker Art Center, Minneapolis, October 22–January 7, 1996. Traveled to Contemporary Arts Museum, Houston, February 17–April 14. Catalogue, text by Richard Flood, Douglas Fogle, Stuart Morgan, Marcelo Spinelli, and Neville Wakefield.

Obsession, The Tannery, London, December.

1996

Glenn Brown, Peter Doig, Jim Hodges, Adriana Varejão, Galerie Ghislaine Hussenot, Paris, January 20–February 24.

21 Days of Darkness, Transmission Gallery, Glasgow, January–February.

Ace! Arts Council Collection new purchases, organized by National Touring Exhibitions. Traveled within Great Britain to Hatton Gallery, Newcastle upon Tyne, March 1–April 13; Harris Museum and Art Gallery, Preston, May 25–July 7; Oldham Art Gallery, July 13–August 25; Hayward Gallery, London, September 19–November 17; Ikon Gallery, Birmingham, January 18–March 9, 1997; Mappin Art Gallery, Sheffield, March 15–April 27; Angel Row Gallery, Nottingham, May 3–June 15; Ormeau Baths Gallery, Belfast, November–December. Brochure, text by Henry Meyric Hughes, Isobel Johnstone, and Ann Jones.

Out of Space, Cole and Cole, Oxford, May–June.

Strange Days, The Agency, London, June–July.

Fernbedienung—Does Television Inform The Way Art Is Made?, Kunstverein, Graz, Austria, September. Catalogue, text by Klemens Gruber, Lynna Joyrick, Theo Lighthart, Jeff Rian, Johann Skocek, Eva Maria Stadler, and Thomas Trummer.

The Jerwood Painting Prize, Lethaby Galleries, Central Saint Martin's College, London, September. Catalogue.

About Vision: New British Paintings in the 1990s, Museum of Modern Art, Oxford, November 10–February 23, 1997. Traveled to Fruitmarket Gallery, Edinburgh, 1997; Laing Art Gallery, Newcastle upon Tyne, 1997–98. Catalogue, text by David Elliott.

1997

Belladonna, Institute of Contemporary Arts, London, January 24–April 12.

A Ilha Do Tesouro (Treasure Island), Fundacao Calouste Gulbenkian, Centro de Art Moderne Jose de Azeredo Perdigao, Lisbon, Portugal, February–May. Catalogue, text by Jorge Molder and Rui Sanches.

Pure Fantasy, Oriel Mostyn, Llandudno, North Wales, May–June.

Glenn Brown, Alex Katz, Katherine Yass, Galerie Barbara Thumm, Berlin, July–August.

Sensation: Young British Artists from the Saatchi Collection, Royal Academy of Arts, London, September 18–December 28. Catalogue, text by Brooks Adams, Lisa Jardine, Martin Maloney, Norman Rosenthal, and Richard Shone.

1998

Group Show, Patrick Painter Inc., Los Angeles, July 9–August 8.

Selected Bibliography

1989

Cork, Richard. "New Art Goes Under The Hammer." *Telegraph Weekend Magazine*, March 11, 1989.

1990

Jennings, Rose. "New Contemporaries, ICA." *City Limits*, January 11, 1990.

1991

Collings, Matthew. "New Contemporaries, ICA." *City Limits*, August 15, 1991.

Dormant, Richard. "Painting With a Message." *The Daily Telegraph*, August 9, 1991.

Kent, Sarah. "New Contemporaries, ICA." *Time Out London*, August 7, 1991.

McEwen, John. "Artists a-plenty." *The Sunday Telegraph*, December 8, 1991.

Norrie, Jan. "B. T. New Contemporaries, Ikon Gallery." *Arts Review*, April 1991.

1992

Lorent, Claude. "Quand L'attitude Devient Art." *Art and Culture*, November 1992.

Palmer, Julie. "Surface Values: A Review, Art and Design." *Contemporary Painting*, Autumn 1992.

1993

Bonami, Francesco. "Vitamin P: The Sound of Painting." *Flash Art* (International Edition), November/December 1993, pp. 37–41.

Beaumont, Peter. "Is Art Dead?" *The Observer*, February 14, 1993.

Bennett, Oliver. "Exhibitionists!" *The Evening Standard Magazine*, May 1993.

Graham-Dixon, Andrew. "Radical Chic and the Schlock of the New." *The Independent*, February 16, 1993.

Harvey, William. "Copycat Crime." *City Limits*, February 4, 1993.

Hilton, Tim. "Familiar Signs of a Misspent Youth." *The Independent on Sunday*, February 2, 1993.

Kent, Sarah. "Awards to the Wise." *Time Out London*, February 3–10, 1993.

Morgan, Stuart. "Confessions from a Body Snatcher." *frieze*, October 1993.

Myers, Terry R. "Painting Invitational." *Flash Art* (International Edition), October 1993, p. 120.

Packer, William. "Creme de la Creme Goes Sour." *The Financial Times*, February 2, 1993.

Pitt, Alex. "Copyright Issues." *Art Monthly*, May 1993.

——. "Whose Art is it Anyway?" *The Observer*, May 9, 1993.

Roberts, James. "Twin Peak: The Barclays Young Artists Award." *frieze*, March/April 1993.

Smith, Roberta. "Painting Invitational at Barbara Gladstone Gallery." *The New York Times*, July 2, 1993, p. C21.

Whitford, Frank. "Blind Men's Bluff." *The Sunday Times*, February 13, 1993.

Wilson, Andrew. "London Winter Round-Up." *Art Monthly*, February 1993.

1995

Archer, Michael. "Licensed to Paint." *Art Monthly*, May 1995, pp. 8–10.

Auty, Giles. "Edge of the black hole." *The Spectator*, April 15, 1995, p. 42.

Brown, Glenn. "Glenn Brown on Willem de Kooning: Paintings, Tate Gallery." *frieze*, May 1995, pp. 54–55.

——. "Glenn Brown on George Condo's Clownmaker. A brush with genius: 20." *The Guardian*, November 14, 1995, p. 9.

Cafopoulos, Catherine. "Glenn Brown at Karsten Schubert." *Arti* (Greece), November/December 1995, pp. 208–11.

Coomer, Martin. "From Here." *Time Out London*, April 19–26, 1995, p. 46.

Cork, Richard. "Bright Young Things at Work and Play." *The Times*, September 26, 1995.

Dormant, Richard. "Funny, but too peculiar." *The Telegraph*, September 20, 1995, p. 6.

Gayford, Martin. "The medium that refused to die." *The Telegraph*, April 12, 1995, p. 19.

Hall, James. "Old Habits Die Hard." *The Guardian*, September 26, 1995, pp. 6–7.

Hilton, Tim. "Review: Fate, hopelessness, little clarity." *The Independent*, April 9, 1995, p. 31.

Hooper, Mark. "Space 1995." *The Face*, November 1995, pp. 84–85.

Hyman, James. "Presences and Spectral Traces." *Galleries*, July 1995, p. 12.

Kent, Sarah. "Glenn Brown, Karsten Schubert." *Time Out London*, July 26, 1995, p. 52.

——. "Pretty Vacant." *Time Out London*, October 4–11, 1995, p. 51.

McEwen, John. "Young British Artists V." *The Sunday Telegraph*, October 1, 1995.

Morgan, Stuart. "Anglo-Saxon Attitudes." *frieze*, March/April 1995, p. 7.

Negrotti, Rosanna. "Spaced Out." *What's On*, October 4–11, 1995, pp. 12–13.

Norman, Geraldine. "Stampede Starts From Here." *The Independent*, April 3, 1995, p. 7.

Packer, William. "Only Artists With Attitude." *Financial Times*, September 30, 1995.

Searle, Adrian. "Any Colour You Like as Long as It's a Joke." *The Independent*, April 4, 1995, p. 21.

Wakefield, Neville. "Quite, Quite Brilliant." *Tate Magazine*, November 1995, pp. 32–39.

——. "Art in the Wrong Place." *The Independent*, October 10, 1995, p. 9.

Wilson, Andrew. "Breaking Content from Form." *Art & Design*, March/April 1995, pp. 7–19.

1996

Anspon, Catherine. "Brilliant! Engages, Energizes at the CAM." *Public News* (Houston), March 6, 1996, pp. 8, 10.

Dannett, Adrian. "Brilliant." *Flash Art*, January/February 1996, pp. 96–97.

Feaver, William. "Crooked Style." *The Observer Review*, November 17, 1996, p. 9.

Feldman, Melissa E. "21 Days of Darkness." *Art Monthly*, April 1996, pp. 38–40.

Findlay, Judith. "21 Days of Darkness." *Flash Art* (International Edition), Summer 1996, p. 99.

Graham-Dixon, Andrew. "On The Surface." *The Independent Tabloid*, November 19, 1996, pp. 4–5.

Hilton, Tim. "The Best Painting in Britain?" *The Independent on Sunday*, November 17, 1996, p. 30.

Johnson, Patricia C. "British exhibit shows attitude, some brilliance." *Houston Chronicle*, February 15, 1996, pp. D1, 6.
Searle, Adrian. "The Best of British Painting?" *The Guardian*, November 1996, pp. 10–11.

1997
Bickers, Patricia. "Sense & Sensation." *Art Monthly*, November 1997, pp. 1–6.
Kent, Sarah. "Sensation." *Time Out London*, September 10–17, 1997.
Street, Catherine. "Belladonna." *On Safari*, Spring 1997.

Ingrid Calame

Born 1965, The Bronx, New York
1985, State College of New York at Buffalo in Siena, Italy
1986, Tyler School of Art in Rome, Italy
1987, State University of New York, Purchase College, New York, BFA
1995, Skowhegan School of Painting and Sculpture, Maine
1996, California Institute of the Arts, Valencia, MFA (Art and Film)
Lives and works in Los Angeles

Selected One-Person Exhibitions
1995
KAPOW! Michael Beauchemin Gallery, Boston, September 23–October 28.

1997
Spalunk . . . , Post, Los Angeles, September 6–October 4.
poonk FOOP, Four Walls, San Francisco, October 17–November 15.

1998
Projected Wall: Ingrid Calame, Rosamund Felsen Gallery, Santa Monica, California, July 11–August 1.

Selected Group Exhibitions
1990
Group Show, Chinatown Space, New York.
Into the '90s, Brooklyn Waterfront Artists' Coalition, New York.

1991
Choice, A.I.R., New York.

1992
Two Person Show, Tower Gallery, Portchester, New York.

1995
Occupato, Bennett Roberts Fine Art, Los Angeles, June 17–August 29.
Video Arts Annual, Los Angeles Center for Photographic Studies at RE:SOLUTION Gallery, Los Angeles.
Works on Paper, McNeese State University, Lake Charles, Louisiana.

1996
After, Post, Los Angeles, February 25–March 30.
Group Show, ACME., Santa Monica, California, September 13–October 12.
Some Dumb Fun, Jessie Metcalf Art Gallery, University of Nevada, Las Vegas.

1997
Drawing, Gallery LASCA, Los Angeles, January 10–February 8.
Summer Invitational, Curt Marcus Gallery, New York, June 6–July 3.
Recent Pictures, ACME., Los Angeles, June 7–July 5.
Spot Making Sense, Grand Arts, Kansas City, Missouri, June 27–August 2. Brochure, text by David Pagel.
Six Choose Six, Visual Arts Gallery, Purchase College, State University of New York, November 10–December 3.

1998
Selections Winter '98, The Drawing Center, New York, January 8–February 14. Brochure, text by Ingrid Calame.
Hot RRRod: Eine Kunstausstellung, Forum Stadtpark, Graz, Austria, February 6–26.
Drawings, Beyond Baroque, Los Angeles, April 2–May 3.
Painting From Another Planet, Deitch Projects, New York, June 5–August 31.
From Here to Eternity, Max Protetch Gallery, New York, July 1–31.

Selected Bibliography
1994
Greenstein, M.A. "Entering the Professional Art Market Without an MFA." *Artweek*, May 1994, p. 17.

1996
Crowley, Matthew. "Cartoons More Than Buffoonery." *Las Vegas Times*, December 4, 1996, p. A5.

1997
Best, Sherry L. "Sensibility or Sense?" *The Pitch*, July 11, 1997.
Hickey, Dave. "Top Ten x 12, The Year in Review." *Artforum*, December 1997, pp. 88–89.
Innaccone, Carmine. "Ingrid Calame at Post." *Art issues.*, November/December 1997, p. 41.
Pagel, David. "Editor's Choice: Art." *BOMB*, Spring 1997, p. 17.
——. "Shifting Images." *Los Angeles Times*, June 20, 1997.
——. "Art Review: 'Landmassed.'" *Los Angeles Times*, September 12, 1997.
Thorson, Alice. "Grand Arts show brings sense and style to the summer season." *The Kansas City Star*, July 4, 1997, p. 24.

1998
Ertl, Barbara. "Hollywood-Träume." *Kronen Zeitung* (Graz, Austria), February 17, 1998, p. 21.
Nigelhell, Franz. "Kulturindustrie and Grazer Verhältnisse." *Neue Zeit*, February 7, 1998, p. 43.
Pagel, David. "Visual Stimulation in L.A.: Paintings from Another Planet." *Flash Art*, Summer 1998, pp. 116–20.
Schjeldahl, Peter. "Ultraloungerie." *The Village Voice*, June 23, 1998.

Fandra Chang

Born 1964, Taipei, Taiwan, Republic of China
1987, Art Center College of Design, Pasadena, California, BFA
Lives and works in Venice, California

Selected One-Person Exhibitions
1992
Fandra Chang, Shea & Bornstein Gallery, Santa Monica, California.

1993
Fandra Chang, Patricia Shea Gallery, Santa Monica, California, April 17–May 15.

1996
Fandra Chang, Shoshana Wayne Gallery, Santa Monica, California, September 7–October 12.

Selected Group Exhibitions
1989
Household Names, Echo Park, California, June 11–17.
Dark As A Space, Marc Richards Gallery, Los Angeles, July 1–29.
i to Eye, Cirrus Gallery, Los Angeles, December 8–January 8, 1990.

1990
nonrePRESENTation, Security Pacific Corporation Gallery at the Plaza, Los Angeles, May 6–June 18. Catalogue, text by Jeremy Gilbert-Rolfe and Colin Gardner.
1990 Phoenix Triennial, Phoenix Art Museum, Arizona, September 8–October 7.
New Edge: Young Los Angeles, Karl Bornstein Gallery, Santa Monica, California.

1991
Five Days, Tom Solomon's Garage, Los Angeles.
Summer Group Show, Shea & Bornstein Gallery, Santa Monica, California.

1992
8 Abstract Variations, Jan Turner Gallery, Los Angeles.

1993
Los Angeles: Not Paintings?, Santa Barbara Contemporary Arts Forum, California, April 3–May 22. Traveled to University of North Texas Art Gallery, Denton, November 15–December 14. Catalogue, text by David Pagel.
Silent Echoes, Tennisport Arts, New York, May 9–July 4.

1994
In Plain Sight: Abstract Painting in Los Angeles, Blue Star Art Space, San Antonio, September 9–October 30. Catalogue, text by Frances Colpitt.
Plane/Structures, Otis College of Art and Design Gallery, Los Angeles, September 10–November 5. Traveled to The Renaissance Society at The University of Chicago, November 20–December 30; Pittsburgh Center for the Arts, February 3–April 12, 1995; Zilkha Gallery, Wesleyan University, Middletown, Connecticut, April 18–May 28; White Columns, New York, October 13–

November 12, 1995; University of North Texas Art Gallery, Denton, November 27–January 28, 1996; Nevada Institute for Contemporary Art, Las Vegas, March–April. Catalogue, text by Dave Hickey, David Pagel, and Joe Scanlan.

Winter Invitational, Patricia Shea Gallery, Santa Monica, California.

1995

Four Generations, Woodbury University Art Gallery, Burbank, California, April 18–May 25. Catalogue, text by Jeremy Gilbert-Rolfe.

Obliquely, Shoshana Wayne Gallery, Santa Monica, California, October 28–November 25.

Painting Outside Painting: 44th Biennial Exhibition of Contemporary American Painting, The Corcoran Gallery of Art, Washington, D.C., December 16–February 19, 1996. Catalogue, text by Terrie Sultan and Terry R. Myers on Chang.

1996

Face-to-Face: Recent Abstract Painting, MIT List Visual Arts Center, Cambridge, Massachusetts, April 13–June 30. Catalogue, text by Katy Kline and Helaine Posner on Chang.

Some Grids, Los Angeles County Museum of Art, June 23–January 5, 1997.

1997

Ambient Suburbs, Post, Los Angeles.

Polly Apfelbaum, Mary Beyt and Fandra Chang, Galerie Ludwig, Krefeld, Germany.

1998

A Common Thread, Littlejohn Contemporary, New York, February 17–March 14.

Exploiting the Abstract, Feigen Contemporary, New York, May 2–June 13. Brochure, text by Shirley Kaneda.

Selected Bibliography

1989

Clearwater, Bonnie. "It's Happening at Home." *The Journal of Art*, September/October 1989.

Curtis, Cathy. "Review." *Los Angeles Times*, July 7, 1989.

O'Brien, John. "Subtleties That Challenge Sight." *Artweek*, July 15, 1989, p. 5.

1990

Curtis, Cathy. "nonrePRESENTation: It's Enough to Make You UnEASY." *Los Angeles Times*, May 15, 1990.

Nilsen, Richard. "The Elegant, the Brutal, and the Puzzling, Triennial Traps Artistic Ferment." *The Arizona Republic*, September 1990, pp. C11, 14.

Scarborough, James. "Engaging Abstraction." *Artweek*, June 7, 1990, p. 13.

1991

Gilbert-Rolfe, Jeremy. "Slaves of L.A. and Others: Young L.A. Artists." *Artspace*, Summer 1991, pp. 72–79.

1992

Gardner, Colin. "Fandra Chang at Shea & Bornstein." *Artforum*, March 1992, p. 114.

——. "Nonrepresentation in Los Angeles." *Tema Celeste*, April/May 1992, pp. 64–69.

Kandel, Susan. "Review." *Arts Magazine*, April 1992.

Pagel, David. "Reviews." *Los Angeles Times*, February 13, 1992, p. F2.

O'Brien, John. "Sum of Parts, 'Open' Season in Los Angeles." *Visions Art Quarterly*, Fall 1992, pp. 27–28.

1993

Crowder, Joan. "Are They or Aren't They?" *Santa Barbara News-Press*, April 16, 1993.

Cutajar, Mario. "Los Angeles: Not Paintings? at the Santa Barbara Contemporary Arts Forum." *Artweek*, May 20, 1993, p. 14.

Darling, Michael W. "Beyond Painting." *The Independent*, April 15, 1993, p. 41.

——. "A Blurring of Definitions." *Artweek*, May 20, 1993, pp. 12–13.

Pagel, David. "Fandra Chang." *Art issues.*, May/June 1993, pp. 16–18.

1994

Arner, Alan G. "Plane show enjoys some flights of fancy." *Chicago Tribune*, December 9, 1994.

Goddard, Dan R. "L.A. Abstract Artists Show View from the Void, Plainly." *San Antonio Express-News*, October 9, 1994.

Green, Richard. "Eye Candy, Modernism Gets Cute in Its Old Age, Planes/Structures." *Los Angeles Reader*, October 21, 1994, pp. 18, 21.

Pagel, David. "Urban Diversions." *Los Angeles Times*, August 6, 1994.

Wasson, Emily Blase. "Abstract painters from West Coast display goods at Blue Star." *The Paisano Plus*, October 4, 1994.

Wilson, William. "Plain/Structures at Otis, Enriching Work." *Los Angeles Times*, September 19, 1994, p. F2.

Zellen, Jody. "Los Angeles: Not Paintings? at the Santa Barbara Contemporary Arts Forum." *Visions Art Quarterly*, Spring 1994, p. 38.

1995

Kapitanoff, Nancy. "Perspectives on Painting." *Los Angeles Times*, April 21, 1995, p. F9.

Pagel, David. "Abstractions Over Time." *Los Angeles Times*, May 4, 1995, p. F4.

Shearing, Graham. "Planes/Structures Requires Altered Behavior." *Tribune Review*, February 10, 1995, p. D3.

1996

Gilbert-Rolfe, Jeremy. "Cabbages, Raspberries, and Video's Thin Brightness." *Art & Design*, May/June 1996, pp. 14–23.

Gohnson-Ross, Robyn. "Empty Frame." *Koan*, February 1996, pp. 8–11.

Hill, Shawn. "Driven to Abstraction." *The Tab*, April 23–29, 1996, p. B5.

Kandel, Susan. "Exploring Enigmatic World Under Glass." *Los Angeles Times*, September 12, 1996, p. F7.

Ostrow, Saul. "History is Now, 'Painting Outside Painting.'" *New Art Examiner*, March 1996, pp. 29–31.

Risatti, Howard. "Review." *Artforum*, April 1996, pp. 105–106.

Sherman, Mary. "Meet Abstract Art 'Face to Face.'" *Boston Sunday Herald*, April 28, 1996, p. 56.

Smith, Roberta. "Testing Limits at the Corcoran." *The New York Times*, January 6, 1996, p. 11.

Spalding, Kelly. "Face to Face: Recent Abstract Painting." *Artsmedia*, June 1996, p. 17.

Temin, Christine. "The Clash of the Abstract." *The Boston Globe*, May 7, 1996, pp. 61, 66.

Tumlir, Jan. "Fandra Chang and Adam Ross at Shoshana Wayne Gallery." *Artweek*, November 1996, pp. 21–22.

1998

Basha, Regina. "Manufacturing Revelations." *art/text*, February–April 1998, pp. 55–59.

Mark D. Cole

Born 1965, Houston

1987, The University of Texas, Austin, BBA

1991, Baylor University, Waco, Texas, JD

Lives and works in Dallas

Selected One-Person Exhibitions

1998

Mark Cole, Haggar Gallery, University of Dallas, April 3–May 10. Catalogue, text by Christine Bisetto.

Selected Group Exhibitions

1995

Expo '95, 500X Gallery, Dallas, January 14–29.

Critic's Choice, Dallas Visual Arts Center, May 12–June 23. Catalogue, text by Don Bacigalupi, Alison de Lima Greene, and William Otton.

1996

Expo '96, 500X Gallery, Dallas, January 6–21.

1997

Expo '97, 500X Gallery, Dallas, January 11–February 2.

Monica Pierce, Mark Cole, Tom Sime, Charlie Uniform Tango, Dallas, April 25–July 6.

Critic's Choice, Dallas Visual Arts Center, May 23–July 3. Catalogue.

1998

Works on Paper '98, San Jacinto College, Houston, April 3–May 1.

A Cool Show, Arlington Museum of Art, Texas, August 8–October 17.

Blunt Object, The David and Alfred Smart Museum of Art, The University of Chicago, September 11–October 25.

Selected Bibliography

1997

Cuellar, Catherine. "X-posing Emerging Talent in the Art World." *Dallas Morning News*, January 10, 1997.

Whitmer, Susan. "Review." *ArtTexNet*, August 1997, p. 1.

1998

Daniel, Mike. "Simply Cool." *Dallas Morning News*, August 7, 1998, p. 51.

Rankin, Jennifer. "Sweet Abstraction." *Arlington Morning News*, August 7, 1998, p. C1.

Tyson, Janet. "Cool Rules: Artworks that say, when in doubt, chill." *Arlington Star Telegram*, August 7–13, p. 20.

Sally Elesby

Born 1942, Abilene, Kansas

1988, State University of New York, Purchase College, BFA

1990, Art Center College of Design, Pasadena, California, MFA

Lives and works in Los Angeles

Selected One-Person Exhibitions

1990

Boundary Lines, W.C. Gallery, Pasadena, California, July 13–15.

Beam Drop, Art Center/Downtown Gallery, Pasadena, California, December 4–16.

1993

Decorated Surfaces, Food House, Santa Monica, California, September 8–27.

1994

Incidental Form, Food House, Santa Monica, California, October 7–29.

1996

Vanitas Paintings for the '90s, Spanish Box, Santa Barbara, California, March 16–April 13.

New Work—Paintings, Bliss, Pasadena, California, April 13–May 5.

1997

Motive Paintings, Gallery LASCA, Los Angeles, March 20–April 19.

1998

Fractal Shadows, Caren Golden Fine Art, New York, January 15–February 21.

Selected Group Exhibitions

1991

Group Show, Marc Richards Gallery, Santa Monica, California, July 26–August 24.

1992

Drawing Show, Bliss, Pasadena, California, July 2–16. Catalogue, text by Adam Ross.

Floored, Bliss, Pasadena, California, July 19–26.

Seven Los Angeles Artists, Los Angeles Contemporary Exhibitions, November 6–December 24.

1993

Sally Elesby, Julian Goldwhite and Larry Mantello, Food House, Santa Monica, California, February 25–March 17.

Food House Visits The Art Store, The Art Store Gallery, Santa Monica, California, May 11–June 5.

Thank You, Food House, Santa Monica, California, June 7–24.

The Zone Show, Sue Spaid Fine Art, Los Angeles, August 2–23.

Germinal Notations, Food House, Santa Monica, California, October 17–November 5.

1994

Current Abstractions, Barnsdall Municipal Art Gallery, Los Angeles, February 22–April 17.

Sally Elesby, Antonio Gonella and Jane Reynolds, Food House, Santa Monica, California, February 23–March 12.

Playfield, Rio Hondo College Art Gallery, Whittier, California, April 18–May 19.

Interdisciplinary, Woodbury University Art Gallery, Burbank, California, May 3–June 3.

Thanks Again, Food House, Santa Monica, California, June 8–25.

Hooked on a Feeling, Kohn Turner Gallery, Los Angeles, July 7–September 2.

Transtextualism, Mark Moore Gallery, Los Angeles, August 6–September 4.

1995

Pretty, Food House, Santa Monica, California, January 6–February 4.

In a Different Light, University Art Museum, University of California at Berkeley, January 11–April 9. Catalogue, text by Nayland Blake, Dan Cameron, Pam Gregg, Harmony Hammond, Richard Hawkins and Dennis Cooper, Lawrence Rinder, Amy Scholder, Nicola Tyson, Simon Watson, and Terry Wolverton.

Lo-Cal, Southern Exposure, San Francisco, March 17–April 15.

Felicity, Jan Baum Gallery, Los Angeles, March 31–May 5.

Flowers, Boritzer/Gray Gallery, Santa Monica, California, May 4–June 5.

1996

Left of Center, Ten in One Gallery, Chicago, January 12–February 17.

Balancing Act, Room, New York, January 18–March 16.

After, Post, Los Angeles, February 25–March 30.

Real Goods, Manhattan Village, Manhattan Beach, California, March 1–31. Catalogue, text by Marilu Knode.

Chalk, Factory Place Gallery, Los Angeles, June 1–29.

Fourteen Days: A Salon, Room, New York, July 10–August 3.

25 Years of Visual Arts at Purchase College, Neuberger Museum of Art, Purchase College, State University of New York, September 15–January 5, 1997. Catalogue, text by Cheryl Cipro Groth.

On and Off the Wall, Guggenheim Gallery, Chapman University, Orange, California, September 24–October 11.

Sally Elesby and Pae White, Four Walls, San Francisco, September 24–October 12.

In the Pocket, Raum für Kunst–Anton Lederer, Graz, Austria, October 2–26. Catalogue, text by Gerhard Gross.

Tangles, Otis College of Art and Design Gallery, Los Angeles, November 2–December 21.

True Bliss, Los Angeles Contemporary Exhibitions, December 5–January 26, 1997.

Skinny Belts and Strappy Sandals, Murray Feldman, Pacific Design Center, Los Angeles, December 6–31.

1997

In the Pocket, Galerie am Molkersteig, Vienna, January 28-February 14. Catalogue, text by Gerhard Gross.

Push: A Painting Show, Miller Fine Art, Los Angeles, April 12–May 10.

May, Crockett Rodeo, Seattle, May 2–25.

A Box, Marcia Mateyka Gallery, Washington, D.C., June 6–July 5.

Spot Making Sense, Grand Arts, Kansas City, Missouri, June 27–August 2. Brochure, text by David Pagel.

Blunt Object, The David and Alfred Smart Museum of Art, The University of Chicago, September 11–October 25.

1998

Deep Forest, Four Walls, San Francisco, January 16–February 14.

Love at the End . . ., Center of Contemporary Art, Seattle, February 7–April 4. Catalogue, text by Susan Kandel and Marilu Knode.

Selected Bibliography

1992

Kandel, Susan. "Sally Elesby." *Los Angeles Times*, December 10, 1992.

1993

Darling, Michael. "Thinned-Out, Pared-Down, Rescaled." *Artweek*, October 7, 1993, p. 12.

Duncan, Michael. "The Zone." *frieze*, November/December 1993.

1994

Darling, Michael. "An Insistent Whimsy." *Artweek*, August 18, 1994, p. 13.

Duncan, Michael. "L.A. Rising." *Art in America*, December 1994, p. 74.

Greene, David A. "Sally Elesby." *Los Angeles Reader*, March 25, 1994, p. 17.

Kandel, Susan. "Current Abstractions." *Art issues.*, May/June 1994, p. 42.

Knight, Christopher. "Needling a Stereotype." *Los Angeles Times*, December 3, 1994, pp. F1, 12.

——. "The Highs Were High and the Lows Were Low." *Los Angeles Times*, December 25, 1994.

Pagel, David. "Hooked on a Feeling." *Los Angeles Times*, July 21, 1994, p. F9.

——. "Transtextualism: Works to Read, See, Feel." *Los Angeles Times*, August 25, 1994.

——. "Feminine Forms." *Los Angeles Times*, October 20, 1994, p. F3.

Tumlir, Jan. "Sally Elesby." *Artweek*, March 24, 1994.

Wilson, William. "Sally Elesby." *Los Angeles Times*, March 18, 1994.

1995

Benish, Barbara. "Sezona v Los Angeles." *atelier*, February 4–16, 1995, p. 9.

Brown, Betty Ann. "'Felicity' at Jan Baum." *Coagula Art Journal*, April 1995.

Darling, Michael. "Pretty at Food House." *Artweek*, March 1995, pp. 38–39.

1996

Blaschy, Barbara D. "Geek Love." *Orange County Weekly*, September 26, 1996.

Curtis, Cathy. "Vertical Inclinations." *Los Angeles Times* (Orange County Edition), September 24, 1996, p. F1.

Duncan, Michael. "Sally Elesby at Bliss and Spanish Box." *Art in America*, November 1996, p. 124.

Iannaccone, Carmine. "Modern Times: The Clown and the Contemporary Sculptor." *L.A. Weekly*, October 4, 1996.

Joyce, Julie. "Sally Elesby." *Art issues.*, Summer 1996, p. 34.

Knight, Christopher. "Can Artists Run Their Own Spaces and Find 'True Bliss'?" *Los Angeles Times*, December 27, 1996.

Stein, Lisa. "Sally Elesby." *Chicago's New City*, February 18, 1996.

Taucher, Claudia. "Kunstlerinnen packen aus." *Kleine Zeitung*, August 29, 1996.

Walsh, Danielle. "Exhibitions Craft a Broader Vision." *The Orange County Register*, September 27, 1996, p. 33.

Wilk, Deborah. "Sally Elesby." *New Art Examiner*, March 1996, pp. 35–36.

Wilson, William. "'Means' Finds New Meanings in Old Schools of Thought." *Los Angeles Times*, September 7, 1996.

1997

Cutajar, Mario. "Art Review." *L.A. Weekly*, April 11, 1997, p. 50.

Darling, Michael. "Sally Elesby." *frieze*, June–August 1997, pp. 88–89.

Howell, George. "Review of 'A Box.'" *Art Papers*, November/December 1997, p. 46.

Knight, Christopher. "Look Out, World, Here They Come!" *Los Angeles Times*, March 31, 1997, p. 63.

Pagel, David. "A Smart, Animated Mix of High, Low Style." *Los Angeles Times*, March 28, 1997, p. F24.

Smith, Richard. "'True Bliss' at LACE." *Artweek*, February 1997, p. 23.

Thorson, Alice. "Sally Elesby." *The Kansas City Star*, July 4, 1997.

1998

Bell, J. Bowyer. "Sally Elesby." *Review*, February 1, 1998.

Duncan, Michael. "Out of the Paste." *Buzz*, February 1998, p. 34.

Kangas, Matthew. "Flower power and frivolities." *The Seattle Times*, February 12, 1998.

Newhall, Edith. "Talent Wired." *New York*, January 26, 1998, p. 64.

Roby, Diane. "Deep Forest: When Urgency Becomes Form." *Artweek*, March 1998, p. 26.

Jeff Elrod

Born 1966, Irving, Texas

1991, University of North Texas, Denton, BFA (Painting and Drawing)

1991–93, The Glassell School of Art, The Museum of Fine Arts, Houston, Core Fellow

Lives and works in Houston

Selected One-Person Exhibitions

1993

Super Elastic Mini-Graphx, Daar Gallery, Amsterdam, November 15.

Super Graphx 'n Such, Rijksakademie Exhibits Gallery, Amsterdam, December 1.

1994

Rustic Dreams, New Gallery, Houston, July 11–August 10.

1995

Killer Painting, Gallery One Three Seven, Houston, July 2–31.

1996

Tragic Fading Supergraphic, Art of this Century, Houston, January 28–March 2.

1997

Analog Paintings, Texas Gallery, Houston, April 2–26.

1998

The Squarepusher, Chinati Foundation, Marfa, Texas, April 24–June 1.

Selected Group Exhibitions

1992

Texas Art Celebration '92, 1600 Smith in Cullen Center, organized by the Assistance League of Houston, February 18–May 7.

1992 Core Fellows Exhibition, The Glassell School of Art, The Museum of Fine Arts, Houston, March 17–April 23. Catalogue.

1993

1993 Core Fellows Exhibition, The Glassell School of Art, The Museum of Fine Arts, Houston, March 16–April 25. Catalogue.

1994

Process•Strategy•Irony, DiverseWorks, Houston, September 10–October 16. Catalogue, text by Aaron Parazette.

Pals of Principals, Commerce Street Artist Warehouse, Houston, November 5–December 15.

1997

Disiptoey, Angstrom Gallery, Dallas, April 5–May 18.

Oktoberfest, Texas Gallery, Houston, October 7–November 22.

1998

Painting: Now and Forever, Part I, Pat Hearn Gallery and Matthew Marks Gallery, New York, June 25–July 31.

Selected Bibliography

1994

Johnson, Patricia C. "One Three Seven: Hey, let's get small." *Houston Chronicle*, July 17, 1994, p. 11.

———. "DiverseWorks Re-discovers Abstraction." *Houston Chronicle*, July 24, 1994, p. D3.

Kalil, Susie. "Soft Core." *Houston Press*, April 9, 1994.

1995

Carroll, Don. "Interview with Anti-Painter Jeff Elrod." *Artlies*, September 1995.

Colpitt, Frances. "Going Against the Grain." *Art in America*, April 1995, pp. 42–47.

Vannucci, Delfina. "Millennium Fever for Aesthetic Outlaws." *Public News* (Houston), December 20, 1995.

1996

Dewan, Shaila. "Graphic Ideas." *Houston Press*, February 22, 1996, p. 35.

Johnson, Patricia C. "Daring, Cynicism, Fun, Hang in Unique Gallery." *Houston Chronicle*, August 4, 1996, p. 12.

1997

Dewan, Shaila. "Pixel Power." *Houston Press*, April 10, 1997, p. 43.

Johnson, Patricia C. "Quick, don't miss these art shows." *Houston Chronicle*, April 19, 1997, p. D2.

Tad Griffin

Born 1966, Houston

1985–87, East Texas State University, Commerce

1987–88, Art Center College of Design, Pasadena, California

1989–91, East Texas State University, Commerce, BFA

Lives and works in Houston

Selected One-Person Exhibitions

1994

A Project for Public Space, Center for Research in Contemporary Art, University of Texas at Arlington, September 17–October 23. Catalogue, text by Karen Emenhiser.

Selected Group Exhibitions

1990

National Collegiate Exhibition and Competition, New York Academy of Art, New York, October.

1991

Cheekwood National Contemporary Painting Competition, Cheekwood Museum of Art, Nashville, Tennessee, October 5–November 17. Catalogue.

1993

The 34th Annual Invitational, Longview Art Museum, Longview, Texas, September 18–October 23. Catalogue, text by Al Harris F.

1993 Texas Biennial Exhibition, organized by The McKinney Avenue Contemporary, Dallas County Fairgrounds, November 20–December 6. Catalogue, text by Chris Cowden, Al Harris F., Benito Huerta, and Marti Mayo.

1994

New Work, Texas Gallery, Houston, February 22–March 26.

Tad Griffin, Tom Moody, John Pomara, David Szafranski, Eugene Binder Gallery, Dallas, Part I: March 4–April 16; Part II: September 9–October 15. Catalogue, text by Tom Moody and John Pomara.
Process•Strategy•Irony, DiverseWorks, Houston, September 10–October 16. Catalogue, text by Aaron Parazette.

1995
1995 New Orleans Triennial, New Orleans Museum of Art, March 25–April 30. Catalogue, text by Dan Cameron.
Texas Abstract: New Painting in the Nineties, ArtPace, San Antonio, November 18–December 22. Traveled within Texas to The McKinney Avenue Contemporary, Dallas, January 5–March 24, 1996; J. Wayne Stark Gallery, Texas A&M University, College Station, April 25–June 9; Museum of the Southwest, Midland, July 10–August 24, 1997; Wayland Baptist University, Plainview, September 2–30; Tyler Museum of Art, January 11–February 22, 1998. Catalogue, text by Frances Colpitt.

1997
Oktoberfest, Texas Gallery, Houston, October 7–November 22.
Works on Paper, Barry Whistler Gallery, Dallas, January 18–February 22.

1998
New to Houston: Recent Additions to Houston Collections, The Museum of Fine Arts, Houston, June 21–August 30.

Selected Bibliography

1993
Emenhiser, Karen. "Coming Together." *Dallas Observer*, December 2–8, 1993, p. 41.
Tyson, Janet. "Texas Biennial." *Fort Worth Star Telegram*, November 23, 1993, pp. E1–2.

1994
Chadwick, Susan. "Texas Artists on View in Provocative Exhibit." *The Houston Post*, March 5, 1994, p. F2.
——. "Geometric Abstractions Bind Together 7 in DiverseWorks Show." *The Houston Post*, September 24, 1994, p. F5.
Frohman, Mark. "Painting As Etiquette." *Artlies*, October/November 1994.
Kalil, Susie. "Abstraction Without Shame." *Houston Press*, October 6, 1994, pp. 34–35.
Kutner, Janet. "Making the Case for Abstract Art." *Dallas Morning News*, March 4, 1994, p. 45.
——. "Four Different Languages." *Dallas Morning News*, March 19, 1994, pp. C1, 13.
Mitchell, Charles Dee. "Art Blitz." *Art in America*, April 1994, pp. 42–47.
Odom, Michael. "Tad Griffin, Tom Moody, John Pomara, David Szafranski." *New Art Examiner*, Summer 1994, pp. 66–67.
Tyson, Janet. "Excellent Offerings." *Fort Worth Star Telegram*, April 6, 1994, pp. E1, 3.

1995
Bookhardt, D. Eric. "The Perennial Triennial." *Gambit* (New Orleans), April 11, 1995, p. 56.
Colpitt, Frances. "Going Against the Grain." *Art in America*, April 1995, pp. 42–47.
Keith, Jr., William E. "Abject Abstraction: The Dumbing Down of Art." *Voices of Art*, December/January 1995, pp. 4–8.
Mitchell, Charles Dee. "Tad Griffin at the Center for Research in Contemporary Art." *Art in America*, February 1995, p. 100.
Moody, Tom. "Tad Griffin." *Artforum*, May 1995, p. 103.
Vetroq, Marcia E. "Report from New Orleans: Dixie Buffet." *Art in America*, September 1995, pp. 61–63.

1996
Davidson, Dick. "Texas Abstracts." *Artlies*, June–September 1996, pp. 46–48.
Goddard, Dan R. "Abstract Art Eschews Emotion." *Arts Writer*, November 26, 1996, p. G3.
Mitchell, Charles Dee. "Of-this-world-abstracts at the MAC." *Dallas Morning News*, February 10, 1996.

Jim Hodges

Born 1957, Spokane, Washington
1980, Fort Wright College, Spokane, Washington, BFA
1986, Pratt Institute, Brooklyn, MFA
Lives and works in New York City

Selected One-Person Exhibitions

1989
Historia Abscondita, Gonzaga University Gallery, Spokane, Washington.

1991
White Room, White Columns, New York, September 11–October 4.

1992
New AIDS Drug, Het Apollohuis, Eidenhoven, Holland.

1993
Jim Hodges, Brooke Alexander, New York, March 25–April 24.

1994
A Diary Of Flowers, CRG Gallery, New York, January 7–February 26.
Everything For You, Interim Art, London, October 21–November 19.

1995
Jim Hodges, Center for Curatorial Studies, Bard College, Annandale-on-Hudson, New York, September 23–December 22.
Jim Hodges, CRG Gallery, New York, October 28–November 25.

1996
States, The Fabric Workshop and Museum, Philadelphia, April 25–June 15.
yes, Marc Foxx, Santa Monica, California, May 18–June 15.

1997
Jim Hodges: No Betweens and More, SITE Santa Fe, March 15–June 22. Brochure.
Jim Hodges, Galerie Ghislaine Hussenot, Paris, September 20–October 11.

1998
Jim Hodges, Kemper Museum of Contemporary Art, Kansas City, Missouri, April 9–June 14. Brochure, text by Dana Self.
Jim Hodges, CRG Gallery, New York, September 11–October 10.

Selected Group Exhibitions

1988
Selections from the Artists File, Artists Space, New York, November 17–January 7, 1989. Catalogue, text by Connie Butler.

1990
Reclamation, Momenta Art Alternatives, Philadelphia.

1991
Black and White, Nancy Hoffman Gallery, New York, June–August.
Lyric: Uses of Beauty at the End of the Century, White Columns, New York.

1992
Healing, Rena Bransten Gallery, San Francisco, May 12–June 13.
An Ode to Gardens and Flowers, Nassau County Museum of Art, Roslyn Harbor, New York.
The Temporary Image, S.S. White Building, Philadelphia.
Update 1992, White Columns, New York.

1993
Sculpture & Multiples, Brooke Alexander, New York, January 8–February 13.
Selections/Spring '93, The Drawing Center, New York, February 27–March 27. Brochure.
Paper Trails: The Eidetic Image, Contemporary American Works on Paper, Krannert Art Museum, University of Illinois, Champaign, March 17–April 18.
Beyond Loss: Art in the Era of AIDS, Washington Project for the Arts, Washington, D.C., April 23–June 13.
Opening Exhibition, Rowles Studio, Hudson, New York, July 14–August 29.
Our Perfect World, Grey Art Gallery & Study Center, New York University, September 14–October 30.
Arachnosphere, Ramnarine Gallery, New York.
Jim Hodges and Bill Jacobson, Paul Morris Fine Art, New York.
The Animal in Me, Amy Lipton Gallery, New York.

1994
A Bouquet for Juan, Nancy Hoffman Gallery, New York, June 4–July 1.
Ethereal Materialism, Apex Art, New York, October 15–November 26.
A Garden, Barbara Krakow Gallery, Boston.
Desire, Charles Cowles Gallery, New York.
It's how you play the game, Exit Art/The First World, New York.
Les fleurs de mon jardin, Galerie Alain Gutharc, Paris.

1995

Sex Sells, Rena Branstem Gallery, San Francisco, January 5–7.

In a Different Light, University Art Museum, University of California at Berkeley, January 11–April 9. Catalogue, text by Nayland Blake, Dan Cameron, Pam Gregg, Harmony Hammond, Richard Hawkins and Dennis Cooper, Lawrence Rinder, Amy Scholder, Nicola Tyson, Simon Watson, and Terry Wolverton.

Material Dreams, Gallery Takashimaya, New York, January 14– March 11.

soucis de pensées, Art: Concept/Oliver Antoine, Nice, France, March 3–April 22.

Mon Voyage à New York, Galerie Elizabeth Valleix, Paris, March 11–April 8.

Avant-Garde Walk à Venezia, 1995 Venice Biennial, June 8–12. Catalogue, text by Marc Pottier.

Late Spring, Marc Foxx, Los Angeles, June 7–July 15.

New Works, Feigen Gallery, Chicago, June 23–August 22.

1996

Glenn Brown, Peter Doig, Jim Hodges, Adriana Varejão, Galerie Ghislaine Hussenot, Paris, January 20–February 24.

Masculine Measures, Jon Michael Kohler Arts Center, Sheboygan, Wisconsin, January 28–May 12.

Material Matters, A.O.I. Gallery, Santa Fe, July–August.

UNIVERSALIS, The 23rd International São Paulo Bienale, October 5–December 8. Catalogue, text by Paul Schimmel.

Swag & Puddle, The Work Space, New York.

1997

Poetics of Obsession, Linda Kirkland Gallery, New York, January 25–February 23.

Gothic, The Institute of Contemporary Art, Boston, April 24–July 6. Catalogue, text by Christoph Grunenberg.

Des Fleurs en Mai, FRAC, Nantes, France, April 25–June 8.

Longing and Memory, Los Angeles County Museum of Art, June 5–September 8. Brochure, text by Lynn Zelevansky.

7th Bienal Internacional de Esculturae Desenho das Caldas da Rainha Bienalt, Portugal, June 7–July 17.

Hanging by a Thread, Hudson River Museum of Westchester, Yonkers, New York, October 3–February 17, 1998. Catalogue, text by Ellen J. Keiter.

Present Tense: Nine Artists In the Nineties, San Francisco Museum of Modern Art, September 13–January 13, 1998. Catalogue, text by Julie Ault, Bill Hayes, and Gary Garrels on Hodges.

Selected Bibliography

1994

Edelman, Robert G. "Jim Hodges." *Artpress*, March 1994, pp. 94–95.

Harris, Susan. "Jim Hodges." *ARTnews*, April 1994, p. 173.

Smith, Roberta. "Jim Hodges." *The New York Times*, February 11, 1994, p. C36.

Upshaw, Reagan. "Jim Hodges at CRG." *Art in America*, May 1994, pp. 109–10.

Weinstein, Matthew. "Jim Hodges at CRG." *Artforum*, May 1994, p. 102.

1995

Canning, Susan M. "Ethereal Materialism." *New Art Examiner*, February 1995, pp. 43–44.

Levin, Kim. "Choices." *The Village Voice*, November 28, 1995.

Smith, Roberta. "The New, Irreverant Approach to Mounting Exhibitions." *The New York Times*, January 6, 1995, p. C25.

——. "Also of Note." *The New York Times*, November 24, 1995, p. C12.

1996

Darling, Michael. "Doodle Dandy, Just Say Yes to Jim Hodges." *Los Angeles Reader*, May 31, 1996, p. 12.

Decter, Joshua. "Jim Hodges." *Artforum*, November 1996, pp. 104–105.

Deitcher, David. "Death in the Marketplace." *frieze*, June–August 1996, pp. 40–45.

Hart, Jane. "Jim Hodges." *ZINGMAGAZINE*, Autumn/Winter 1996/1997.

Kandel, Susan. "Jim Hodges." *Los Angeles Times*, June 6, 1996.

Killam, Brad. "Jim Hodges." *New Art Examiner*, September 1996.

1997

Clemmer, David. "Jim Hodges at SITE Santa Fe." *Flash Art* (International Edition), Summer 1997, p. 98.

Darling, Michael. "Longing and Memory." *L.A. Weekly*, June 20–26, 1997.

Knight, Christopher. "Beguiled by 'Longing and Memory.'" *Los Angeles Times*, June 7, 1997.

McClure, Lissa. "Jim Hodges." *Review*, February 1, 1997.

McKenna, Kristine. "The Contemporary Not Temporary at LACMA." *Los Angeles Times*, June 7, 1997.

1998

Cotter, Holland. "Messages Woven, Sewn or Floating in the Air." *The New York Times*, January 9, 1998, p. E37.

Grundberg, Andy. "Present Tense: Nine Artists in the Nineties." *Artforum*, February 1998, p. 87.

Laffer, Christine. "Present Tense: Nine Artists in the Nineties." *Art Papers*, March/April 1998, p. 36.

Zimmer, William. "Works That Are Made From Textiles." *The New York Times*, January 18, 1998, p. 18.

Callum Innes

Born 1962, Edinburgh

1980–84, Grays School of Art, Aberdeen

1984–85, Edinburgh College of Art, Post Graduate DIP

Lives and works in Edinburgh

Selected One-Person Exhibitions

1986

Callum Innes, Artspace Gallery, Aberdeen.

1988

Callum Innes, 369 Gallery, Edinburgh.

1990

Callum Innes, Frith Street Gallery, London.

Callum Innes, Jan Turner Gallery, Los Angeles.

1991

Callum Innes, Frith Street Gallery, London.

Callum Innes, Galerie Patrick de Brock, Antwerp.

1992

Callum Innes, Institute of Contemporary Arts, London, April 16–May 24. Catalogue.

Callum Innes, Scottish National Gallery of Modern Art, Edinburgh, November 13–January 3, 1993.

Callum Innes, Galerie nächst St. Stephan, Rosemarie Schwartzwälder, Vienna.

1993

Callum Innes, Frith Street Gallery, London.

Callum Innes, Galerie Bob van Orsouw, Zurich.

Callum Innes, Jan Turner Gallery, Los Angeles. Catalogue.

Callum Innes, Galerie Patrick de Brock, Antwerp.

1994

Callum Innes, Frith Street Gallery, London.

1995

Callum Innes, Mackintosh Museum, Glasgow School of Art.

Callum Innes, Galerie Gilbert Brownstone and Cie, Paris.

Callum Innes, Galerie M & R Fricke, Düsseldorf.

Callum Innes, Galerie Bob van Orsouw, Zurich. Catalogue, text by Friedrich Meschede.

Callum Innes, Angel Row Gallery, Nottingham, England. Catalogue, text by Adrian Searle.

Callum Innes, Galeria Paolo Gentili, Florence.

1996

Callum Innes, Frith Street Gallery, London.

Callum Innes, Patrick de Brock Gallery, Knokke, Belgium.

Callum Innes (1990–1996), Inverleith House, Royal Botanic Garden Edinburgh, August 10–October 6. Catalogue, text by Mel Gooding.

Callum Innes, Galerie Slewe, Amsterdam.

1997

Callum Innes, Sean Kelly Gallery, New York, February 28–April 12.

Callum Innes, Kunsthaus Zurich.

Callum Innes, Galerie M & R Fricke, Düsseldorf and Berlin.

1998

Callum Innes, Ikon Gallery, Birmingham, England.

Callum Innes, Galerie Bob van Orsouw, Zurich.

Callum Innes, Frith Street Gallery, London, January 17–March 5.

Callum Innes, Brownstone & Corréard, Paris.

Selected Group Exhibitions

1989

Fruitmarket Open, Fruitmarket Gallery, Edinburgh.

Group Show, 369 Gallery, Edinburgh.

Scatter, Third Eye Centre, Glasgow.

1990

The British Art Show 1990, MacLellan Galleries, Glasgow. Traveled to Leeds City Art Gallery, Leeds; Hayward Gallery, London. Catalogue, text by Caroline Collier, Andrew Nairne, and David Ward.

1991

Kunst Europa, Kunstverein Freiburg, Germany. Catalogue.

Painting Alone, Pace Gallery, New York. Catalogue, text by Rainer Crone and David Moos.

1992

Abstrakte Malerei zwischen Analyse und Synthese, Gallerie nächst St. Stephan, Vienna. Catalogue.

1993

Callum Innes/Perry Roberts: Works on Paper, Frith Street Gallery, London.

Coalition (Roderick Buchanan, Yang Jie Chang, Callum Innes, Huang Yong Ping), Centre for Contemporary Arts, Glasgow. Catalogue, text by Andrew Nairne.

John Moore's, Walker Art Gallery, Liverpool. Catalogue.

New Voices, organized by Arts Council of Great Britain World Touring Exhibition. Traveled to Centre de Conferences Albert Borchette, Brussels; Musée National d'Histoire et d'Art, Luxembourg; Taksim Art Gallery, Istanbul; State Fine Arts Gallery, Ankara, Turkey; State Painting and Sculpture Museum, Izmir, Turkey. Catalogue.

Prospect '93, Frankfurter Kunstverein,Germany. Catalogue.

Wonderful Life, Lisson Gallery, London.

1994

Collezione Agostino e Patrizia Re-Rebaudengo, Turin, Italy; La Galleria Civice di Modena, Modena, Italy. Catalogue.

Delit d'initiés, Galerie Gilbert Brownstone & Cie, Paris.

Idea Europe, Palazzo Pubblico, Siena, Italy. Catalogue.

Lead and Follow: The Continuity of Abstraction, Atlantis Gallery, London. Catalogue.

New Voices, Centre d'Art Santa Monica, Barcelona, and Museo de Bellos Artes, Bilbao, Spain. Catalogue.

Paintmarks, Kettles Yard, Cambridge, England. Traveled to City Art Gallery, Southampton, and Mead Gallery, Coventry. Catalogue.

Seeing the Unseen, The Invisible Museum, Peter Fleissig Collection, London. Catalogue.

1995

Architecture of The Mind, Barbara Farber Gallery, Amsterdam, April 11–May 24. Catalogue, text by David Moos.

From Here, Waddington Galleries and Karsten Schubert, London, March–April. Catalogue, text by Andrew Wilson.

The Turner Prize 1995, Tate Gallery, London, November 1–December 3. Brochure, text by Virginia Button.

The Jerwood Painting Prize, Royal Scottish Academy, Edinburgh, and Royal Academy, London.

The Mutated Painting, Galerie Martina Detterer, Frankfurt.

New Abstraction, Kohn Turner Gallery, Los Angeles.

The Punter's Art Show, BBC Project, The Orchard Gallery, Derry, Ireland.

1996

About Vision: New British Paintings in the 1990s, Museum of Modern Art, Oxford, November 10–February 23, 1997. Traveled within Great Britain to Fruitmarket Gallery, Edinburgh, 1997; Laing Art Gallery, Newcastle upon Tyne, 1997–98. Catalogue, text by David Elliott.

Kleine Welten, Galerie M & R Fricke, Düsseldorf.

1997

Best of the Season, The Aldrich Museum of Contemporary Art, Ridgefield, Connecticut, September 14–January 4, 1998. Catalogue, text by Harry Philbrick.

Abstractions Provisoires, Musée d'Art Moderne de St. Etienne, France.

Selected Bibliography

1990

Beaumont, Mary Rose. "Callum Innes at Frith Street." *Arts Review* (London), April 6, 1990, p. 181.

Feaver, William. "Notices: The British Art Show." *Vogue*, May 1990, pp. 22–23.

1991

Archer, Michael. "Callum Innes at Frith Street Gallery." *Artforum*, December 1991, p. 118.

Renton, Andrew. "Callum Innes at Frith Street Gallery." *Flash Art*, November/December 1991, p. 138.

Searle, Adrian. "Review of Frith Street Gallery exhibition." *Time Out London*, October 9, 1991.

Slotover, Matthew. "Callum Innes." *frieze*, December/January 1991/92, pp. 16–17.

1992

"Callum Innes Receives FIAR Award." *Flash Art* (International Edition), January/February 1992, p. 153.

Cork, Richard. "Galleries: London." *The Times*, May 1992.

Feaver, William. "Review of ICA Exhibition." *The Observer*, May 1992, p. 112.

Hilton, Tim. "A Mark Made and Abstracted." *The Guardian*, April 23, 1992.

McEwen, John. "Review of ICA Exhibition." *The Sunday Telegraph*, April 26, 1992.

1993

Batchelor, David. "Callum Innes/Perry Robert: Works on Paper." *frieze*, September/October 1993, pp. 61–62.

Feaver, William. "Callum Innes." *ARTnews*, May 1993, p. 112.

Gale, Iain. "In the studio . . . Iain Gale meets Callum Innes." *The Independent*, September 1993.

Wilson, Andrew. "Callum Innes: A Quality of Detachment." *Forum International*, March/April 1993, pp. 87–89.

1994

Barnes, Rachel. "Light and Air: Review of Paintmarks at Kettles Yard." *The Daily Telegraph*, August 10, 1994.

Feaver, William. "Callum Innes at Frith Street." *The Observer*, May 15, 1994.

——. "Callum Innes at Frith Street." *ARTnews*, September 1994, pp. 182–83.

Godfrey, Tony. "Callum Innes and Juan Uslé." *Untitled*, Summer 1994.

Searle, Adrian. "Callum Innes and Juan Uslé at Frith Street Gallery." *Time Out London*, June 1, 1994.

1995

Hall, Charles. "Towards a broader picture." *The Times*, August 11, 1995, p. 32.

Henry, Clare. "Red Dots in the Sunrise." *The Herald*, November 25, 1995.

Kent, Sarah. "Seen and heard." *Time Out London*, November 8, 1995, p. 45.

MacMillan, Ian. "Less is More." *Modern Painters*, Winter 1995, pp. 20–22.

1996

Corner, Lena. "Demolition Man." *The Big Issue*, March 25–31, 1996.

Feldman, Melissa E. "Callum Innes at Frith Street." *Art in America*, October 1996, p. 128.

Gale, Iain. "Exhibitions London." *The Independent*, May 10, 1996.

Hilton, Tim. "The Best Painting in Britain?" *Independent on Sunday*, November 17, 1996, p. 30.

McEwen, John. "Our abstracted, natural world." *The Sunday Telegraph*, September 8, 1996, p. 8.

——. "It's Young, It's British, It's Cool." *The Sunday Telegraph*, November 17, 1996.

1997

Hilton, Tim. "Cool for Hamsters." *Independent on Sunday*, November 23, 1997.

Morley, Simon. "Light as." *Contemporary Visual Arts*, Winter 1997, pp. 30–37.

1998

Burton, Jane. "Callum Innes, Frith Street." *ARTnews*, May 1998, pp. 182, 184.

Emil Lukas

Born 1964, Pittsburgh

1986, Edinboro University, Pennsylvania, BFA
Lives and works in Stockertown, Pennsylvania

Selected One-Person Exhibitions

1986

Emil Lukas, Mendelson Gallery, Pittsburgh.

1987

Emil Lukas, Mendelson Gallery, Pittsburgh.

1988

Emil Lukas, Pinta Galleria D'Arte Contemporanea, Genoa, Italy.

1989

Emil Lukas, Mendelson Gallery, Pittsburgh.

1990

Emil Lukas, Althea Viafora Gallery, New York, November 3–28.

1992

Emil Lukas, Tom Solomon's Garage, Los Angeles, June 6–28.

Emil Lukas, Galerie Nova, Pontresina, Switzerland, December 19–January 23, 1993.

1993

Emil Lukas, John Post Lee Gallery, New York, February 4–27.

1994

Emil Lukas: When Limbs Rub, Tom Solomon's Garage, Los Angeles, April 23–May 28.

Emil Lukas: Makings of the Small, Bravin Post Lee Gallery, New York, November 17–December 24.

1995

Emil Lukas, Studio la Cittá, Verona, Italy, April. Catalogue, text by Luigi Meneghelli.

Recent Work, Haines Gallery, San Francisco, September 5–October 7.

1996

Emil Lukas, Bravin Post Lee Gallery, New York, October 10–November 9.

1997

Emil Lukas, Haines Gallery, San Francisco, January 28–March 8.

Emil Lukas, Guerlain Foundation, Les Musnuls, France.

Emil Lukas, Studio la Cittá, Verona, Italy.

1998

Emil Lukas, Studio la Cittá, Verona, Italy, April–May. Catalogue, text by Mario Bertoni.

Emil Lukas, Galerie Shroeder, Cologne.

Selected Group Exhibitions

1987

New Attitudes: Recent Pennsylvania Abstraction, Southern Alleghenies Museum of Art, Pittsburgh, October 23–November 30. Catalogue, text by Michael J. Allison.

Simonetta Fadda, Emil Lukas, Ivano Sossella, Cesare Viel, Pinta Galleria D'Arte Contemporanea, Genoa, Italy, December 22–January 15, 1988.

1989

Selections 46, The Drawing Center, New York, September 9–October 21.

1990

Work on Paper, Paula Allen Gallery, New York, June 19–July 13.

A Question of Paint, Hallwalls Contemporary Arts Center, Buffalo, New York, September 21–November 2. Brochure, text by Charles Wright, Jr.

1991

Small Works, 80 Washington Square East Galleries, New York, February 3–March 9.

Ornament: Ho Hum All Ye Faithful, John Post Lee Gallery, New York, December 11–January 11, 1992.

Casual Ceremony, White Columns, New York.

James Hyde, Emil Lukas, Vik Muniz, Mendelson Gallery, Pittsburgh.

1992

Collector's Choice of Emerging Artists, Ruth Vered Gallery, East Hampton,New York, September–November.

10 Steps, Horodner Romley Gallery, New York, November 13–December 12.

New Address, Muranushi-Lederman, New York.

The Hole Is Part of The Sum, Michael Klein Gallery, New York.

1993

Painting as Paradigm, Stark Gallery, New York, January 5–30.

Major Medical: Invasive Procedures of Contemporary Art, City Without Walls, Newark, New Jersey, January 28–March 12.

Hyper-CATHEXIS: Layers of Experience, Stux Gallery, New York, March 27–April 24.

Between, John Post Lee Gallery, New York, September 10–October 9.

Windows and Doors, Holly Solomon Gallery, New York.

1994

Possible Things, Bardamu Gallery, New York, January 20–February 26.

Practicamenta Argento, Studio la Cittá, Verona, Italy, September–October.

Critical Mass, Yale University Art Gallery, New Haven, December 5–17. Traveled to The McKinney Avenue Contemporary, Dallas, January 20–February 26, 1995. Catalogue, text by Charles Long.

Inner Circle, Tom Solomon's Garage, Los Angeles.

60 Drawings from Art Hotel, The Drawing Room, Amsterdam.

1995

Down The Garden Path, The Work Space, New York, March 25–May 13.

From Nature, Haines Gallery, San Francisco, May 4–June 17.

La Belle et La Bête, Musée d'Art Moderne de la Ville de Paris, October 6–November 19. Catalogue, text by Lynn Gumpert.

The Use of Evidence, Contemporary Art Museum, University of South Florida, Tampa, October 30–December 22. Catalogue.

A Drawing, Bravin Post Lee Gallery, New York, November 21–December 23.

1996

The Collection of Panza di Biumo: Artisti Degli Anni '80 e '90, Museo d'Arte Moderna e Contemporanea di Trento, Trent, Italy, September 12–December 8.

Rick Arnitz and Emil Lukas, Galerie Zenit, Heineskjerning Og Zenit, Frederiksberg, Denmark, October 5–26.

Painting in an Expanding Field, Ursan Gallery, Bennington, Vermont.

1997

Matters of the Heart, Haines Gallery, San Francisco, February 14–March 30.

Onomatopoeia, Studio la Cittá, Verona, Italy, July 5–September 27. Catalogue, text by Anthony Iannacci.

Obsession + Devotion, Haines Gallery, San Francisco, October 15–November 15.

1998

Emil Lukas, Jonathan Seliger, Daniel Weiner, Bravin Post Lee Temporary, New York, March 19–April 25.

Landscape and Memory, Haines Gallery, San Francisco, May 28–July 3.

Selected Bibliography

1992

Braff, Phyllis. "7 Artists With Bright Futures." *The New York Times*, September 13, 1992, p. 18.

Faust, Gretchen. "Casual Ceremony." *Arts Magazine*, March 1992, p. 79.

Kandel, Susan. "Unraveling a Mystery at Thomas Solomon's Garage." *Los Angeles Times*, June 5, 1992.

Kuoni, Gisela. "Emil Lukas, die Entstenhung einer Ausstellung." *Sunder Zeituna*, March 1992.

Smith, Roberta. "Casual Ceremony." *The New York Times*, January 3, 1992, p. C28.

1993

Deggiovanni, Piero. "Luca Caccioni/Emil Lukas." *Tema Celeste*, November 1993.

Levin, Kim. "Choices." *The Village Voice*, February 17, 1993.

Lohaus, Stella. "Review." *Forum International,* Spring 1993.

Meneghelli, Luigi. "Alle sorgenti mistiose dell'arte." *L'Arena*, October 11, 1993.

Seward, Keith. "Emil Lukas at John Post Lee Gallery." *Artforum*, May 1993, p. 107.

1994

Choon, Angela. "Openings: Art that Springs from New Terrain." *Art & Antiques*, May 1994.

Cohen, Michael. "Emil Lukas at Tom Solomon's Garage." *Flash Art* (International Edition), Summer 1994, pp. 126–27.

Kandel, Susan. "Lukas' Alternative Scenario Playhouse." *Los Angeles Times*, May 27, 1994.

Levin, Kim. "Voices." *The Village Voice*, December 6, 1994.

1995

Baker, Kenneth. "Things Stacked Up at Haines." *San Francisco Chronicle*, September 16, 1995.

Bauer, Julia. "The Local Artist Rediscovers in Realism The Natural Way—In Suburbia." *The Express Times*, March 25, 1995, p. 1.

Scarabelli, Luca. "Emil Lukas, Vegitali Ignoti." *Quaderno d'Arte Contemporanea*, Winter 1995/1996.

1996

Meneghelli, Luigi. "Tanto per farsi un'idea dell'arte actuale." *L'Arena*, November 6, 1996.

1997

Baker, Kenneth. "Emil Lukas at Haines Gallery." *ARTnews*, May 1997, p. 170.

Bonetti, David. "Biological Approach to Art." *San Francisco Examiner*, February 1997.

Koplos, Janet. "Emil Lukas at Bravin Post Lee." *Art in America*, February 1997, pp. 101–102.

Fabian Marcaccio

Born 1963, Rosario de Santa Fe, Argentina
1980–83, University of Philosophy, Rosario de Santa Fe
Lives and works in New York

Selected One-Person Exhibitions

1992

Inter-Painting, Jason Rubell Gallery, Palm Beach, Florida, November 7–December 5. Catalogue, text by Jason Rubell.

1993

The Altered Genetics of Painting, John Post Lee Gallery, New York, March 4–27. Catalogue, text by Meyer Raphael Rubinstein.
Mutual Betrayal, Barbara Farber Gallery, Amsterdam, May 25–July 3. Catalogue.
Unpaintables, Anders Tornberg Gallery, Lund, Sweden.

1994

On Unpaintables, Galerie Thaddaeus Ropac, Paris, February 26–April 3.
New Painting Management, Galerie Rolf Ricke, Cologne, November 11–December 21.

1995

Paint-Zone, Bravin Post Lee Gallery, New York, March 25–April 22.
Paint-Zone, L.A. Louver Gallery, Venice, California, October 28–November 25.

1996

Fabian Marcaccio, Barbara Farber Gallery, Amsterdam, June 2–22. Catalogue, text by Barry Schwabsky.
Fabian Marcaccio: With-ject Brazil/Con-jecto Brasil, Galeria Camargo Vilaça, São Paulo, August 6–30. Catalogue, text by Carlos Basualdo.
Fabian Marcaccio, Studio la Cittá, Verona, Italy.

1997

Paintants, Baumgartner Galleries, Washington, D.C., February 28–April 6.
Paintants #2, Schmidt Contemporary Art, St. Louis, Missouri, April 26–May 21.
Fabian Marcaccio, Galeria Diaz, Madrid.
Survey Exhibition, Museo Alejandro Otero, Caracas, Venezuela.

1998

Con-jecto Argentina, Galeria Ruth Benzacar, Buenos Aires, March 25–April 25.
Paintant-Compounds, Galerie Rolfe Ricke, Cologne, April 24–June 16.
With-jecT Spain (Con-jecto Expaña), Galeria Joan Prats, Barcelona, and Galeria Salvador Diaz, Madrid, April–May. Catalogue, text by Fernando Castro Flórez, Raphael Rubinstein, and David Ryan.
Paintants #3, Mario Diacono Gallery, Boston, May 2–28.

Selected Group Exhibitions

1986

Trends, Museum of Contemporary Hispanic Art, New York, July 10–August 10.

1988

Artists in the Marketplace, The Bronx Museum of Art, New York, June 9–July 31.
Jornadas de la Critica, Spinto Center, Buenos Aires.
Sei Incisori, Palazzo Bounaccorsi, Italy.

1989

Invitational, Stux Gallery, New York, January 11–28.
Ideas and Images From Argentina, The Bronx Museum of Art, New York, October 3–January 28, 1990. Catalogue, text by Jorge Glusberg.
Translations, Castle Naudary, France.

1990

Group Exhibition, Althea Viafora Gallery, New York, December 11–January 9, 1991.
International Bienial of Paper Art, Hoesch Museum, Duren, Germany.
Paradigma '80s–'90s, Jacob Karpio Gallery, San Jose, Costa Rica.

1991

Invitational, Stux Gallery, New York, January 16–February 9.
Summer Review '91, Stux Gallery, New York, June 19–August 15.
Ornament: Ho Hum All Ye Faithful, John Post Lee Gallery, New York, December 11–January 11, 1992.
Group Exhibition, Jacob Karpio Gallery, San Jose, Costa Rica. Catalogue, text by Reynaldo Laddaga.
Group Exhibition, New Era Space, New York.

1992

Fabian Marcaccio and Daniel Wiener, John Post Lee Gallery, New York, January 17–February 22.
How It Is, Tony Shafrazi Gallery, New York, February 1–29.
Recent Abstract Painting, Schmidt Contemporary Art, St. Louis, Missouri, March 14–April 8.
Multiple Grounds Part II, Systema Galleries, Baarn, The Netherlands, April 11–May 24.
Slow Art, Institute for Contemporary Art, P.S. 1 Museum, New York, April 26–June 21.
Contextures & Constructures, Rubenstein/Diacono, New York, May 9–30.
Niente Nuovo, Studio la Cittá, Verona, Italy, May 15–July 30. Catalogue, text by Anthony Iannacci.
James Hyde, Jody Lomberg, Fabian Marcaccio, Arena Gallery, New York, June 2–27.
Kinder! Macht Neues!, Galerie Rolf Ricke, Cologne, June 13–August 22.
Off Balance, Jason Rubell Gallery, Palm Beach, Florida, June–July.
A New American Flag, Max Protetch Gallery, New York, October 24–January 9, 1993.
Cultural Fabrication, John Good Gallery, New York.
Erwartung, Munic Museum, Rosario de Santa Fe, Argentina.
Theoretically Yours, The Museum of Aosta, Italy. Catalogue, text by Patricia Collins & Richard Milazzo.
Who's Afraid of Duchamp, Minimalism and Passport Photography, Annina Nosei Gallery, New York.

1993

The Brushstroke: Painting in the '90s, Ruth Bloom Gallery, Los Angeles, January 21–February 20.
Needlepoint, Embroidery, Macrame, and Crochet, Postmasters Gallery, New York, February 13–March 13. Catalogue, text by Patricia Collins & Richard Milazzo.
The Post-Dialectical Index, Sala Comunale Palazzo Constanzi, Trieste, Italy, February 13–March 4. Traveled to Lattuada Studio, Milan, Italy, June 1–July 15; Horodner Romley Gallery, New York, June 15–July 15. Catalogue, text by Robert Morgan.
Tool Box, Studio la Cittá, Verona, Italy, March 21. Catalogue, text by Anthony Iannacci.
Plötslich Ist Eine Zeit Hereingebrochen, In Der Alles Möglich Sein Sollte Part 3, Kunstverein Ludwigsburg, Germany, April 18–May 16.
Irony & Ecstacy, Salama-Caro Gallery, London, April 21–May 29. Catalogue, text by Klaus Ottman.
Herr Schleirmachers Sista Dröm, Galerie Nordenhake, Stockholm, May 14.
Group Show, Baumgartner Galleries, Washington, D.C., July.
Teddy and Other Stories, Claudio Bottello Arte, Turin, Italy. Traveled to Galleria In Arco, Turin, Italy. Catalogue, text by Luca Beatrice and Cristiana Parrella.

1994

Reveillon '94, Stux Gallery, New York, January 8–February 12.
Conditioning Painting, Galerie Nächt St. Stephan, Vienna, January 28–March 19.
The Brushstroke and Its Guises, New York Studio School, March 7–April 16.
Drawings: Lasker, Marcaccio, Nozkowski, Stephan, Bravin Post Lee Gallery, New York, April 23–May 21.
Painting Language, L.A. Louver Gallery, Venice, California, August 23–September 24.
Revisioning The Familiar, Zilkha Gallery, Wesleyan University, Middletown, Connecticut, August 30–October 2. Catalogue, text by Ayako Nezu and Elizabeth Toohey.
Practicamente Argento, Studio la Cittá, Verona, Italy, September–October.
On Paper, Schmidt Contemporary Art, St. Louis, Missouri, October 15–November 14.
De-Pop, Cummings Art Center, Connecticut College, New London, November 9–December 9.
Fractured Seduction, Artifact Gallery, Tel Aviv. Catalogue, text by Maia Damianovic.
Possible Things, Bardamu Gallery, New York.

1995

Mesotica, Museo de Arte e Diseno Contemporáneo, San Jose, Costa Rica, January 18–March 15.
On Target, Horodner Romley Gallery, New York, January 21–February 25.
The Mutated Painting, Galerie Martina Detterer, Frankfurt, February 25–May 5.
Pittura-Immedia, Neue Galerie am Landesmuseum Joanneum, Graz, Austria, March 11–April 18. Catalogue, text by Peter Weibel.
Architecture of The Mind, Barbara Farber Gallery, Amsterdam, April 11–May 24. Catalogue, text by David Moos.

New York Abstract, Contemporary Arts Center, New Orleans, April 29–June 25. Catalogue, text by Lew Thomas.
Outside You, Baumgartner Galleries, Washington, D.C., May 24–June 30. Catalogue, text by David Moos.
Transatlantica, Museo Alejandro Otero, Caracas, Venezuela, June 9–October 8. Catalogue, text by Ruth Auerbach, María Luz Cárdenas, Fernando Castro Florez, and Raphael Rubinstein.
Unveiled Painting, Kunstraum Wien, Vienna, September 16–October 22. Brochure, text by Klaus Dieter Zimmer.
Art at the Edge: Tampering, High Museum of Art, Atlanta, October 10–January 7, 1996. Catalogue, text by Susan Krane.
Una Nuova Tradizione Americana, Galeria Oddi Baglioni, Rome, October 24.
The Use of Evidence, Contemporary Art Museum, University of South Florida, Tampa, November 3–December 22. Catalogue.
Painting Outside Painting: 44th Biennial Exhibition of Contemporary American Painting, The Corcoran Gallery of Art, Washington, D.C., December 16–February 19, 1996. Catalogue, text by Terrie Sultan and David Pagel on Marcaccio.
70-80-90, Museo Nacional de Bellas Artes, Buenos Aires, December–January. Catalogue, text by Jorge Glusberg.

1996
Alice's Looking Glass: A Glimpse At the Non-Linear, Apex Art, New York, March 7–April 6. Catalogue, text by Mary Beyt.
Pratiques Abstraites, Galerie Thaddaeus Ropac, Paris, March 19–April 20.
Transformal, Secession, Vienna, March 22–April 25. Catalogue, text by Maia Damianovic.
Face-to-Face: Recent Abstract Painting, MIT List Visual Arts Center, Cambridge, Massachusetts, April 13–June 30. Catalogue, text by Katy Kline and Helaine Posner on Marcaccio.
Form als Ziel mündet immer in Formalismus, Galerie Rolf Ricke, Cologne, June 7–August 10.
Bare Bones, TZ Art & Co., New York, June 25–September 5.
Photographism, Pratt Institute, New York, September 21–November 2.
New York Abstraction, MacDonald Stewart Art Centre, University of Guelph, Ontario, Canada, October 24–January 10, 1997.
Reconditioned Abstraction, Forum For Contemporary Art, St. Louis, Missouri, November 15–January 4, 1997. Catalogue, text by Martin Ball and Mel Watkin.
Grito, Museo Nacional de Bellas Artes, Galeria Século XXI, Rio de Janeiro, November 26–January 22, 1997.
The Artist and The Book, Baumgartner Galleries, Washington, D.C., December 6–January 8, 1997.
Painting in an Expanding Field, Ursan Gallery, Bennington College, Vermont.
Without Frontiers, Museo Alejandro Otero, Caracas, Venezuela.
Works on Paper, Galerie Rolf Ricke, Cologne, Germany.

1997
Pintura, Galeria Joan Prats, Barcelona, February–March.
After the Fall: Aspects of Abstract Painting since 1970, Newhouse Center for Contemporary Art, Snug Harbor Cultural Center, Staten Island, New York, March 27–September 7. Catalogue, text by Lilly Wei.
Frankensteinian, Caren Golden Fine Art, New York, May 29–July 3.
In-Form, Bravin Post Lee Gallery, New York, June 4–July 19.
Theories of The Decorative: Abstraction and Ornament in Contemporary Painting, Inverleith House, Edinburgh, August 9–October 5, and the Ulrich Museum of Art, Wichita, Kansas, October 30–December 30. Catalogue, text by David Moos.
Vertical Painting, Institute for Contemporary Art, P.S. 1 Museum, New York, August 16–October 26.
Stepping Up, Andrew Mummery Gallery, London, September 18–October 25.
technological drift, Lawing Gallery, Houston, October 18–November 15.
ca-ca poo-poo, Kölnischer Kunstverein, Cologne, November 8–January 11, 1998.
De Visiones y de Ritmos, Centro Cultural Parque de España, Rosario de Santa Fe, Argentina, November 11–30. Catalogue, text by Eleonora Traficante.
Moving Toward the Millennium, Schmidt Contemporary Art, St. Louis, Missouri, December 12–January 30, 1998.
Face à Face, Galerie Thaddaeus Ropac, Paris.
Portraits, Galerie Ropac, Salzburg, Austria.

1998
Spectacular Optical, Thread Waxing Space, New York, May 28–July 18.
Fabian Marcaccio and Jessica Stockholder, Goetz Foundation, Munich, Germany, Fall.

Selected Bibliography

1992
Adams, Brooks. "Slow Art. Painting in New York Now: P.S. 1." *Art in America*, October 1992, pp. 154–55.
Collins, Patricia, and Richard Milazzo. "Fabian Marcaccio: A Talk With Collins & Milazzo (Doubletalk)." *Tema Celeste*, Fall 1992, p. 93.
Kaneda, Shirley. "Profiles and Positions: An Interview with Fabian Marcaccio." *BOMB*, Fall 1992, p. 12.
Mahoney, Robert. "Fabian Marcaccio and Daniel Weiner." *Arts Magazine*, April 1992, p. 92.
Morsiani, Paola. "New York." *Juliet*, April/May 1992.
Rubinstein, Raphael. "Fabian Marcaccio and Daniel Weiner at John Post Lee Gallery." *Flash Art* (International Edition), Summer 1992, p. 114.
Smith, Roberta. "A Conceptual Face-Off at 2 Whitney Branches." *The New York Times*, June 26, 1992, p. C22.
Smolik, Noemi. "Kinder Macht Neues." *Artforum*, December 1992, p. 105.
Tager, Alisa. "Fabian Marcaccio and Daniel Weiner." *Tema Celeste*, April/May 1992, p. 93.

1993
Curto, Guido. "Teddy and Other Stories at Claudio Botello and In Arco Turin." *Flash Art* (Italian Edition), April 1993.
Drolet, Owen. "Fabian Marcaccio at John Post Lee Gallery." *Flash Art* (International Edition), May/June 1993, p. 86.
Ebony, David. "Fabian Marcaccio at John Post Lee Gallery." *Art in America*, October 1993, p. 136.
Fleming, Lee. "Summer Show at Baumgartner." *The Washington Post*, August 7, 1993.
Iannacci, Anthony. "Tool Box." *Segno*, May/June 1993, p. 54.
Kahn, Eve. "The Next Generation." *Art & Auction*, April 1993.
Pinchback, Daniel. "Fabian Marcaccio at John Post Lee Gallery." *Art & Antiques*, March 1993, p. 21.
Schwabsky, Barry. "Fabian Marcaccio at John Post Lee Gallery." *Artforum*, Summer 1993, pp. 109–10.
Smith, Roberta. "Fabian Marcaccio at John Post Lee Gallery." *The New York Times*, March 19, 1993, p. C22.

1994
Carrier, David. "Fine Young Cannibal: Fabian Marcaccio." *Artforum*, September 1994, pp. 84–87.
Hofleitner, Johanna. "Conditional Painting." *Flash Art*, May/June 1994, p. 123.
Moos, David. "What you can do for pop to what pop can do for you." *art/text*, January 1994, p. 42.
Rubinstein, Raphael. "Private Eyes." *ARTnews*, January 1994, p. 89.
——. "Abstraction in a Changing Environment." *Art in America*, October 1994, pp. 102–109.
Saltz, Jerry. "A Year in The Life: Tropic of Painting." *Art in America*, October 1994, p. 99.

1995
Benjamin, Andrew. "Fabian Marcaccio: Rehearsing Complex Painting." *Journal of Philosophy and the Visual Arts*, no. 6 (1995), p. 45.
Damianovic, Maia. "Image Without Family." *Tema Celeste*, Winter 1995, pp. 44–49.
Pagel, David. "Paradox Adds Strength to 'Paint-Zone.'" *Los Angeles Times*, November 9, 1995, p. F4.
Rubinstein, Raphael. "Full Circle." *Art in America*, May 1995, pp. 108–109.

1996
Damianovic, Maia. "Painting On The Horns of A Dilemma (the hybrid quality of recent painting)." *Art Press*, March 1996, pp. 30–36.
Esman, Abigail. "Fabian Marcaccio at Barbara Farber Gallery, Amsterdam." *Art Nexus*, October–December 1996, pp. 149–50.
Gilbert-Rolfe, Jeremy. "Cabbages, Raspberries, and Video's Thin Brightness." *Art & Design*, May/June 1996, pp. 14–23.
Hill, Shawn. "Driven to abstraction: List Center exhibit showcases the work of 10 artists." *The Tab*, April 23–29, 1996, p. 5B.
Lamoree, Jhim. "Fabian Marcaccio at Barbara Farber Gallery, Amsterdam." *Flash Art* (International Edition), November/December 1996, p. 114.
Levin, Kim. "Capsule Review of 'Bare Bones' at TZ Art." *The Village Voice*, June 25, 1996.
Moos, David. "Architecture of the Mind: Machine Intelligence and Abstract Painting." *Art & Design*, May/June 1996, pp. 54–63.

Risatti, Howard. "Painting Outside Painting." *Artforum*, April 1996, pp. 105–106.
Sherman, Mary. "Meet abstract art 'Face-to-Face.'" *Boston Sunday Herald*, April 16, 1996, pp. 56–57.
Smith, Roberta. "Testing Limits at the Corcoran." *The New York Times*, January 6, 1996, p. 11.
Temin, Christine. "Review of Face-to-Face: Recent Abstract Painting, List Center." *The Boston Globe*, May 7, 1996, pp. 61, 66–67.

1997
Basualdo, Carlos. "Fabian Marcaccio: Tents of War." *Art Nexus*, April–June 1997, pp. 54–58.
Risatti, Howard. "Fabian Marcaccio at Baumgartner Galleries." *Artforum*, Summer 1997, pp. 141–42.
Rubinstein, Raphael. "Abstraction Out of Bounds." *Art in America*, November 1997, pp. 104–15.
Smith, Roberta. "In-Form at Bravin Post Lee Gallery." *The New York Times*, July 4, 1997, p. C24.
——. "More Spacious and Gracious, Yet Still Funky At Heart." *The New York Times*, October 31, 1997, p. E31.
Wilson, Janet. "Fabian Marcaccio at Baumgartner." *ARTnews*, June 1997, p. 131.

1998
Anton, Saul. "Inform at Bravin Post Lee." *art/text*, March 1998, pp. 96–97.

Beatriz Milhazes

Born 1960, Rio de Janeiro
1981, Curso de Comunicacao Social/FACHA
1983, Escola de Artes Visuais do Parque Lage
Lives and works in Rio de Janeiro

Selected One-Person Exhibitions

1985
Beatriz Milhazes, Galeria Cesar Ache, Rio de Janeiro, September.

1987
Beatriz Milhazes, Galeria Cesar Ache, Rio de Janeiro, May.

1988
Beatriz Milhazes, Galeria Suzana Sassoum, São Paulo, August.

1989
Beatriz Milhazes, Pasargada Arte Contemporânea, Recife, Brazil, January.

1990
Beatriz Milhazes, Galeria Saramenha, Rio de Janeiro, August.

1991
Beatriz Milhazes, Subdistricto Comercial de Arte, São Paulo, May. Catalogue, text by Luiz Ernesto.

1993
Beatriz Milhazes, Sala Alternativa Artes Visuales, Caracas, Venezuela, September, and Galeria Camargo Vilaça, São Paulo, November–December. Catalogue, text by Stella Teizeira de Barros.

1994
Beatriz Milhazes, Galeria Ramis F. Barquet, Monterrey, Mexico, May. Catalogue, text by Paulo Herkenhoff.
Beatriz Milhazes, Paço Imperial, Rio de Janeiro, August.
Beatriz Milhazes: Pinturas, Galeria Anna Maria Neimeyer, Rio de Janeiro, September 15–October 1.

1995
Project FINEP, Paço Imperial, Rio de Janeiro, January.
Beatriz Milhazes, Dorothy Goldeen Gallery, Los Angeles, June.

1996
Beatriz Milhazes, Edward Thorp Gallery, New York, March.
Beatriz Milhazes, Centro de Artes Calouste Gulbenkian, Rio de Janeiro, August.
Beatriz Milhazes, Galeria Camargo Vilaça, São Paulo, October. Catalogue, text by Adriano Pedrosa.

1997
Beatriz Milhazes, Barbara Farber Gallery, Amsterdam, April.
Beatriz Milhazes, Elba Benitez Galeria, Madrid, May.
Beatriz Milhazes: Recent Paintings, Edward Thorp Gallery, New York, November 15–January 10, 1998.
Beatriz Milhazes, 1989/1993, Museo Alfredo Anderson, Curitiba, Brazil.

1998
Beatriz Milhazes, Galerie Natalie Obadia, Paris, April–June.

Selected Group Exhibitions

1983
Salão Nacional de Artes Plásticas, Museu de Arte Moderna, Rio de Janeiro, March.
Pintura, Pintura, Fundacao Casa Rui Barbosa, Rio de Janeiro, May.

1984
Arte na Rua 2, Museu de Arte Contemporânea, São Paulo, May.
Como Vai Você Geraçoa 80?, Parque Lage, Rio de Janeiro, June.

1985
Arte Construção, Galeria do Centro Empresarial, Rio de Janeiro, January.
Salão Nacional de Artes Plásticas, Museu de Arte Moderna, Rio de Janeiro, April.

1986
Territorio Ocupado, Parque Lage, Rio de Janeiro, January.
4 Pintores, Galeria de Arte UFF, Niteroi, Brazil, February.
Novas Impressões, GB Arte, Rio de Janeiro, February.
Bienal Latino Americana de Arte sobre Papel, Buenos Aires, May.
El Escrete Voador, Guadalajara, Mexico, June.

1987
Salão Paulista de Arte Contemporânea, Pavilhão da Bienal, São Paulo, April.

1988
Dois a Dois, Galeria do Consulado Geral da Argentina, Rio de Janeiro, October.
Salão Nacional de Artes Plásticas, Funarte, Rio de Janeiro, October.
Subindo a Serra, Palácio das Artes, Belo Horizonte, Brazil, November.

1989
I Bienal Internacional de Cuencas, Equador, June.
O Mestre e a Mostra, Parque Lage, Rio de Janeiro, July.
Canale, Fonseca, Milhazes, Pizarro, Zerbini, Museu de Arte Contemporânea, São Paulo, Brazil. Traveled to Museu Municipal de Arte, Curitiba, Brazil, August.
Rio Hoje, Museu de Arte Moderna, Rio de Janeiro, October.

1990
O Rosto e a Obra, Galeria de IBEU, Rio de Janeiro, January.
Projeto Árqueos, Fundição Progresso, Rio de Janeiro, August.
Prêmio Brasília de Artes Plásticas, Museu de Arte de Brasília, November.

1991
BR/80—A Pintura dos Anos 80, Casa França–Brazil, Rio de Janeiro, May.
Brasil: La Nueva Generacion, Museo de Bellas Artes, Caracas, Venezuela, June.

1992
Eco-Arte, Museu de Arte Moderna, Rio de Janeiro, June.
América, Sala Alternativa, Caracas, Venezuela, October.
João Sataminni/Subdistrito, Casa das Rosas, São Paulo, November.
A Caminho do Museu: Coleção Jeão Leão Sataminni, Paço Imperial, Rio de Janeiro, December.

1993
A Caminho do Museu, Centro Cultural São Paulo, March.
Brasil Contemporâneo, Casa da Imagem, Curitiba, Brazil, May.
A Escolha do Artista, Paço Imperial, Rio de Janeiro, August.
Encontros e Tendências, Museu de Arte Contemporânea da Universidade de São Paulo, August.
Gravuras, Espaço Namour, São Paulo, August.
Coleção Gilberto Chateaubriand, Museu de Arte Moderna, Rio de Janeiro, September.

1994
Encuentro Interamericano de Artes Plásticas: Dialogo sobre Siete Puntos, Museo de Guadalajara, Mexico, May.
Pequelo Formatos Latinoamericanos, Luigi Marrozzini Gallery, San Juan, Puerto Rico, June.
The Exchange Show: Twelve Painters from San Francisco and Rio de Janeiro, Yerba Buena Center for the Arts, San Francisco, June 23–August 28, and Museu de Arte Moderna, Rio de Janeiro, October 6–November 19. Catalogue, text by Anne Trueblood Brodzky and Marcus de Lontra Costa.

1995

Anos 80: O Palco da Diversidade, Museu de Arte Moderna, Rio de Janeiro. Traveled to Galeria de Arte Sesi, São Paulo, May.

Regards d'Amerique Latine, Galerie Regard, Geneva, Switzerland, May.

Group Show, Galeria Camargo Vilaça, São Paulo, July.

Transatlântica: The America-Europa Non Representativa, Museo Alejandro Otero, Caracas, Venezuela, July.

Panorama da Atual Arte Brasileira, Museu de Arte Moderna, São Paulo, Brazil. Traveled to Museu de Arte Moderna, Rio de Janeiro, October.

1995 Carnegie International, Carnegie Museum of Art, Pittsburgh, November 5–February 18, 1996. Catalogue, text by Richard Armstrong and Stella de Teizeira de Barros on Milhazes.

1996

Excesso, Paço das Artes, São Paulo, October.

Brasil Contemporâneo, Casa da America Latina, Madrid.

Coleção João Sattamini, Museu de Arte Contemporânea de Nierid, Brazil.

Impressões Itinerantes, Palácio das Artes, Belo Horizonte, Brazil.

Ouro de Artista, Galeria Casa Triângulo, São Paulo.

Pequenas Mãos, Paço Imperial, Rio de Janeiro. Traveled to Centro Cultural Alumni, São Paulo.

Yole, Milhazes, Duarte, Museo Alejandro Otero, Caracas, Venezuela.

1997

New Editions and Works on Paper, Betsy Senior Gallery, New York, April.

Theories of the Decorative: Abstraction and Ornamentation in Contemporary Painting, Inverleith House, Edinburgh, Scotland, August 9–October 5, and the Ulrich Museum of Art, Wichita, Kansas, October 30–December 30. Catalogue, text by David Moos.

Desde el Cuerpo: Alegorias de lo Feminino, Museo de Bellas Artes, Caracas, Venezuela.

1998

Sala Especial, Salão Nacional de Artes, Museu de Arte Moderna, Rio de Janeiro, January.

Decorative Strategies, Center for Curatorial Studies, Bard College, Annandale-on-Hudson, New York, April 5–19.

hanging, Galeria Camargo Vilaça, São Paulo, May. Catalogue.

Everyday, 11th Biennial of Sydney, Australia, September 17–November 8. Catalogue, text by Jonathan Watkins.

Selected Bibliography

1994

Sada, Paulo. "Beatriz Milhazes." *Art Nexus*, October–December 1994, p. 121.

1995

Adams, Brooks. "Carnegie International." *Art in America*, December 1995, p. 33.

Pagel, David. "A Carnegie Blast." *New York Observer*, October 18, 1995.

Vogel, Carol. "Inside Art." *The New York Times*, June 23, 1995, p. C26.

Wallis, Stephen. "In Review." *Art & Antiques*, January 1995, p. 80.

1996

Ebony, David. "Beatriz Milhazes at Edward Thorp." *Art in America*, November 1996, pp. 109–10.

Schwabsky, Barry. "Beatriz Milhazes." *Artforum*, May 1996, pp. 96–97.

Smith, Roberta. "Beatriz Milhazes at Edward Thorp Gallery." *The New York Times*, March 22, 1996, p. C27.

———. "The Gallery Doors Open to the Long Denied." *The New York Times*, May 26, 1996, p. 1.

1997

Cotter, Holland. "Beatriz Milhazes at Edward Thorp Gallery." *The New York Times*, December 5, 1997, p. E33.

Mumford, Steve. "Beatriz Milhazes." *Review*, December 1, 1997, p. 25.

Olmo, Santiago B. "Beatriz Milhazes." *Art Nexus*, October–December 1997, pp. 151–52.

Smith, Roberta. "Across 30 Years, Sculptural Solidity." *The New York Times*, October 31, 1997, p. E33.

Takashi Murakami

Born 1962, Tokyo

1986, Tokyo National University of Fine Arts and Music, graduated, Japanese Traditional Painting (Nihon-ga)

1988, Tokyo National University of Fine Arts and Music, MA

1993, Tokyo National University of Fine Arts and Music, Ph.D.

Lives and works in Tokyo and New York

Selected One-Person Exhibitions

1989

Takashi Murakami, Gallery Ginza Surugadai, Tokyo.

1991

Takashi Murakami, Röntgen Kunst Institut, Tokyo, August–September.

Takashi Murakami, Gallery Aries, Tokyo, September–October. Catalogue, text by Noi Sawaragi.

It's That I am Against Acceptance of It, Hosomi Gallery Contemporary, Tokyo, December 3–21. Brochure, text by Minami Yusuke.

Takashi Murakami, Aoi Gallery, Osaka.

1992

Wild, Wild, Röntgen Kunst Institut, Tokyo, February 14–March 18.

1993

A Very Merry Unbirthday!, Hiroshima City Museum of Contemporary Art, June 19–July 18. Catalogue.

A Romantic Evening, Gallery Cellar, Nagoya.

Takashi Murakami, Nasubi Gallery, Tokyo.

1994

Which is Tomorrow?—Fall in Love—, The Bathhouse, Shiraishi Contemporary Art Inc., Tokyo, June 17–July 16. Catalogue.

Azami, Kikyo, Ominaeshi, Aoi Gallery, Osaka.

Fujisan, Gallery Koto, Okayama.

1995

Crazy Z, The Bathhouse, Shiraishi Contemporary Art Inc., Tokyo, October 24–November 18.

Niji, Gallery Koto, Okayama.

Takashi Murakami, Emmanuel Perrotin, Paris.

Takashi Murakami, Yngtingagatan 1, Stockholm.

1996

A Very Merry Unbirthday, To You, To Me!, Ginza Komatsu, Tokyo.

Konnichiwa, Mr. DOB, Kirin Plaza, Osaka.

Takashi Murakami, Feature, Inc., New York.

Takashi Murakami, Gallery Koto, Okayama.

Takashi Murakami, Gavin Brown's Enterprise, New York.

727, Tomio Koyama Gallery, Tokyo.

7272, Aoi Gallery, Osaka.

1997

Takashi Murakami, Center for the Arts, State University of New York at Buffalo, April 10–July 13. Brochure, text by Tom Folland.

Takashi Murakami, Blum & Poe, Santa Monica, California, July 17–August 16.

Takashi Murakami, Emmanuel Perrotin, Paris.

1998

Takashi Murakami, Blum & Poe, Santa Monica, California.

Takashi Murakami, Feature, Inc. New York.

Takashi Murakami, Tomio Koyama Gallery, Tokyo.

Selected Group Exhibitions

1991

Jan Hoet in Tsurugi, Tsurugi-cho, Ishikawa.

Jan Hoet's Vision, Art Gallery Artium, Fukuoka.

1992

Anomaly, Röntgen Kunst Institut, Tokyo. Catalogue.

1st Transart Annual Painting/Crossing, Bellini Hill Galley, Yokohama.

Nakamura and Murakami, Metaria Square Hotel, Osaka.

Nakamura and Murakami, Space Ozone, Seoul, July 4–25. Traveled to Project Room, Shiraishi Contemporary Art Inc., Tokyo, August 28–September 19. Catalogue, text by Min Nishihara.

Tama Vivant '92, Seed Hall, Shibuya Seibu, Tokyo.

1993

Art Today '93 Neo Japanology, Sezon Museum of Modern Art, Karuizawa, Nagano.

Beyond "Nihon-ga"—An Aspect of Contemporary Japanese Painting, Tokyo Metropolitan Art Museum.

The Exhibition for Exhibitions, Kyoto Shijo Gallery.

February 1st Festival, Malaria Art Show Vol. 1, Tokyo.

00 Collaboration, Sagacho Exhibit Space, Tokyo.

1994

Lest We Forget: On Nostalgia, The Gallery at Takashimaya, New York, May 18–July 9, 1994. Catalogue, text by Lynn Gumpert and Thomas Sokolowski.

Shinjuku Syonen Art, Shinjuku Kabuki-cho, Tokyo.

VOCA '94, The Ueno Royal Museum, Tokyo.

1995

Cutting Up, Max Protetch Gallery, New York.

Incidental Alterations: P.S.1 Studio Artists 1994–95, The Angel Orensanz Foundation, New York. Catalogue.

Japan Today, Louisiana Museum of Modern Art, Humlebaek, Denmark; Traveled to Kunstnernes Hus, Oslo; Liljevalchs Konsthall, Stockholm; Waino Aaltonen Museum of Art, Turku, Finland; MAK, Vienna, Austria. Catalogue, text on Murakami by Tone O. Nielsen.

Transculture, Palazzo Giustiniani Lolin, 46th Venice Biennale, June 11–September 4, organized by The Japan Foundation and Fukutake Science and Culture Foundation. Traveled to Naoshima Museum of Contemporary Art, Okayama, Japan. Catalogue, text by Fumio Nanjo and Dana Friis-Hansen.

1996

The Second Asia-Pacific Triennial of Contemporary Art, Queensland Art Gallery, South Brisbane, Australia, September 27–January 19, 1997. Catalogue, text by Midori Matsui.

Ironic Fantasy, The Miyagi Museum of Art, Sendai.

Romper Room, Thread Waxing Space, New York. Traveled to DiverseWorks, Houston, September 19–October 11, 1997. Catalogue, text by Danielle Chang.

Sharaku Interpreted by Japan's Contemporary Artists, The Japan Foundation Forum, Tokyo.

Tokyo Pop, The Hiratsuka Museum of Art, Kanagawa, Japan. Catalogue.

1997

Flying Buttress Please, Torch Gallery, Amsterdam.

Hiropon Show '97: Tokyo Underground Visual Show, Shop 33, Tokyo.

Japanese Contemporary Art Exhibition, The National Museum of Contemporary Art, Seoul.

Need for Speed, Grazer Kunstverein, Austria.

Singularity in Plurality, Yokohama Civic Art Gallery, Kanagawa. Catalogue.

Super Body, Tomio Koyama Gallery, Tokyo.

1998

Cities on the Move, Secession, Vienna, and capcMusée d'art contemporain de Bordeaux, France. Catalogue, edited by Hou Hanru and Hans Ulrich Obrist.

So what? Exhibition of Contemporary Japanese Art, Ecole Nationale Superleure des Beaux-Arts, Paris.

Selected Bibliography

1992

Friis-Hansen, Dana. "Empire of Goods: Young Japanese Artists and Commodity Culture." *Flash Art* (International Edition), March/April 1992, pp. 78–81.

——. "Takashi Murakami: R.P." Brochure, Shiraishi Contemporary Art, Inc., March 1992.

Sawaragi, Noi, and Fumio Nanjo. "Dangerously Cute." *Flash Art*, March/April 1992, pp. 75–81.

1994

Bellars, Peter. "If you can't beat 'em." *Asahi Evening News*, July 17, 1994.

1996

Higa, Karen. "Some Thoughts on National and Cultural Identity: Art by Contemporary Japanese and Japanese American Artists." *Art Journal*, Fall 1996, pp. 6–13.

1997

Matsui, Midori. "Tokyo Pop." *Flash Art* (International Edition), November/December 1997, p. 110.

Pagel, David. "Paintings in Midst of Generational Conflict." *Los Angeles Times*, August 1, 1997, p. F28.

Sawaragi, Noi. "Takashi Murakami." *World Art*, Summer 1997, p. 76.

1998

Friis-Hansen, Dana. "Takashi Murakami." *Grand Street* (New York), Summer 1998, p. 221.

Molinari, Guido. "Takashi Murakami." *Flash Art* (International Edition), March/April 1998, p. 106.

Pagel, David. "Art Review." *Los Angeles Times*, July 3, 1998, p. 26.

Aaron Parazette

Born 1960, Ventura, California

1987, University of South Florida, Tampa, BA

1990, The Claremont Graduate School, California, MFA

1990–92, The Glassell School of Art, The Museum of Fine Arts, Houston, Core Fellow

Lives and works in Houston

Selected One-Person Exhibitions

1991

Not Perfect, Davis/McClain Gallery, Houston, July 13–November 1.

Empty Abstraction, Lloyd Shin Gallery, Chicago, September 27–October 17.

1992

Paintings with Subtitles, Davis/McClain Gallery, Houston, July 9–August 8.

1993

New Paintings, Kim Light Gallery, Los Angeles, October 23–November 24.

1994

New Paintings, Texas Gallery, Houston, October 4–November 5.

1997

Pleasure Provision, Texas Gallery, Houston, March 5–29.

Selected Group Exhibitions

1991

1991 Core Fellows Exhibition, The Glassell School of Art, The Museum of Fine Arts, Houston, March 14–April 25. Catalogue.

1992

Texas Art Celebration '92, 1600 Smith in Cullen Center, organized by the Assistance League of Houston, February 18–May 7.

1992 Core Fellows Exhibition, The Glassell School of Art, The Museum of Fine Arts, Houston, March 17–April 23. Catalogue.

1993

Traditional Forms/Insidious Visions, The Glassell School of Art, The Museum of Fine Arts, Houston, January 19–March 1.

Summer Reading, Texas Gallery, Houston, August 3–28.

Deluge, Lyons Weir Gallery, Chicago, December 10–January 4, 1994.

Raw, Graham Gallery, Albuquerque.

Small Works, Works Gallery, South Coast Plaza, Costa Mesa, California.

1994

Forging Ahead, Center for Research in Contemporary Art, University of Texas at Arlington, February 25–April 9. Catalogue, text by Al Harris F.

Inquiring Mind, Conduit Gallery, Dallas, March 25–April 23.

Exquisite Corpse, The McKinney Avenue Contemporary, Dallas, October 26–November 27.

Faith in Doubt, Center for the Arts, State University of New York at Buffalo, October 28–December 22. Catalogue, text by Al Harris F. and Karen Emenhiser.

1995

Irreverent Homage, Bucknell University, Lewisberg, Pennsylvania, January 16–February 26. Catalogue, text by Lynn Cazaban.

Analogs of Modernism, DARE at The McKinney Avenue Contemporary, Dallas, April 7–May 21. Catalogue, text by Tom Moody.

Summer Serial, Texas Gallery, Houston, July 1–August 26.

The Home Show, University of Texas at San Antonio Art Gallery, July 13–September 1. Catalogue, text by Frances Colpitt.

Contact: The 114th Annual Exhibition, San Francisco Art Institute, October 12–November 12. Catalogue, text by David Izu.

Wallpaper Works, Contemporary Arts Museum, Houston, November 17–January 7, 1996. Catalogue, text by Stephanie Smith.

Texas Abstract: New Painting in the Nineties, ArtPace, San Antonio, November 18–December 22. Traveled within Texas to The McKinney Avenue Contemporary, Dallas, January 5–March 24, 1996; J. Wayne Stark Gallery, Texas A&M University, College Station, April 25–June 9; Museum of the Southwest, Midland, July 10–August 24, 1997; Wayland Baptist University, Plainview, September 2–30; Tyler Museum of Art, January 11–February 22, 1998. Catalogue, text by Frances Colpitt.

1996

Buttered Side Up, Hallwalls Contemporary Arts Center, Buffalo, New York, September 21–November 2. Traveled to The Koffler Gallery, North York, Ontario, Canada, June 19–August 10, 1997. Catalogue, text by Karen Emenhiser.

True Bliss, Los Angeles Contemporary Exhibitions, December 5–January 26, 1997. Catalogue, text by Julie Joyce and David A. Greene.

1997

Disiptoey, Angstrom Gallery, Dallas, April 5–May 18.

Equal Pay, Revolution Summer Gallery, Houston, June 7–29.

Post-Pop, Post-Pictures, The David and Alfred Smart Museum of Art, The University of Chicago, August 22–September 21. Catalogue, text by Courtenay Smith.

Primary Colors, Barbara Farber Gallery/Rob Jurka, Amsterdam, October 5–November 6.

Oktoberfest, Texas Gallery, Houston, October 7–November 22.

1998

On the Beach at Galveston, Galveston Arts Center, Texas, June 6–July 12.

Done in Texas, Musée de l'Echevinage, Saintes, France, July 8–October 31.

Selected Bibliography

1991

Chadwick, Susan. "Art of Change." *The Houston Post*, March 26, 1991, p. D1.

Johnson, Patricia C. "Variety the Hallmark of 'Introductions.'" *Houston Chronicle*, July 20, 1991, p. 4.

Ludlam, Jane. "Summertime News." *Houston Press*, July 25, 1991.

1992

Chadwick, Susan. "Artistic to the Core: Some Promising Young Talent at Glassell Exhibit." *The Houston Post*, March 24, 1992, p. C1.

——. "Introductions 1992 Has Some Winners." *The Houston Post*, July 21, 1992.

Johnson, Patricia C. "'Introductions' Offers Uneven Mix." *Houston Chronicle*, July 22, 1992, p. 1.

Kalil, Susie. "Soft Core." *Houston Press*, April 9, 1992.

——. "In the Abstract." *Houston Press*, April 30, 1992.

——. "Word and Pictures." *Houston Press*, August 6, 1992.

McBride, Elizabeth. "Houston's Artists." *Public News* (Houston), September 2, 1992, p. 14.

Ziebell, Rob. "The People Who Make Houston, Houston." *Houston Metropolitan*, August 1992.

1994

Chadwick, Susan. "Texas Artists on View in Provocative Exhibit." *The Houston Post*, March 5, 1994, p. F2.

Huntington, Richard. "Something Funny Happens to Contemporary Art." *The Buffalo News*, November 22, 1994.

Kalil, Susie. "Abstraction without Shame." *Houston Press*, October 6, 1994, pp. 34–35.

Licata, Elizabeth. "Artitorial." *Artvoice*, November 23, 1994.

1995

Colpitt, Frances. "Going Against the Grain." *Art in America*, April 1995, pp. 42–47.

Goddard, Dan R. "Abstract Art Eschews Emotion." *San Antonio Express News*, November 26, 1995, p. G3.

Huntington, Richard. "Our Critic's Review." *The Buffalo News*, January 1, 1995.

Isola, Marina. "Four Play." *The Met*, April 27, 1995, p. 39.

Johnson, Patricia C. "Serious Series." *Houston Chronicle*, July 30, 1995, p. 12.

Mitchell, Charles Dee. "Sampling Past Art Elements for the Present." *The Dallas Morning News*, April 7, 1995.

——. "Aaron Parazette at Texas Gallery." *Art in America*, April 1995, p. 115.

Vannucci, Delfina. "Wallpaper as Wall Hanging." *Public News*, November 29, 1995, pp. 12–13.

1996

Huntington, Richard. "Visual Pleasure." *The Buffalo News*, October 11, 1996.

Knight, Christopher. "Can Artists Run Their Own Spaces and Find 'True Bliss'?" *Los Angeles Times*, December 27, 1996.

Mitchell, Charles Dee. "Of-this-world-abstracts at the MAC." *Dallas Morning News*, February 10, 1996.

1997

Auerbach, Lisa. "True Bliss at LACE." *L.A. Weekly*, January 2, 1997.

Colpitt, Frances. "Aaron Parazette at Texas Gallery." *Art in America*, July 1997, pp. 98–99.

Dewan, Shaila. "Light and Darkness." *Houston Press*, March 20, 1997, p. 49.

Mitchell, Charles Dee. "Rogueish Gallery." *Dallas Morning News*, May 16, 1997.

Richard Patterson

Born 1963, Leatherhead, Surrey, England

1982–83, Watford College of Art & Design, England, Foundation Course

1983–86, Goldsmiths' College, London, BA Honors (Fine Art)

Lives and works in London

Selected One-Person Exhibitions

1995

Richard Patterson, Anthony d'Offay Gallery, London, June 1–July 8.

1997

Richard Patterson, Anthony d'Offay Gallery, London, September 12–October 18. Catalogue, text by Stuart Morgan.

Selected Group Exhibitions

1988

Freeze, Surrey Docks, London. Catalogue, text by Jeffrey Ian.

1996

Ace! Arts Council Collection new purchases, organized by National Touring Exhibitions. Traveled within Great Britain to Hatton Gallery, Newcastle upon Tyne, March 1–April 13; Harris Museum and Art Gallery, Preston, May 25–July 7; Oldham Art Gallery, July 13–August 25; Hayward Gallery, London, September 19–November 17; Ikon Gallery, Birmingham, January 18–March 9, 1997; Mappin Art Gallery, Sheffield, March 15–April 27; Angel Row Gallery, Nottingham, May 3–June 15; Ormeau Baths Gallery, Belfast, November– December. Brochure, text by Henry Meyric Hughes, Isobel Johnstone, and Ann Jones.

Faustrecht der Freiheit, Sammlung Volkmann, Kunstsammlung Gesa, April 14–May 27. Traveled to Neuer Museum, Westerberg Bremen, June 22–September 15.

Answered Prayers, Contemporary Fine Arts, Berlin, April 16–May 11.

Portrait of the Artist, Anthony d'Offay Gallery, London, April 25–June 14.

About Vision: New British Paintings in the 1990s, Museum of Modern Art, Oxford, November 10–February 23, 1997. Traveled to Fruitmarket Gallery, Edinburgh, 1997; Laing Art Gallery, Newcastle upon Tyne, 1997–98. Catalogue, text by David Elliott.

1997

Package Holiday, New British Art in the Orphiuchus Collection, The Hydra Workshop, Greece, July 26–September 30. Catalogue.

Pictura Britannica: Art from Britain, Museum of Contemporary Art, Sydney, August 22–November 30. Traveled to the Art Gallery of South Australia, Adelaide, December 1–February 1, 1998; City Gallery Wellington, New Zealand, February 23–April 26, 1998. Catalogue, text by David Barrett, Tony Bennett, Patricia Bickers, Patrick J. Boylan, Kobena Mercer, Bernice Murphy, Nilos Papastergiadis, Stephen Snoddy, and John A. Walker.

Sensation: Young British Artists from the Saatchi Collection, Royal Academy of Arts, London, September 18–December 28. Catalogue, text by Brooks Adams, Lisa Jardine, Martin Maloney, Norman Rosenthal, and Richard Shone.

False Impressions, The British School at Rome. Catalogue.

1998

Head First: Portraits from the Arts Council Collection, The City Gallery Leicester, January 17–February 28. Traveled within Great Britain to City Art Gallery, Southampton, April 9–May 31; Abbot Hall Gallery, Kendal, June 10–September 13; Hatton Gallery, Newcastle upon Tyne, September 26–November 8; Victoria Art Gallery, Bath, January 16–February 28, 1999, Graves Art Gallery, Sheffield, March 6–April 18; Ferens Art Gallery, April–June.

Selected Bibliography

1988

Craddock, Sasha. "The Fast Dockland Track to Simplicity." *The Guardian*, September 13, 1988.

1995

Maloney, Martin. "London's Wannabe Art Scene." *Flash Art* (International Edition), October 1995, pp. 60–61.

Wilson, Andrew. "Gerhard Richter, Richard Patterson." *Art Monthly*, July 1995.

1996

Cork, Richard. "Paint your bandwagon." *The Times*, December 31, 1996.

Hilton, Tim. "The Best Painting in Britain?" *The Independent on Sunday*, November 17, 1996, p. 30.

Linton, Norbert. "Open Plan." *The Royal Academy Magazine*, Autumn 1996, pp. 60–63.

Shone, Richard. "London and Edinburgh: contemporary exhibitions." *The Burlington Magazine*, July 1996, pp. 472–74.

1997

Coomer, Martin. "Richard Patterson." *Time Out London*, September 21, 1997.

Del Re, Gianmarco. "Richard Patterson." *Flash Art* (International Edition), November/December 1997, p. 115.

Herbert, Martin. "Richard Patterson." *Time Out London*, September 10, 1997.

Kent, Sarah. "Sensation." *Time Out London*, September 10, 1997.

Lambeth, Andrew. "Fashion Parade." *The Spectator*, January 4, 1997, pp. 40–41.

Maloney, Martin. "Richard Patterson's Young Minotaur." *Frank*, November 1997.

Monique Prieto

Born 1962, Los Angeles

1987, University of California, Los Angeles, BFA
1992, California Institute of the Arts, Valencia, BFA
1994, California Institute of the Arts, Valencia, MFA
Lives and works in Los Angeles

Selected One-Person Exhibitions

1994

Paintings, ACME., Santa Monica, California, November 16–December 23.

1995

Monique Prieto, ACME., Santa Monica, California, October 6–November 4.

1996

Monique Prieto, Bravin Post Lee Gallery, New York, April 13–May 11.

Monique Prieto, ACME., Santa Monica, California, October 18–November 16.

1997

Monique Prieto, Virginia Commonwealth University, Richmond, January 17–March 2.

Monique Prieto, ACME., Los Angeles, November 21–December 20.

1998

Monique Prieto, Robert Prime, London, March 19–May 9.

Selected Group Exhibitions

1987

Juried Exhibition, Wight Gallery, University of California, Los Angeles.

1989

Corazón Mexicana, Bacilia Hernandez Gallery, Long Beach, California.

1994

Temporary, The Museum of Contemporary Art, Los Angeles.

1995

Uta Barth, Chris Finley, Joyce Lightbody, Monique Prieto, Jennifer Steinkamp, ACME., Santa Monica, California, July 12–August 12.

1996

Chalk, Factory Place Gallery, Los Angeles, June 1–29.

Painting All-Over, Again, Ayuntamiento de Zaragoza, Spain, September 5–30. Catalogue, text by Saul Ostrow.

The Speed of Painting, Pat Hearn Gallery, New York, September 7–October 13.

Stream of Consciousness, University Art Museum, University of California at Santa Barbara, September 28–November 10. Catalogue, text by Elizabeth Brown.

Trans/Inter/Post: Hybrid Spaces, Art Gallery, University of California at Irvine, October 15–November 23.

The New Narrative Abstraction, The Art Gallery at Brooklyn College, LaGuardia Hall, New York, November 13–December 20.

1997

Group Exhibition, ACME., Santa Monica, California, June 7–July 5.

1997 Biennial, Orange County Museum of Art, Newport Beach, California, April 19–June 8. Catalogue, text by Bruce Guenther.

Spot Making Sense, Grand Arts, Kansas City, Missouri, June 27–August 2. Brochure, text by David Pagel.

Selected Bibliography

1995

Knight, Christopher. "Canvassing the Year of Brilliance." *Los Angeles Times*, December 31, 1995, p. 60.

Pagel, David. "Marriage of Two Techniques Yields Fresh Style." *Los Angeles Times*, November 2, 1995, p. F8.

1996

Cooper, Jacqueline. "Monique Prieto." *New Art Examiner*, January 1996, pp. 41–42.

Crowder, Joan. "Conscious Raising." *Santa Barbara News-Press*, October 11, 1996, p. 11.

Curtis, Cathy. "Distinguishing Marks." *Los Angeles Times* (Orange County Edition), October 22, 1996, p. F1.

Darling, Michael. "Monique Prieto." *Art issues.*, January/February 1996, p. 41.

Knight, Christopher. "Riding Tradition's Currents to a Higher Consciousness." *Los Angeles Times*, October 10, 1996.

Levin, Kim. "Choices." *The Village Voice*, May 1, 1996.

Pagel, David. "Monique Prieto." *BOMB*, Summer 1996.

——. "Discovering Joy in Colorful 'Big Picture.'" *Los Angeles Times*, October 31, 1996.

Rubinstein, Raphael. "Monique Prieto at Bravin Post Lee." *Art in America*, December 1996, pp. 100–101.

Saltz, Jerry. "The Speed of Painting." *Time Out New York*, October 3–10, 1996, p. 25.

Smith, Roberta. "Monique Prieto." *The New York Times*, May 10, 1996.

1997

Curtis, Cathy. "Inextricable References." *Los Angeles Times* (Orange County Edition), May 6, 1997, p. F6.

Dubin, Zan. "Painter Monique Prieto's Birth of a Notion." *Los Angeles Times* (Orange County Edition), June 4, 1997, pp. F2, 5.

Frank, Peter. "Monique Prieto." *L.A. Weekly*, December 12–18, 1997, p. 164.

Hickey, Dave. "Top Ten x 12: The Year in Review." *Artforum*, December 1997, pp. 88–89.

Knight, Christopher. "Look Out, World, Here They Come!" *Los Angeles Times*, March 30, 1997, pp. 63–64.

Pagel, David. "Adding a Splash of Fun to Abstraction." *Los Angeles Times*, December 5, 1997.

Scott Richter

Born 1943, Atlanta

1965, Parsons School of Design, New York
1971, The New School, New York, BFA
Lives and works in Weston, Connecticut

Selected One-Person Exhibitions

1980

Scott Richter, Eugenia Cuculon Gallery, New York.

Scott Richter, Camielle Strauss Gallery, Caracas, Venezuela.

1981

Scott Richter, Hamilton Art Gallery, Elmira College, New York.

1983

Object of Desire Series, Institute for Contemporary Art, P.S. 1 Museum, New York, September 25–November 20.

Scott Richter, Luise Ross Gallery, New York, November 1–19.

1985

Scott Richter, Zabriski Gallery, New York, September 18–October 19.

Scott Richter, Valencia College, Orlando, Florida, October 14–November 20.

1987

Scott Richter, Curt Marcus Gallery, New York, May 1–27.

1988

Scott Richter, University of Massachusetts at Amherst, October 31–December 13.

1989

Scott Richter, Pittsburgh Center for the Arts, February 4–March 19.

Scott Richter, Fuller/Grose Gallery, San Francisco, March 2–April 3.

False Prophet, Curt Marcus Gallery, New York, September 14–October 14.

1990

Scott Richter, Beth Urdang Gallery, Boston, September 7–October 13.

1992

Scott Richter, John Stoller Gallery, Minneapolis, March 2–April 26.

Future/Hope ÷ Futility/X, Curt Marcus Gallery, New York, March 5–28.

1994

Counterpoint, The Thorne Gallery, Keene State College, New Hampshire, November 4–December 11.

1996

Scott Richter, Craig Krull Gallery, Santa Monica, California, March 9–April 13.

Selected Group Exhibitions

1984

Invitational Exhibition, Grace Borgenicht Gallery, New York, May 23–June 22.

Group Show, Condeso/Lawler Gallery, New York, September 8–29.

Young Americans, Galerie Bellman, New York, October 2–November 3.

1985

Winter Show, Gallery Nature Morte, New York, January 1–29.

Figures: Sculpture in the Auditorium, Institute for Contemporary Art, P.S. 1 Museum, New York, January 13–March 10.

Figure It Out, Laguna Gloria Art Museum, Austin, Texas, February 16–April 7.

The Mystery Show, Jersey City Museum, New Jersey, April 19–June 28.

Affiliations: Recent Sculpture and Its Antecedents, Whitney Museum of American Art at Stamford, Connecticut, June 28–August 24.

Body and Soul, Contemporary Arts Center, Cincinnati, September 6–October 12. Catalogue, text by Sarah Rogers-Lafferty.

Not Just Black and White, New York Cultural Center, New York, November 3–28.

The Psyche and the Human Form, The Sculpture Center, New York, November 5–30.

Irregulars: Wall Works, Henry Street Settlement, New York, November 30–January 6, 1986.

1986

After Nature, Germans Van Eck Gallery, New York, February 1–22. Brochure, text by Steven Henry Madoff.

Contemporary Primitivism, Laguna Gloria Art Museum, Austin, Texas, February 28–April 11.

Group Show, Lawrence Oliver Gallery, Philadelphia, March 12–April 11.

Group Show, Gallery Nature Morte, New York, September 1–24.

The Figure Abstracted: Intimated Presences, Robeson Center Gallery, Rutgers University, Newark, New Jersey, September 18–October 31.

Selection of 20th Century Three-Dimensional Portraits, Cleveland Center for Contemporary Arts, November 30–January 12, 1987. Catalogue, text by Mary S. Myers.

Sculpture on the Wall, The Aldrich Museum of Contemporary Art, Ridgefield, Connecticut, December 6–February 15, 1987. Brochure, text by Martha Scott.

Inaugural Exhibition, Curt Marcus Gallery, New York.

1987

Synthesis, Fuller/Goldeen Gallery, San Francisco, July 1–August 1.

Contemporary Drawing, Collegiate School, New York.

1988

Avant-Garde in the Eighties, Los Angeles County Museum of Art, April 25–July 12. Catalogue, text by Howard N. Fox.

Figures: Form and Fiction, Everson Museum of Art, Syracuse, New York, September 23–November 11. Catalogue, text by Dominique Nahas and Tom Finkelpearl.

Figurative Impulses, Santa Barbara Museum of Art, California, October 15–January 1, 1989. Catalogue, text by Nancy Doll.

Sculptors on Paper: New Work, Madison Art Center, Wisconsin, December 5–January 31, 1989.

Group Show, Greenville County Museum of Art, Greenville, South Carolina.

1989

The Emerging Figure, The Norton Gallery of Art, West Palm Beach, Florida, January 28–March 19. Catalogue, text by Bruce Weber and Douglas Dreishpoon.

10 Gallery Artists, Nina Freudenheim Gallery, Buffalo, New York.

1991

Stark Contrast, Trenkman Gallery, New York, October 21–November 17.

1993

Paper Trails: The Eidetic Image, Contemporary American Works on Paper, Krannert Art Museum, University of Illinios, Champaign, March 17–April 18.

Three Gallery Artists, Nina Freudenheim Gallery, Buffalo, New York, April 24–May 22.

10 x 10, TZ Art & Co., New York.

1994

Color, TZ Art & Co., New York.

Sculpture, Nina Freudenheim Gallery, Buffalo, New York.

1995

Drawings, Nina Freudenheim Gallery, Buffalo, New York.

1996

The Landscape Reclaimed, The Aldrich Museum of Contemporary Art, Ridgefield, Connecticut, September 15–January 5, 1997. Catalogue, text by Nancy Princenthal.

Beyond the Picture Plane, Connecticut Commission of the Arts, Hartford.

1997

Ten Artists/Ten Visions, DeCordova Museum, Lincoln, Massachusetts, June 14–September 1. Catalogue, text by Nick Copasso.

Table Tops: Morandi to Mapplethorpe, California Center for the Arts Museum, Escondido, September 21–January 21. Catalogue, text by Reesey Shaw.

WOMEN WOMEN WOMEN: Artists, Objects, Icons, Greenville County Museum of Art, Greenville, South Carolina, November 12–April 26, 1998. Catalogue, text by Joanna Isaak.

1998

Saturation, Mills Gallery, Boston Center for the Arts, May 15–July 26.

Selected Bibliography

1982

Eder, Bruce. "At Greenspace: Figures." *ArtsWeekly*, December 1, 1982, p. 23.

Lichenstein, Therese. "Group Show: Nature Morte." *Arts Magazine*, November 1983, p. 40.

Upshaw, Reagan. "Figuratively Sculpting at P.S. 1." *Art in America*, March 1982, p. 142.

Watkins, Eileen. "Exhibits at Robeson Gallery in Newark Take Figurative Look at the Human Figure." *The Jersey Journal*, March 1982, p. 143.

1984

Glueck, Grace. "Invitational Exhibition." *The New York Times*, June 1, 1984, p. C23.

Kramer, Kathryn. "Lifesigns." *Arts Magazine*, February 1984, p. 18.

Levin, Kim. "Art." *The Village Voice*, June 12, 1984, p. 68.

1985

Brenson, Michael. "The Human Form in the Work of 12 Sculptors." *The New York Times*, February 1, 1985, p. C24.

——. "Art." *The New York Times*, September 27, 1985, p. C28.

Dishman, Laura Stewart. "Works of Scott Richter Comprise a Powerful Show." *The Orlando Sentinel*, November 12, 1985.

Levin, Kim. "Art." *The Village Voice*, October 15, 1985, p. 70.

Masters, Greg. "Scott Richter." *Arts Magazine*, November 1985, p. 142.

Princenthal, Nancy. "Young Americans." *ARTnews*, January 1985, pp. 141–42.

Raynor, Vivian. "Jersey City: Mystery Show." *The New York Times*, June 2, 1985, p. C24.

Watkins, Eileen. "Jersey City Museum Exhibit Explores Modern Mystery." *The Jersey Journal*, May 24, 1985, p. 143.

Westfall, Stephen. "Scott Richter." *Art in America*, December 1985, p. 124.

1986

Brenson, Michael. "Sculpture Breaks the Mold of Minimalism." *The New York Times*, November 23, 1986, p. C1.

Dishman, Laura Stewart. "Body & Soul Bursting With Profound Intimacy." *The Orlando Sentinel*, August 4, 1986.

Madoff, Steven Henry. "Sculpture Unbound." *ARTnews*, November 1986, pp. 103–109.

Mahoney, Robert. "Major Works." *Arts Magazine*, March 1986, p. 137.

Raynor, Vivian. "Intimations of Figures at Newark's Robeson Center Gallery." *The New York Times*, October 12, 1986, p. C36.

1987

Baker, Kenneth. "Minimalism and Runaway Wit." *The San Francisco Chronicle*, July 11, 1987, p. 38.

Kaplan, Steven. "Head, Heart, & Hands." *Art Finder*, Spring 1987, pp. 96–97.

Reece, Margaret B. "Aldrich Museum of Contemporary Art/Sculpture on the Wall." *ART/New England*, April 1987.

1988

Chayat, Sherry. "Sculpture Exhibit at Everson Comments about Dehumanization." *Syracuse Herald-Journal*, September 22, 1988.

——. "Body Language." *Syracuse Herald American*, October 9, 1988.

Crowder, Joan. "An Attitude Toward the Figurative." *The Santa Barbara News Press*, November 18, 1988, pp. 25–26.

Woodard, Josef. "California 'Figurative Impulses.'" *Sculpture*, March/April 1988, p. 32.

——. "Abstracting the Figure." *Artweek*, December 10, 1988, p. 9.

——. "Figuratively Speaking." *The Independent*, December 22, 1988, p. 73.

1989

Crowder, Joan. "As Canvas Dries." *The Santa Barbara News Press*, January 15, 1989, p. 19.

Gibson, Eric. "Donald Judd: the end of sculpture." *The New Criterion*, April 1989, p. 53.

Kimmelman, Michael. "Scott Richter." *The New York Times*, September 30, 1989, p. C28.

Kohen, Helen L. "Art Note." *The Miami Herald*, January 29, 1989, p. 7K.

Pennela, Florence. "Emerging Ideas." *Poughkeepsie Journal*, April 28, 1989, p. 1D.

1990

De Vuono, Frances. "Scott Richter." *ARTnews*, January 1990, p. 162.

Johnson, Ken. "Scott Richter at Curt Marcus." *Art in America*, January 1990, pp. 163–64.

Princenthal, Nancy. "Scott Richter." *Art in America*, September 1992, pp. 124–25.

Stapen, Nancy. "Minimalism with a Modern Touch." *The Boston Globe*, October 4, 1990.

1996

Zimmer, William. "Landscape Returns to the Foreground." *The New York Times*, October 13, 1996, p. 32.

1997

Pincus, Robert. "A Feast for Eyes Laid Out on 'Tabletops.'" *San Diego Union-Tribune*, October 12, 1997.

1998

Millis, Christopher. "Foot-thick mounds of paint highlight 'Saturation.'" *South End News*, July 2, 1998, pp. 11–12, 15.

Pae White

Born 1963, Pasadena, California

1981, Scripps College, Claremont, California, BA

1990, Skowhegan School of Painting and Sculpture, Maine

1991, Art Center College of Design, Pasadena, California, MFA

Lives and works in Pasadena, California

Selected One-Person Exhibitions

1989

Pae White, Bliss, Pasadena, California, September 22–October 13.

1993

Pae White, Shoshana Wayne Gallery, Santa Monica, California, February 5–March 7.

1995

Summer Work, Shoshana Wayne Gallery, Santa Monica, California, September 15–October 21.

1997

Animal Flood, I–20, New York, April 12–May 11.

Selected Group Exhibitions

1990

Mixed Media and Messages, Lang Art Gallery, Scripps College, Claremont, California, May 2–22.

1991

The Lick of the Eye, Shoshana Wayne Gallery, Santa Monica, California.

Sam Durant, Ed Suman, Andrew Winer and Pae White, Parker Zanic Gallery, Los Angeles.

1992

Detour, International House, New York, April 24–May 27. Catalogue, text by Alisa Tager.

Summer Show, Shoshana Wayne Gallery, Santa Monica, California.

Victor Estrada, Charles Long, Lisa Yuskavage and Pae White, Elizabeth Koury, New York, September 10–October 3.

Recent Purchases From the Roseview Collection, Roseview Museum, Los Angeles, November 22–December 13.

1993

Victor Estrada, Pae White, Christof Kohlhofer, Shoshana Wayne Gallery, Santa Monica, California, February 5–March 7.

The Imp of the Perverse, Sally Hawkins Gallery, New York, February 27–April 3.

Sugar N' Spice, Long Beach Museum of Art, California, February 28–May 23. Catalogue, text by Noriko Gamblin.

Cherry Bomb, Southern Exposure, San Francisco, April 30–May 23.

Home Alone, Bliss, Pasadena, California, June 19–July 3.

TIMES, Anderson O'Day Gallery, London, June 30–July 10.

Into the Lapse, 1301, Santa Monica, California, August 6–12.

1994

The Art of Seduction, The Center Gallery at Miami-Dade Community College, Florida, January 20–March 4. Catalogue, text by Bonnie Clearwater.

Watt, Witte de With and Kunsthal, Rotterdam,The Netherlands, February 19–March 27. Catalogue.

Bad Girls II, The New Museum, New York, March 5–April 10.

al dente, Caren Golden Fine Art, New York, May 18–June 25.

Pure Beauty, The American Center, Paris, June 7–August 15. Traveled to The Museum of Contemporary Art, Los Angeles, September 24–January 8, 1995.

Transtextualism, Mark Moore Gallery, Santa Monica, California, August 6–September 1.

Against Nature, Art Center College of Design, Pasadena, California, September 10–18.

Plane/Structures, Otis College of Art and Design Gallery, Los Angeles, September 10–November 5. Traveled to The Renaissance Society at The University of Chicago, November 20–December 30; Pittsburgh Center for the Arts, February 3–April 12; Zilkha Gallery, Wesleyan University, Middletown, Connecticut, April 18–May 28, 1995; White Columns, New York, October 13–November 12; University of North Texas Art Gallery, Denton, November 27–January 28, 1996; Nevada Institute for Contemporary Art, Las Vegas, March–April. Catalogue, text by Dave Hickey, David Pagel, and Joe Scanlan.

Notational Photography, Petzel/Borgmann and Metro Pictures, New York, September 17–October 15.

Identity: The Logic of Appearance, Krinzinger Gallery, Vienna, September 30–November 19.

1995

HAWAII, with Jorge Pardo, Friedrich Petzel Gallery, New York, January 21–February 25.

The Message is the Medium, Castle Gallery, College of New Rochelle, New York, February 12–April 7.

Youth Culture Ate My Dog (but I don't really mind), TBA, Chicago, April 8–May 20.

Neotoma, Otis College of Art and Design Gallery, Los Angeles, September 16–November 4.

Saturday Night Fever, Tom Solomon's Garage, Los Angeles.

Smells Like Vinyl, Roger Merians Gallery, New York.

1996

Ginny Bishton, Richard Hawkins, Pae White, Richard Telles Gallery, Los Angeles, May 4–June 1.

Mod Squad, Spanish Box, Santa Barbara, California, May 18–June 8.

Landscape Reclaimed, The Aldrich Museum of Contemporary Art, Ridgefield, Connecticut, September 15–January 5, 1997. Catalogue, text by Nancy Princenthal.

Sally Elesby/Pae White, Four Walls, San Francisco, September 24–October 12.

Just Past: The Contemporary in MOCA's Permanent Collection, The Museum of Contemporary Art, Los Angeles, September 29–January 19, 1997.

Open House, Williamson Gallery, Art Center College of Design, Pasadena, California, October 20–December 20.

True Bliss, Los Angeles Contemporary Exhibitions, December 5–20. Catalogue, text by Julie Joyce.

1997

New Grounds: Prints and Multiples, Contemporary Art Museum, University of South Florida, Tampa, January 11–March 8. Catalogue, text by Hank Hine and Margaret Miller.

Filler, Shoshana Wayne Gallery, Santa Monica, California, February 1–March 1.

Ten Los Angeles Artists, Stephen Wirtz Gallery, San Francisco, February 5–March 1.

Her Eyes are a Blue Million Miles, Three Day Weekend in Mälmo, Sweden, July 11–14, and Three Day Weekend in London, July 24–31.

Enterprise, The Institute of Contemporary Art, Boston, July 23–September 28. Catalogue, text by Christoph Grunenberg.

(re)Mediation: The Digital in Contemporary American Printmaking, 1997 Ljublijana Biennial of Graphic Arts, Slovenia. Traveled to Contemporary Art Museum, University of South Florida, Tampa, August 17–October 10. Brochure, text by Jade Dillinger and Margaret Miller.

No Small Feet, Rhona Hoffman Gallery, Chicago, September 12–October 18.

Best of the Season, The Aldrich Museum of Contemporary Art, Ridgefield, Connecticut, September 14–January 4, 1998. Catalogue, text by Harry Philbrick.

Elusive Paradise: Los Angeles Art from the Permanent Collection, The Museum of Contemporary Art, Los Angeles, October 5–May 17, 1998. Brochure, text by by Kerry Brougher, Connie Butler, and Stacia Payne.

1998

Love at the End of the Tunnel, or the Beginning of a Smart New Day, Center of Contemporary Art, Seattle, February 7–April 4.

The Unreal Person, Huntington Beach Art Center, California, April 26–June 14.

Flaming June, works on paper, inc., Los Angeles, June 13–July 25.

PhotoImage: Printmaking '60s to '90s, Museum of Fine Arts, Boston, July 6–27.

Hirsch Farm Project Now: Speculative Environment, Theme Song and Wisconsin Open House, Museum of Contemporary Art, Chicago, July 18–October 18. Brochure, text by Amada Cruz.

In the Polka Dot Kitchen, Otis College of Art and Design Gallery, Los Angeles, and The Armory Center for the Arts, Pasadena, California, October 3–November 21.

Selected Bibliography

1991

Gilbert-Rolfe, Jeremy. "Slaves of L.A., and Others." *Artspace*, Summer 1991, p. 72.

Kandel, Susan. "L.A. in Review." *Arts Magazine*, November 1991, p. 97.

Rugoff, Ralph. "Missing Persons." *L.A. Weekly*, August 2, 1991, p. 7.

1992

Relyea, Lane. "Politically Correct/Incorrect." *Artspace*, July/August 1992, pp. 28–30.

1993

Anderson, Michael. "Sugar N' Spice." *Art issues.*, May/June 1993, p. 39.

Barrie, Lita. "A Forest of Toys." *Visions*, Winter 1993, pp. 23–24.

Curtis, Cathy. "Nice N' Subversive." *Los Angeles Times* (Orange County Edition), March 18, 1993, p. 4.

Frank, Peter. "Intriguing Works by New Generation of Women Artists. . . " *Long Beach Press Telegram*, March 12, 1993, p. 14.

Kandel, Susan. "Pae White." *Art issues.*, September/October 1993, p. 43.

King, Debra. "Women's Perspective in Art." *Westart*, March 28, 1993, p. 3.

Lillington, David. "Times." *Metropolis*, no. 4 (1993), pp. 47–49.

Myers, Terry R. "Girlfriend in a Coma: Notes on a Proposed Exhibition." *Blocnotes*, Spring 1993, pp. 12–13.

Pagel, David. "The Strange House That Pae White Built." *Los Angeles Times*, February 19, 1993, p. F20.

——. "Interview with Pae White." *BOMB*, Summer 1993, pp. 12–14.

Roth, Charlene. "Kitchen Fiction." *Artweek*, May 20, 1993, p. 24.

1994

Barden, Lane. "In the Eye of the Beholder." *Artweek*, November 17, 1994, p. 10.

Breerette, Geneviéve. "Tout nouveau, tout beau." *Le Monde*, June 8, 1994.

Colas, Sandrine. "pure beauty." *Galeries* (France), June 1994, p. 4.

Koshalek, Richard. "American Center in Paris." *Art Press*, June 1994, p. 20.

Kraft, Scott. "But Will the French Thank Us?" *Los Angeles Times*, June 5, 1994, p. 6.

Muchnic, Suzanne. "Bliss, Food House, and Hello Artichoke." *ARTnews*, May 1994, p. 125.

Tumlir, Jan. "A Conversation With Pae White, artist." *Artweek*, November 17, 1994, p. 11.

Turner, Elisa. "Seducing Viewers With Questions of Art." *The Miami Herald*, January 30, 1994, p. 10.

——. "The Art of Seduction." *ARTnews*, Summer 1994, pp. 184–85.

Van den Boogerd, Dominic, and David Lillington. "It's Real, But Very Fucked Up." *Metropolis*, March 1994.

Wilson, William. "Pure Beauty: Irony Becomes Stale Second Time Around." *Los Angeles Times*, September 28, 1994.

1995

Auerbach, Lisa Anne. "Table Games." *Los Angeles Reader*, March 31, 1995, p. 13.

Clothier, Peter. "Pure Beauty." *ARTnews*, February 1995, p. 132.

Kandel, Susan. "Seductive Mystery." *Los Angeles Times*, September 28, 1995, p. F10.

O'Brien, John. "New Alternatives." *Art Papers*, November/December 1995, p. 29.

Pagel, David. "Pae White." *Art issues.*, November/December 1995, p. 44.

1996

Muchnic, Suzanne. "Pae White, John O'Reily." *ARTnews*, February 1996, p. 142.

Smith, Roberta. "Testing Limits at the Corcoran." *The New York Times*, January 6, 1996, p. 11.

1997

Duehr, Gary. "Beam up to the ICA's Enterprise." *The Tab*, July 29–August 4, 1997, p. 2B.

Hill, Shawn. "The pursuit of absence." *Bay Windows*, August 28, 1997, p. 30.

Huffstutter, P.J. "Digital Fine Art." *Daily News*, January 20, 1997, p. B1.

Lunenfeld, Peter. "Jennifer Steinkamp, Light in Space." *art/text*, August–October 1997, pp. 58–63.

Millis, Christopher. "All too clear." *The Boston Phoenix*, August 4, 1997, p. 14.

Scanlan, Joe. "Pae White." *frieze*, November/December 1997, pp. 89–90.

Silver, Joanne. "Work in Progress: International Artists Try Out Some New Ideas at the ICA." *Boston Herald*, July 25, 1997, pp. S11, 13.

Temin, Christine, "Christoph Grunenberg is bringing the world to the ICA." *The Boston Sunday Globe*, July 13, 1997.

——. "'Enterprise' Invites Viewers to Pitch In." *The Boston Globe*, August 1, 1997, pp. D1, 8.

Vogel, Carol. "Inside Out." *The New York Times*, April 25, 1997, p. C27.

Zimmer, William. "A Gallery Sampler at the Aldrich." *The New York Times*, December 14, 1997, p. 20.

1998

Curtis, Cathy. "Dressing the Flesh." *Los Angeles Times*, May 12, 1998, p. F2.

Dawson, Angela. "Into the Streets." *Adweek*, February 23, 1998.

Tumlir, Jan. "The Nouveau Objet." *art/text*, May–July 1998, pp. 40–43.

Selected Readings

Essays and Articles

Colpitt, Frances. "Going Against the Grain." *Art in America*, April 1995, pp. 42–47.

Danto, Arthur C. "Art after the End of Art." *Artforum*, April 1993, pp. 62–69.

Gilbert-Rolfe, Jeremy. "Cabbages, Raspberries, and Video's Thin Brightness." *Art & Design*, May/June 1996, pp. 14–23.

Lawson, Thomas. "Last Exit: Painting." *Artforum*, October 1981, pp. 40–47.

"Painting in the Age of Artificial Intelligence." Special issue. *Art & Design*, no. 5/6 (June 1996): pp. 6–92.

Pagel, David. "Visual Stimulation in L.A.: Paintings from Another Planet." *Flash Art*, Summer 1998, pp. 116–20.

Rubinstein, Raphael. "Abstraction Out of Bounds." *Art in America*, November 1997, pp. 104–15.

Schapiro, Meyer. "Recent Abstract Painting." Paper presented at the annual meeting of the American Federation of Arts, Houston, April 5, 1957. Reprint. In *Modern Art: 19th and 20th Centuries: Collected Papers*, pp. 213–26. New York: George Braziller, 1978.

"Special Focus: The Condition of Painting," *Contemporary Visual Arts* (London), no. 15 (1997).

Wei, Lilly. "Talking Abstract." *Art in America*, July 1987, pp. 80–97.

——. "Talking Abstract: Part Two." *Art in America*, December 1987, pp. 112–29, 171.

Exhibition Catalogues

1997 Biennial. Text by Bruce Guenther. Newport Beach, California: Orange County Museum of Art, 1997.

About Vision: New British Painting in the 1990s. Text by David Elliott. Oxford: Museum of Modern Art, 1996.

Abstraction in the Twentieth Century: Total Risk, Freedom, Discipline. Text by Mark Rosenthal. New York: Solomon R. Guggenheim Museum, 1996.

After the Fall: Aspects of Abstract Painting since 1970. Text by Lilly Wei. Staten Island, N.Y.: Newhouse Center for Contemporary Art, Snug Harbor Cultural Center, 1997.

Analogs of Modernism. Text by Tom Moody. Dallas: DARE at The McKinney Avenue Contemporary, 1995.

Critiques of Pure Abstraction. Text by Mark Rosenthal. New York: Independent Curators Incorporated, 1995.

Endgame: Reference and Simulation in Recent Painting and Sculpture. Text by Yves-Alain Bois, Thomas Crow, Hal Foster, David Joselit, Bob Riley and Elisabeth Sussmman. Boston: Massachusetts Institute of Technology and The Institute of Contemporary Art, 1986.

Face-to-Face: Recent Abstract Painting. Text by Katy Kline, Ron Platt, and Helaine Posner. Cambridge, Mass.: MIT List Visual Arts Center, 1996.

The Great Decade of American Abstraction: Modernist Art 1960 to 1970. Text by E.A. Carmean, Jr. Houston: The Museum of Fine Arts, Houston, 1974.

hanging. São Paulo: Galeria Camargo Vilaça, 1998.

The Image of Abstraction. Text by Kerry Brougher. Los Angeles: The Museum of Contemporary Art, 1988.

Los Angeles: Not Paintings? Text by David Pagel. Santa Barbara, Calif.: Santa Barbara Contemporary Arts Forum, 1993.

More than Minimal: Feminism and Abstraction in the '70s. Text by Whitney Chadwick, Kate Linker, Lucy Lippard, Leah Schroder, and Susan L. Stoops. Waltham, Mass.: Rose Art Museum, Brandeis University, 1996.

The New Sculpture 1965–75: Between Geometry and Gesture. Text by Richard Armstrong, John G. Hanhardt, and Robert Pincus-Witten. New York: Whitney Museum of American Art, 1990.

Out of Actions: between performance and the object, 1949–1979. Text by Guy Brett, Hubert Klocker, Shinichiro Osaki, Kristine Stiles, and Paul Schimmel. Los Angeles: The Museum of Contemporary Art, 1998.

Painting Machines: Industrial Image and Process in Contemporary Art. Text by Ana de Az´carate, Anthe Constantinidou, Leslie Goldman, Karen Gramm, Caroline A. Jones, Alice Kim, Renato Rodrigues da Silva with C. A. J., and Isabell Sobin. Boston: Boston University Art Gallery, 1997.

Painting Outside Painting: 44th Biennial Exhibition of Contemporary American Painting. Text by Terrie Sultan, Maia Damianovic, Eleanor Heartney, Julie Joyce, Jeff Kelley, Leslie King-Hammond, Judith Russi Kirshner, Terry R. Myers, Klaus Ottmann, David Pagel, Barry Schwabsky, and Kathleen Shields. Washington, D.C.: The Corcoran Gallery of Art, 1995.

Painting—The Extended Field. Text by Sven-Olov Wallenstein. Stockholm: Magasin 3 Stockholm Konsthall, and Malmö: Rooseum Center for Contemporary Art, 1996.

Patterns of Excess. Text by Ingrid Schaffner. Glenside, Pa.: Beaver College Art Gallery, 1997.

Pictura Britannica: Art from Britain. Text by David Barrett, Patricia Bickers, Patrick J. Boylan, Kobena Mercer, Bernice Murphy, Nikos Papastergiadis, Stephen Snoddy, and John A. Walker. Sydney: Museum of Contemporary Art, 1997.

Post-Abstract Abstraction. Text by Eugene Schwartz. Ridgefield, Conn.: The Aldrich Museum of Contemporary Art, 1987.

Reconditioned Abstraction. Text by Martin Ball and Mel Watkin. St. Louis: Forum for Contemporary Art, 1996.

Post-Pop, Post-Pictures. Text by Courtenay Smith. Chicago: The David and Alfred Smart Museum of Art, The University of Chicago, 1997.

Re:Fab Painting Abstracted, Fabricated and Revised. Text by Rochelle Feinstein, Shirley Kaneda, Margaret A. Miller, W.J.T. Mitchell, and Christine Van Schoonbeck. Tampa, Fla.: Contemporary Art Museum, University of South Florida, 1996.

Repicturing Abstraction. Text by Arthur C. Danto, Chris Gregson, Steven S. High, H. Ashley Kistler, and Richard Waller. Richmond, Va.: Richmond Curatorial Project, 1995.

Sensation: Young British Artists from the Saatchi Collection. Text by Brooks Adams, Lisa Jardine, Martin Maloney, Norman Rosenthal, and Richard Shone. London: Royal Academy of Arts, 1997.

Sense and Sensibility: Women Artists and Minimalism in the Nineties. Text by Lynn Zelevansky. New York: The Museum of Modern Art, 1994.

The Spiritual in Art: Abstract Painting 1890–1985. Text by Carel Blotkamp, Judi Freeman, and Maurice Tuchman. Los Angeles: Los Angeles County Museum of Art, 1986.

Spot Making Sense. Text by David Pagel. Kansas City, Mo.: Grand Arts, 1997.

Sunshine & Noir: Art in L.A. 1960–1997. Text by Anne Ayres, Laura Cottingham, Mike Davis, Russell Ferguson, William R. Hackman, Timothy Martin, Lars Nittve, and Peter Schjeldahl. Denmark: Louisiana Museum of Modern Art, Humlebaek, 1997.

Texas Abstract: New Painting in the Nineties. Text by Francis Colpitt. San Antonio: ArtPace Foundation for Contemporary Art, 1995.

Books

Bois, Yves-Alain, et al. *Painting As Model*. Boston: M.I.T. Press, 1990.

Carrier, David. *The Aesthete in the City: The Philosophy and Practice of Abstract Painting in the 1980s*. University Park, Pa.: Pennsylvania State University Press, 1994.

Danto, Arthur C. *After the End of Art: Contemporary Art and the Pale of History*. Princeton, N.J.: Princeton University Press, 1997.

Fer, Briony. *On Abstract Art*. New Haven, Conn., and London: Yale University Press, 1997.

Foster, Hal, ed. *The Anti-Aesthetic: Essays on Postmodern Culture*. Port Townsend, Wash.: Bay Press, 1983.

Halley, Peter. *Collected Essays 1981–87*. New York: Gallery Bruno Bischofberger, 1988.

Hickey, Dave. *The Invisible Dragon: Four Essays on Beauty*. Los Angeles: The Foundation for Advanced Critical Studies, 1993.

Lippard, Lucy. *Six Years: The Dematerialization of the Art Object from 1966 to 1972*. New York: Praeger Publishers, Inc., 1973.

McEvilley, Thomas. *The Exile's Return: Toward a Redefinition of Painting for the Post-Modern Era*. Cambridge, England: Cambridge University Press, 1993.

Sandler, Irving. *The Triumph of American Painting: A History of Abstract Expressionsim*. New York: Harper & Row Publishers, 1970.

Stiles, Kristine, and Peter Selz, eds. *Theories and Documents of Contemporary Art: A Sourcebook of Artists' Writings*. Berkeley: University of California Press, 1996.

Contemporary Arts Museum

Board of Trustees

Staff

Dana Friis-Hansen is senior curator at the Contemporary Arts Museum where he has organized exhibitions such as *Richard Long: Circles, Cycles, Mud, Stones* and *Sugimoto*. From 1991–95 he was Associate Curator at Nanjo & Associates, a contemporary arts organization in Tokyo, where he organized *TransCulture* for the 1995 Venice Biennale.

David Pagel is an L.A.-based critic who writes for the *Los Angeles Times*. He is a Visiting Scholar at The Claremont Graduate University and an adjunct curator at the Institute of Visual Arts at the University of Wisconsin–Milwaukee. He is also contributing editor to *BOMB* and *Art issues*.

Raphael Rubinstein lives in New York where he is a senior editor at *Art in America*. His recent publications include a selection of his art criticism translated into French, *Peintures Croisées* (L'Harmattan), and a collection of poems, *The Basement of the Café Rilke* (Hard Press).

Peter Schjeldahl is a columnist for *The Village Voice* and a contributing editor of *Art in America*. He has worked as a regular art critic for *The New York Sunday Times, Vanity Fair,* and *7 Days*. He is the author of *The Hydrogen Jukebox: Selected Writings, 1978–1991, The 7 DAYS Art Columns,* and *Columns & Catalogues*.

Copy Editor: Polly Koch
Associate Editor: Paula Webb
Publication Coordinators: Alexandra Irvine and Lynn M. Herbert
Design: Don Quaintance, Public Address Design, Houston
Production Assistant: Elizabeth Frizzell
Typography: Public Address Design; composed in Apollo and Formata
Printing: Meridian Printing, East Greenwich, Rhode Island
Color separations/halftones: Elite Color, Providence, Rhode Island

Photography

All photographs courtesy the artists unless noted in caption or list below.

ACME., Sant Monica, California: pp. 78–79
Mitchell Algus Gallery, New York: p. 32 (top)
Angles Gallery, Santa Monica, California: pp. 22, 44–45
Blum & Poe, Santa Monica, California: pp. 72–73
The Eli and Edythe L. Broad Collection: p. 17 (right)
Brownstone, Corréard & Cie, Paris: p. 31 (center)
CRG Gallery, New York: p. 20 (right), p. 62
Geoffrey Clements; courtesy VAGA, New York, NY: p. 32 (center, left)
D'Amelio Terras Gallery, New York: pp. 42–43
Bevan Davies; courtesy Max Protetch Gallery, New York: p. 32 (center, right)
Anthony d'Offay Gallery, London: pp. 12, 76–77
Paula Goldman: p. 24
Marian Goodman Gallery, New York: p. 32 (bottom)
Gorney Bravin & Lee, New York: p. 69
Sean Kelly Gallery, New York: pp. 64–65
Yves Klein Archives: p. 30 (top)
Erich Koyama: p. 83
Curt Marcus Gallery, New York: p. 18
Lehmann Maupin: p. 50
Philippe Migeat; courtesy Musée National d'Art Moderne, Paris; ©Centre G. Pompidou: pp. 29 (bottom), 31 (top)
The Museum of Fine Arts, Houston: p. 59
©1991 Hans Namuth Estate, Collection Center for Creative Photography, University of Arizona: p. 14
Bacci Orazio; courtesy Archivio Opera Piero Manzoni: p. 30 (bottom)
Patrick Painter, Inc.: p. 48
Private Collection: p. 29 (top)
The Saatchi Gallery, London: pp. 20 (left), 49
Masaaei Sekiya; courtesy the artist: p. 29 (center)
Shoshana Wayne Gallery, Santa Monica, California: p. 53
Harry Shunk: p. 30 (center)
Orin Slor: frontispiece, p. 56
Holly Solomon Gallery, New York: p. 33 (right)
Sonnabend Gallery, New York: p. 16
Richard Stoner; courtesy The Andy Warhol Museum, Pittsburgh: pp. 17 (left), 33 (left)
Grant Taylor; courtesy the artist and Rosamund Felsen Gallery, Santa Monica: p. 33 (center)
Edward Thorp Gallery, New York: pp. 38–39, 70–71
Texas Gallery, Houston: front cover, pp. 58, 60–61, 74–75
Copyright©1998: Whitney Museum of American Art: p. 31 (bottom)
Zindman/Fremont, NY; courtesy CRG Gallery, New York: p. 63